THE EVERYTHING

HEALTHY CASSEROLE COOKBOOK

Dear Reader,

Stop what you are doing, take a deep breath, and realize that even in today's busy world, there's time to slow down a bit and savor healthful and delicious food. This book will help guide you in planning one-dish meals that are chock-full of the whole grains, fruits, vegetables, and lean proteins that your body needs to stay healthy. Even better, once these dishes are assembled and bubbling away in the oven, you can use those extra few moments of hands-off cooking time to enjoy as you wish.

As a registered dietitian, I often hear new clients worry that they have to make drastic changes to their diet and lifestyle in order to be healthier. And while change is sometimes warranted, those first steps toward living a healthier lifestyle have to fit your routine and taste preferences. You might start by cooking the recipes in this book that seem the most familiar to you. Then once you grow comfortable in the kitchen, you can begin trying new ingredients and recipes.

Have fun experimenting in the kitchen and enjoy the delicious food you've created!

In good health,

Kris Widican, MS, RD, LDN

Welcome to the EVERYTHING® Series!

These handy, accessible books give you all you need to tackle a difficult project, gain a new hobby, comprehend a fascinating topic, prepare for an exam, or even brush up on something you learned back in school but have since forgotten.

You can choose to read an Everything® book from cover to cover or just pick out the information you want from our four useful boxes: e-questions, e-facts, e-alerts, and e-ssentials.

We give you everything you need to know on the subject, but throw in a lot of fun stuff along the way, too.

We now have more than 400 Everything® books in print, spanning such wide-ranging categories as weddings, pregnancy, cooking, music instruction, foreign language, crafts, pets, New Age, and so much more. When you're done reading them all, you can finally say you know Everything®!

QUESTION

Answers to
common questions

FACT

Important snippets
of information

ALERT

Urgent
warnings

ESSENTIAL

Quick
handy tips

PUBLISHER Karen Cooper

DIRECTOR OF ACQUISITIONS AND INNOVATION Paula Munier

MANAGING EDITOR, EVERYTHING® SERIES Lisa Laing

COPY CHIEF Casey Ebert

ASSISTANT PRODUCTION EDITOR Jacob Erickson

ACQUISITIONS EDITOR Lisa Laing

ASSOCIATE DEVELOPMENT EDITOR Hillary Thompson

EDITORIAL ASSISTANT Ross Weisman

EVERYTHING® SERIES COVER DESIGNER Erin Alexander

LAYOUT DESIGNERS Colleen Cunningham, Elisabeth Lariviere, Ashley Vierra, Denise Wallace

Visit the entire Everything® series at *www.everything.com*

THE
EVERYTHING®
HEALTHY CASSEROLE COOKBOOK

Kris Widican, MS, RD, LDN

Aadamsmedia

Avon, Massachusetts

*This book is dedicated to every time-pressed
cook who loves food and wants to
eat healthfully.*

An Everything® Series Book.
Everything® and everything.com® are registered trademarks of F+W Media, Inc.

Published by Adams Media, a division of F+W Media, Inc.
57 Littlefield Street, Avon, MA 02322 U.S.A.
www.adamsmedia.com

Nutritional statistics by Nicole Cormier, RD

Contains material adapted and abridged from:
The Everything® Calorie Counting Cookbook, by Paula Conway, copyright © 2008 by F+W Media, Inc., ISBN 10: 1-59869-416-2, ISBN 13: 978-1-59869-416-1; *The Everything® Diabetes Cookbook, 2nd Edition*, by Gretchen Scalpi, RD, CDN, CDE, copyright © 2010, 2002 by F+W Media, Inc., ISBN 10: 1-4405-0154-8, ISBN 13: 978-1-4405-0154-8; *The Everything® Healthy College Cookbook*, by Nicole Cormier, RD, copyright © 2010 by F+W Media, Inc., ISBN 10: 1-4405-0411-3, ISBN 13: 978-1-4405-0411-2; *The Everything® Healthy Cooking for Parties Book*, by Linda Larsen, copyright © 2008 by F+W Media, Inc., ISBN 10: 1-59869-925-3, ISBN 13: 978-1-59869-925-8; *The Everything® Italian Cookbook*, by Dawn Altomari, BPS, copyright © 2005 by F+W Media, Inc., ISBN 10: 1-59337-420-8, ISBN 13: 978-1-59337-420-4; *The Everything® Low-Cholesterol Cookbook*, by Linda Larsen, copyright © 2008 by F+W Media, Inc., ISBN 10: 1-59869-401-4, ISBN 13: 978-1-59869-401-7; *The Everything® Meals on a Budget Cookbook*, by Linda Larsen, copyright © 2008 by F+W Media, Inc., ISBN 10: 1-59869-508-8, ISBN 13: 978-1-59869-508-3; *The Everything® Mexican Cookbook*, by Margaret Kaeter, copyright © 2004 by F+W Media, Inc., ISBN 10: 1-58062-967-9, ISBN 13: 978-1-58062-967-6; *The Everything® One-Pot Cookbook, 2nd Edition*, by Pamela Rice Hahn, copyright © 2009, 1999 by F+W Media, Inc., ISBN 10: 1-59869-836-2, ISBN 13: 978-1-59869-836-7; *The Everything® Potluck Cookbook*, by Linda Larsen, copyright © 2009 by F+W Media, Inc., ISBN 10: 1-59869-990-3, ISBN 13: 978-1-59869-990-6; *The Everything® Sugar-Free Cookbook*, by Nancy T. Maar, copyright © 2008 by F+W Media, Inc., ISBN 10: 1-59869-408-1, ISBN 13: 978-1-59869-408-6; *The Everything® Vegan Cookbook*, by Jolinda Hackett with Lorena Novak Bull, RD, copyright © 2010 by F+W Media, Inc., ISBN 10: 1-4405-0216-1, ISBN 13: 978-1-4405-0216-3; *The Everything® Whole-Grain, High-Fiber Cookbook*, by Lynette Rhorer Shirk, copyright © 2008 by F+W Media, Inc., ISBN 10: 1-59869-507-X, ISBN 13: 978-1-59869-507-6.

ISBN 10: 1-4405-2932-9
ISBN 13: 978-1-4405-2932-0
eISBN 10: 1-4405-3000-9
eISBN 13: 978-1-4405-3000-5

Printed in the United States of America.

10 9 8 7 6 5 4 3 2 1

Library of Congress Cataloging-in-Publication Data
is available from the publisher.

*This book is available at quantity discounts for bulk purchases.
For information, please call 1-800-289-0963.*

Contents

Acknowledgments

My thanks go out to all of my family and friends who have been kind enough to taste an endless stream of casseroles. Your feedback has been priceless!

Introduction

THE MENTION OF CASSEROLES might bring to mind a mixture of twentieth-century convenience foods that are baked together in the oven. However, casseroles have enjoyed a place in history since the invention of earthenware cooking vessels.

Food historians believe the word *casserole* originated from the Classical Greek word for cup, *kuathos*, which over centuries morphed into the Old French word *casse*, before becoming the word *casserole*. Eventually, the term came to mean both a style of cooking where food is slowly baked in a low oven and the container in which the food is baked.

Although they are humble in nature, and often used as a means of stretching expensive ingredients to feed many, casseroles have evolved to incorporate regional food preferences and can be an elegant and healthful addition to any meal.

It's easy to make healthy and satisfying casseroles by incorporating a mix of whole grains, lean meats, vegetarian meat replacements, fresh vegetables, and herbs with a judicious use of convenience products, including canned beans, boxed broths, or canned chopped tomatoes.

Most casseroles are bound by a sauce or gravy, which eliminates the need for fatty ingredients to keep them moist. All that's usually needed is a light mist of nonstick spray, and you are ready to assemble.

While casseroles are often main-dish fare, almost everything from appetizers to desserts can be made into a casserole—often with fantastic results. There are few better ways to show off the sweetness of summer corn and tomatoes or the juiciness of ripe berries than to bake them into a casserole.

Use these recipes for inspiration, and bring your creativity to the kitchen. Enjoy!

CHAPTER 1

An Introduction to Healthy Casserole Cooking

Imagine having time to tuck into a good book, catch up on household chores, or take a breather from a hectic day at work—all while dinner bubbles and browns away in the oven. It's easy to do just that when you incorporate wholesome slow-cooked foods, such as casseroles, into your eating plan. This chapter will guide you through the process of making healthful one-dish meals from the bottom up. Learn about how to select cooking equipment to make your time in the kitchen more efficient, how to stock your pantry with casserole-friendly ingredients, and how to make any traditional casserole recipe healthier.

Kitchen Equipment

The right-sized casserole dish and a few handy pieces of kitchen equipment can simplify your time in the kitchen and make cooking more enjoyable. Take inventory, and make a list of pieces you might need to add to your collection before you start to cook.

FACT

It's estimated that more than 80 percent of American homes have Pyrex products, a popular producer of casserole dishes. Legend has it that the idea for Pyrex glassware came from the wife of a Corning Glass Works scientist, who wanted ovensafe dishes that were as sturdy as the railroad signal lanterns her husband produced.

Casserole Dishes and Baking Pans

Don't worry if you don't have every casserole dish called for in this list—you can often substitute one dish for another if you adjust the cooking time. If you are using a deeper dish than what is called for in the recipe, add a few minutes to the cooking time. If you are using one that is shallower, reduce the cooking time by a few minutes. Casserole dishes come in various shapes, materials, and colors, but here's a list of the basic sizes you might want to include in your kitchen for everyday cooking.

1-Quart (4-Cup) Casserole

This size dish is great for appetizers, side dishes, and smaller main course casseroles. A 6-inch soufflé dish or a 9-inch pie plate holds approximately the same volume.

1½-Quart (6-Cup) Casserole

Most often made of glass and measuring 8" × 8", this workhorse dish is often used for cooking starches, vegetable dishes, or smaller casseroles. Substitute a 10-inch pie plate, an 8-cup casserole, or a 7-inch soufflé dish.

2-Quart (8-Cup) Casserole

This casserole dish is usually made of metal, and slightly deeper and wider at 9" × 9" than the square glass casserole dish. Use it for side dishes, smaller desserts, or moderate-sized main dishes. If you don't have this pan, use an 8-inch soufflé dish or an 8" × 8" glass square pan as a substitute.

3-Quart (12-Cup) Casserole

Usually made of glass with 9" × 13" dimensions, this dish is perfectly sized to feed a crowd! It is often sold as part of a set with the 8" × 8" glass baking dish, and some may even come with plastic lids that snap on for transporting and storing casseroles.

If buying a metal pan of this size, look for sturdy, heavyweight models. In many recipes a 3-quart Dutch oven may be substituted.

3-Quart Dutch Oven

Made of either ovenproof stainless steel or enameled cast iron, this lidded pot is essential for braising meats and vegetables or other dishes where keeping moisture inside the pot is necessary. Unlike other casserole dishes, this pot can go directly from the stove burners to the oven.

5-Quart (or Larger) Dutch Oven

Made of the same materials as the 3-quart Dutch oven, and used for similar cooking applications, this pot simply holds more volume. Use for potlucks or parties where you'll have a crowd.

Other Handy Kitchen Tools

Owning multiple sets of commonly used kitchen items, such as measuring spoons, bowls, or rubber spatulas, helps you reduce the amount of time you spend washing these items between tasks. Other tools, including food processors and mandolins, make quick work of thinly slicing and shredding vegetables. Consider adding the following:

- A can opener
- A vegetable peeler
- A few plastic or wooden cutting boards of various sizes for cutting and chopping food

- Several wooden spoons, heatproof rubber spatulas, and whisks for mixing
- A small paring knife, a large chef's knife, and a serrated bread knife
- Mixing bowls made of a nonreactive material such as glass or stainless steel
- An assortment of pots and pans for stovetop cooking
- A few sturdy, low-rimmed baking sheets
- Dry and liquid measuring cups of various sizes
- Measuring spoons
- A metal colander for draining pasta and rinsing fruits and vegetables
- A mandolin for slicing or shredding foods
- A box grater for shredding cheeses or vegetables
- A food processor for shredding, slicing, or mixing ingredients

One of the most important pieces of equipment used in making casseroles is your oven. Check that yours is running at the proper temperature by investing in an oven thermometer. If it's high or low, you can make adjustments to the cooking time accordingly.

Casserole Cooking Tips and Tricks

Casseroles may take a little work up front, but the great thing is that once they are assembled, they can be baked at any time. Even better, their flavors often improve once they've had time to blend after a rest in the refrigerator.

Make Ahead

Most casseroles can be assembled ahead of the time you plan to bake them without much change in the recipe. Simply wrap the prepared casserole tightly in plastic wrap or cover with a tight-fitting lid and store in the refrigerator until you are ready to bake it.

For those recipes that have biscuit, crumble, or cobbler toppings, it's often wise to prepare and add the toppings just prior to baking so that they do not become soggy. In some cases, as when preparing fresh bread crumbs, you can make the topping at the time you assemble the casserole, store it separately, and add it to the casserole just prior to baking.

A cold casserole taken right out of the refrigerator may require up to 20 minutes of additional baking time. Check the casserole to make sure it is thoroughly cooked through by taking its temperature. It should reach a safe internal temperature of 165°F or higher in the center. If the temperature of the center is lower than 165°F, the casserole needs more time in the oven.

Freezing

The best casseroles to freeze are those that have a lot of moisture in them, as freezing tends to make foods dry. Lasagnas with lots of sauce, stews, and braised dishes tend to freeze especially well. And, generally, unbaked casseroles tend to freeze better than baked casseroles. If you do plan on freezing a casserole that has been baked, it's helpful to divide it into single portion sizes before freezing so that you can defrost only the portion you plan on eating at one sitting.

You can freeze a casserole directly in the pan it is to be cooked in, but this takes up a lot of space in the freezer (plus you lose the use of your pan for the duration that the casserole is frozen). Alternatively, line your casserole dish with nonstick foil or foil that has been sprayed with nonstick spray, then assemble and freeze it as usual. Once the casserole is frozen, you can pop it out of the dish and store the casserole "cube" wrapped and labeled in the freezer.

To cook frozen casseroles, defrost them overnight in the refrigerator (do not defrost them on the counter), then bake as directed in the recipe.

Reheating

Reheat only the portion of the casserole you intend on eating at one sitting. This will prevent the rest of the casserole from becoming dry and help to prevent the growth of bacteria on the uneaten portion of the food.

Use a microwave on the reheat setting or the oven set to a lower temperature than the casserole was originally baked at to reheat casseroles. Remember to let the casserole sit for a minute or two after microwaving so that the food can heat through evenly.

Healthy Cooking Guidelines

Most nutrition and health professionals agree that a healthy eating plan is one that includes a variety of fruits and vegetables, whole grains, lean meats and poultry, seafood, low-fat or fat-free dairy, eggs, beans and peas, and nuts and seeds. It also limits the amount of sodium, solid fats, added sugars, and refined grains you eat to a small amount every day.

FACT

Fiber is a type of carbohydrate that your body can't digest. Diets high in fiber have been shown to help maintain bowel health, lower blood cholesterol levels, aid in weight loss, and control blood sugar levels. Fiber is found in vegetables, fruits, whole grains, and legumes.

Of course, within this basic framework of healthful eating, there are endless ways to individualize eating plans to make them vegetarian, vegan, dairy-free, wheat-free, or simply to suit your personal taste. It's easier to manage what you eat when you cook at home, and with a little know-how you can put together some truly satisfying, delicious, and healthy meals.

Carbohydrates

With all the debate surrounding carbohydrates over the last few years, you might think that avoiding them altogether is the solution for maintaining a healthy weight. In fact, carbohydrates are the body's primary source of fuel. You need them in your eating plan so that your brain, central nervous system, muscles, intestines, and kidneys can function properly. The United States Department of Agriculture recommends that between 45 and 65 percent of the calories in our eating plan come from carbohydrates.

Food scientists break carbohydrates into two groups: simple and complex. Simple carbohydrates include sugar molecules such as fructose, dextrose, glucose, and sucrose. Complex carbohydrates are three or more sugar molecules strung together to form a chain. Instead of getting hung up on these terms (they don't tell the whole picture of how your body uses either type of molecule anyway), just remember to stick with mostly whole food sources of carbohydrates. Whole grains (grains that contain the endosperm, germ, and bran), legumes, fruits, and vegetables are examples of whole food carbohydrates. Not only do they supply you with energy, they are also an important source of vitamins and minerals. In contrast, refined products such as white rice, white flour, or simple sugars have these vitamins and minerals stripped from them during the refining process.

Protein

You use the protein from your diet to build and repair tissue, make hormones and enzymes, build a healthy immune system, and for energy when you don't have enough carbohydrates in your system. The USDA suggests that 10 percent to 35 percent of calories come from protein. Proteins are made of amino acids—nine of which you can't make in your own body and are therefore called "essential." Animal protein from meat, fish, eggs, and milk are considered to be "complete" proteins because they contain all nine essential amino acids.

Vegetable proteins (with the exception of soy) are considered to be incomplete proteins and must be eaten in combination so as to provide the full array of essential amino acids. An example of this would be to combine rice with beans in a single meal. Whole grains, legumes, nuts, seeds, and vegetables all contain protein.

Fats

The USDA recommends that about 20 percent to 35 percent of calories in your diet come from fat. You need this amount in your diet for normal growth and development, energy, absorption of the fat-soluble vitamins (A, E, D, and K), and cushioning of your organs.

Saturated fat typically comes from animal sources (milk, butter, meat, and cheese) but may also be found in some tropical oils. It is solid at room temperature and should not exceed 7 percent of the total calories you eat every day. A high intake of saturated fat can raise blood cholesterol.

Trans fats are made during the process of hydrogenation, where hydrogen is added to liquid vegetable oils to make them solid for commercial use as stick margarine and shortenings. These fats raise LDL ("bad") blood cholesterol. The American Heart Association recommends limiting trans fat to less than 1 percent of total daily caloric intake.

Polyunsaturated and monounsaturated fats are considered to be among the healthier types of fat. They come from plant-based sources including plant oils (safflower, olive, and corn), avocados, nuts, and seeds. There is evidence to suggest that these oils, when used in place of saturated fats in the diet, can help reduce blood cholesterol levels.

Cholesterol

Cholesterol is a waxy substance that occurs naturally in all parts of your body. It's used to produce many hormones, to make the bile acids that help you digest fat, and to make vitamin D.

Your liver makes cholesterol, but it can also be obtained from your diet (this type of cholesterol is called dietary cholesterol, which comes from animal products). Too much cholesterol in your blood can lead to a condition called atherosclerosis—the buildup of fat and cholesterol in the walls of arteries. The 2010 Dietary Guidelines for Americans suggest limiting dietary cholesterol to less than 300 milligrams per day.

Vitamins and Minerals

Eating a wide variety of foods while staying within your calorie needs will generally supply your body with most of the vitamins and minerals it needs for optimal health. Some groups of people—vegans who don't eat animal protein, or pregnant or nursing mothers, for example—may need additional supplementation of key nutrients. Discuss your diet and health concerns with your doctor and registered dietitian to determine if you should consider taking supplements or make modifications to your present diet.

Sodium

Sodium is an essential nutrient and is needed in very small quantities for normal body functioning unless substantial losses occur through sweating. There's good evidence that increased sodium intake leads to higher blood pressure, while a reduction in sodium in the diet helps to reduce blood pressure.

The 2010 Dietary Guidelines for Americans recommends reducing sodium intake to less than 2,300 milligrams per day, and to less than 1,500 milligrams for African Americans and those who have hypertension, diabetes, or chronic kidney disease, or are older than age fifty-one.

Sugars

Sugars occur naturally in foods like fruits, vegetables, and dairy products; however, for most people to stay within their calorie needs, they need to limit the amount of added sugars they eat. Foods with added sugars include sodas, sweets, and many snack foods, sauces, and condiments. Read ingredient labels carefully and choose wisely.

Adapting Traditional Casserole Recipes to Make Them Healthier

There are infinite ways to modify traditional casserole recipes that use high-fat, high-sugar, and low-nutrient convenience foods to make them healthier and ensure they have great taste.

Starches

Most casserole recipes that call for white rice, plain pasta, or bread crumbs made from white bread can easily be converted so that they incorporate brown or wild rice, whole-wheat pasta, or whole-wheat bread crumbs. This will help to increase the fiber and nutrient content of the casserole. The cooking time and amount of liquid or sauce in the casserole may need to be increased slightly.

For different flavor and texture, try incorporating another type of grain such as quinoa, wheat berries, or barley into recipes you already use—you might just be on your way to creating another casserole favorite!

Condensed Soups

Condensed soups give traditional casseroles a silky, creamy texture, help keep them moist, and add lots of flavor. Unfortunately, they are often high in fat and sodium. Think about substituting fat-free or low-fat evaporated milk in place of creamy soups. Use tomato sauce or vegetable purées instead of vegetable soup bases. Or thicken low-sodium broths and stocks with flour, potato starch, or cornstarch before adding them to recipes.

Vegetables

Adding vegetables to casseroles will not only improve their fiber and nutrient content but also boost flavor and make the casserole much more interesting.

ESSENTIAL

Some vegetables give off a lot of water during cooking, which isn't a problem when adding them to braises or stews, but may make layered casseroles soupy. Usually par-cooking vegetables prior to adding them to casseroles will help release some of the moisture. If that doesn't work, it may be necessary—as with vegetables like spinach—to squeeze them dry by hand.

Using fresh vegetables in casseroles is always a good choice, but many canned and frozen vegetables will do in a pinch. Some, including canned tomatoes, might even be sweeter because they are picked at the height of ripeness. Be aware that some frozen vegetables give off a lot of water, so adjust cooking times and other ingredients accordingly.

Fat

Instead of using butter, shortening, or lard as directed in some casserole recipes, consider substituting monounsaturated and polyunsaturated fats. For those recipes that call for full-fat dairy products, try reducing the amount that you use or use lower-fat versions of those same products. Trim the visible fat from meat and poultry, and choose lean ground meats over fattier grinds.

Sodium

Control the amount of sodium that goes into your casserole recipes by choosing low-salt or salt-free products such as broths, sauces, or canned tomatoes, and adding less salt during cooking. Instead use boldly flavored salt-free spice blends and fresh herbs to punch up flavor and add some color.

CHAPTER 2

Breakfast and Brunch

Baked Scrambled Eggs

These eggs are easy to make when feeding a crowd. They bake up light and fluffy in the oven and give you plenty of time to prepare other sides.

INGREDIENTS | SERVES 12

¼ cup butter

20 large egg whites

10 large egg yolks

1 teaspoon salt

1¾ cups fat-free milk

1. Preheat the oven to 350°F and lightly spray a 9"× 13" casserole dish with nonstick spray.

2. In a glass measuring cup, heat the butter in the microwave until melted.

3. In a separate bowl, whisk the eggs, salt, and milk.

4. Pour the melted butter and then the eggs into the casserole.

5. Bake, uncovered, for 8 minutes, then stir. Bake for 10–15 more minutes or until eggs are set.

PER SERVING Calories: 136 | Fat: 8.8g | Protein: 12g | Sodium: 365mg | Fiber: 0g | Carbohydrates: 1.8g | Sugar: 0g

Parmesan, Prosciutto, and Asparagus Oven Omelet

This omelet is a take on the classic American ham and cheese omelet. Because Parmesan cheese and prosciutto are boldly flavored and slightly salty, you can use less, reduce the amount of added salt in the egg mixture, and save on calories.

INGREDIENTS | SERVES 6

1 pound asparagus, trimmed and chopped

12 large egg whites

6 large egg yolks

1 cup fat-free milk

4 ounces prosciutto, thinly sliced

⅓ cup shredded Parmesan cheese

¼ cup finely chopped basil

¼ teaspoon salt

¼ teaspoon pepper

1. Preheat the oven to 375°F and lightly spray a 9" × 13" casserole dish with nonstick spray.

2. Place the asparagus and 1 tablespoon water into a microwave-safe bowl. Cover the bowl with plastic wrap and steam the asparagus on the high setting until crisp-tender, about 1 minute. Drain the asparagus and allow to cool.

3. Whisk the egg whites, yolks, milk, prosciutto, Parmesan, basil, salt, and pepper together in a large bowl. Add the cooled asparagus and stir. Pour into the prepared casserole dish.

4. Bake the omelet, uncovered, on the middle rack until it is set in the center, 45–50 minutes.

PER SERVING Calories: 216 | Fat: 12g | Protein: 20g | Sodium: 515mg | Fiber: 1.6g | Carbohydrates: 6g | Sugar: 1.6g

Better Baked Oats with Warm Spices and Apricots

Feel free to substitute your favorite combination of dried fruit, nuts, seeds, and spices to customize this cozy breakfast treat.

INGREDIENTS | SERVES 6

3 cups old-fashioned rolled oats

3¾ cups fat-free milk

½ cup chopped dried apricots

¼ cup shelled pumpkin seeds, toasted

½ teaspoon cinnamon

½ teaspoon ground cardamom

¼ teaspoon salt

1. Spray an 8" × 8" baking dish with nonstick spray and preheat the oven to 350°F.

2. Combine the oats, milk, apricots, pumpkin seeds, cinnamon, cardamom, and salt in a large bowl; stir to combine. Pour into prepared casserole dish.

3. Bake on the middle rack of the oven until all the liquid is absorbed, about 25–30 minutes. Serve hot.

PER SERVING Calories: 433 | Fat: 9.6g | Protein: 22g | Sodium: 180mg | Fiber: 9.7g | Carbohydrates: 67g | Sugar: 5.8g

Sweet Ricotta Strata with Plumped Fruit

Similar to a bread pudding, but not quite as sweet, this breakfast strata tastes great when served alongside a fresh berry salad. Plump the fruit by soaking it in hot, boiling water for 10 minutes, then drain.

INGREDIENTS | SERVES 6

6 large egg whites

3 large egg yolks

1 tablespoon sugar

¼ teaspoon salt

4 cups cubed whole-wheat baguette

½ cup plumped dried cherries, chopped

½ cup plumped dried currants

½ cup part-skim ricotta cheese, drained

Fresh Berry Salad

Combine a half pint each of washed fresh blueberries, raspberries, and blackberries. Add 2 teaspoons of chopped fresh mint. Gently mix to combine and serve.

1. Spray an 8" × 8" casserole dish with nonstick spray. Whisk the egg whites, egg yolks, sugar, and salt together in a large bowl.

2. Stir in the baguette, cherries, currants, and ricotta; pour into prepared casserole dish.

3. Place a heavy weight on top of the strata so that the custard mixture can soak into the bread. Refrigerate for at least 1 hour and up to 1 day.

4. When ready to bake the strata, preheat the oven to 325°F. Place the strata on the middle rack and bake until the center is set and cooked through, about 1 hour.

PER SERVING Calories: 204 | Fat: 5.5g | Protein: 12g | Sodium: 204mg | Fiber: 2.5g | Carbohydrates: 28g | Sugar: 15g

Better Baked Oats

The oats, spices, fruit, and nuts in this recipe plump pleasingly in the oven and allow you hands-free time to do other things on hectic mornings. If you can't find apple pie spice, substitute a mixture of cinnamon, ginger, cloves, and nutmeg.

INGREDIENTS | SERVES 6

3 cups old-fashioned rolled oats
3¾ cups fat-free milk
½ cup raisins
¼ cup toasted walnut pieces
1½ teaspoons apple pie spice mix
¼ teaspoon salt

Rolled Oats

Rolled oats are cereal grains that have been flattened and steamed so that they cook faster. Oatmeal contains soluble fiber, which lowers your "bad" (LDL) cholesterol without changing your "good" (HDL) cholesterol.

1. Spray an 8" × 8" baking dish with nonstick spray and preheat the oven to 350°F.

2. Combine the oats, milk, raisins, walnut pieces, spice mix, and salt in a large bowl; stir to combine. Pour into prepared casserole dish.

3. Bake on the middle rack of the oven until all the liquid is absorbed, about 25–30 minutes. Serve hot.

PER SERVING Calories: 285 | Fat: 6.6g | Protein: 9.5g | Sodium: 297mg | Fiber: 3.8g | Carbohydrates: 50g | Sugar: 18g

Baked Barley Porridge with Blueberries and Walnuts

If you want to reduce the cooking time slightly, toast the barley the night before and soak overnight in the water and milk. The next morning, continue with the recipe as directed.

INGREDIENTS | SERVES 4

1 tablespoon unsalted butter
1 cup pearled barley, rinsed
2 cups water
2 cups fat-free milk
½ cup chopped walnut pieces, toasted
¼ cup brown sugar
¼ teaspoon salt
½ cup fresh or frozen blueberries

Barley

This nutty and pleasantly chewy grain is high in a dietary fiber called beta-glucan, which helps to lower cholesterol. It is also a very good source of selenium and manganese.

1. Spray an 8" × 8" casserole dish with nonstick spray and preheat the oven to 350°F.

2. Melt the butter over medium heat in a small saucepan, then add the barley and stir frequently until it begins to toast and smell nutty. Immediately add the water and milk; bring to a boil, then turn off the heat.

3. Add the walnut pieces, brown sugar, and salt and pour mixture into the prepared casserole dish.

4. Bake, uncovered, on the middle oven rack for 35 minutes. Stir once, add the blueberries, and bake for an additional 10–15 minutes until the barley is plumped and tender.

PER SERVING Calories: 404 | Fat: 13g | Protein: 11g | Sodium: 219mg | Fiber: 9.4g | Carbohydrates: 63g | Sugar: 15g

Roasted Mixed-Berry Compote

Serve this berry compote as a hot topping for pancakes or French toast, or cooled as a topping for Greek yogurt and granola. Substitute fresh berries if they are in season.

INGREDIENTS | SERVES 4

1 cup frozen strawberries
1 cup frozen raspberries
1 cup frozen blueberries
½ cup orange juice
1 tablespoon grated orange zest from 1 orange
1 tablespoon honey

1. Spray an 8" × 8" casserole dish with nonstick spray and preheat the oven to 350°F.

2. Combine strawberries, raspberries, blueberries, orange juice, orange zest, and honey together in the casserole dish. Cover tightly with foil and bake on center rack until berries begin to break down, about 30 minutes.

3. Remove foil and bake an additional 10–15 minutes until the berry mixture thickens.

PER SERVING Calories: 86 | Fat: 0.69g | Protein: 1.6g | Sodium: 1.8mg | Fiber: 4g | Carbohydrates: 21g | Sugar: 15g

Baked Barley Porridge with Cheddar Cheese, Chives, and Apples

Soy sauce is an unexpected ingredient in this recipe, but adds a welcomed savory flavor and nutty color to the porridge.

INGREDIENTS | SERVES 4

1 tablespoon unsalted butter
1 cup pearled barley
2 cups water
2 cups fat-free milk
½ cup chopped dried apples
1 tablespoon reduced-sodium soy sauce
½ cup shredded reduced-fat Cheddar cheese
2 tablespoons chopped chives

1. Spray an 8" × 8" casserole dish with nonstick spray and preheat the oven to 350°F.

2. Melt the butter over medium heat in a small saucepan, then add the barley and stir frequently until it begins to toast and smell nutty. Immediately add the water and milk; bring to a boil, then turn off the heat.

3. Stir in the apples and soy sauce and pour into the prepared dish. Sprinkle the cheese over the barley mixture and bake, uncovered, on the middle rack until the barley is tender, about 45 minutes.

4. Remove from the oven, stir, and sprinkle the chives over the top. Serve hot.

PER SERVING Calories: 322 | Fat: 5.5g | Protein: 17g | Sodium: 501mg | Fiber: 9g | Carbohydrates: 53g | Sugar: 6.7g

Maple Oven French Toast

This version of French toast easily feeds a crowd and saves you the trouble of individually pan-frying each serving (not to mention saving calories and fat to boot). Look for freshly baked, unsliced loaves of bread in the bakery department of your supermarket.

INGREDIENTS | SERVES 6

1 (16-ounce) loaf soft-crust whole-wheat bread
3 large eggs
1½ cups milk
3 tablespoons maple syrup
2 teaspoons vanilla extract

1. Spray a 9" × 13" casserole dish with nonstick spray. Slice the bread into thick slices, then slice the bread into halves. Shingle the bread slices in overlapping layers in the casserole.

2. Whisk together the eggs, milk, maple syrup, and vanilla and pour the custard over the bread. Cover the casserole dish with plastic wrap and weigh the top down for at least 1 hour and up to 1 day so that the custard can soak into the bread.

3. Preheat the oven to 425°F. Bake the French toast, uncovered, on the middle oven rack until the custard is set and the top of the casserole is golden, 25–30 minutes.

PER SERVING Calories: 283 | Fat: 5.6g | Protein: 12g | Sodium: 474mg | Fiber: 4.6g | Carbohydrates: 48g | Sugar: 6g

Banana and Chocolate Chip Oven French Toast

This is a great make-ahead dish for guests that are arriving early in the morning. Assemble it the night before and pop it into the oven as your guests arrive.

INGREDIENTS | SERVES 6

1 (16-ounce) loaf soft-crust whole-wheat bread
1 ripe banana, peeled and sliced
⅓ cup chocolate chips
3 large eggs
1½ cups milk
3 tablespoons brown sugar
2 teaspoons vanilla extract

1. Spray a 9" × 13" casserole dish with nonstick spray. Slice the bread into thick slices, then slice the bread into halves. Shingle the bread slices with the banana slices and chocolate chips in overlapping layers in the casserole.

2. Whisk together the eggs, milk, brown sugar, and vanilla and pour the custard over the bread. Cover the casserole dish with plastic wrap and weigh the top down for at least 1 hour and up to 1 day so that the custard can soak into the bread.

3. Preheat the oven to 425°F. Bake the French toast, uncovered, on the middle oven rack until the custard is set and the top of the casserole is golden, 25–30 minutes.

PER SERVING Calories: 366 | Fat: 9.2g | Protein: 12g | Sodium: 476mg | Fiber: 5.3g | Carbohydrates: 62g | Sugar: 16g

Country Breakfast Casserole with Vegetarian Sausage

Vegetarian breakfast sausage is found in the refrigerator section of the natural groceries aisle in your supermarket. Lightlife's Gimme Lean is a brand of ground sausage that's easy to crumble, but other brands will work just as well if you break them up with a few pulses in the food processor.

INGREDIENTS | SERVES 6

2 tablespoons olive oil

1 large sweet onion, diced

1 large green bell pepper, diced

8 ounces vegetarian sausage, crumbled

12 large egg whites

6 large egg yolks

1 cup fat-free milk

2 tablespoons chopped parsley

½ teaspoon salt

¼ teaspoon pepper

½ cup shredded extra-sharp, reduced-fat Cheddar cheese

TVP: Flavor, No Cholesterol

Textured vegetable protein, or textured soy protein, is the main ingredient in most vegetarian sausage brands and many meatless "meat" products. Though it is typically made from defatted soy flour, other ingredients may be added depending on the brand. It is naturally cholesterol-free (because it is a vegetarian product) and easily assumes the flavor of whatever seasonings you add to it.

1. Preheat the oven to 375°F and lightly spray a 9" × 13" casserole dish with nonstick spray.

2. Heat 1 tablespoon of the olive oil over medium-high heat in a nonstick skillet and sauté the onion and pepper until softened, about 5 minutes. Spread the vegetable mixture on the bottom of the casserole dish in an even layer.

3. Heat the remaining 1 tablespoon oil over medium-high heat in the skillet and sauté the vegetarian sausage until lightly golden, breaking up large pieces with the back of a wooden spoon, about 10 minutes. Spread the sausage over vegetable mixture in an even layer.

4. Whisk the egg whites, yolks, milk, parsley, salt, and pepper together in a large bowl. Pour over the vegetables and sausage, then sprinkle cheese on top.

5. Bake the casserole, uncovered, on the middle rack until it is set in the center, 45–50 minutes.

PER SERVING Calories: 300 | Fat: 17g | Protein: 26g | Sodium: 976mg | Fiber: 2g | Carbohydrates: 10g | Sugar: 2g

Spinach and Mushroom Oven Omelet

Serve this hearty omelet with toasted whole-grain bread and fresh fruit. For an extra kick of flavor, sprinkle a few tablespoons of chopped chives over the top before serving.

INGREDIENTS | SERVES 6

2 tablespoons olive oil

1 (16-ounce) package button mushrooms, sliced

3 scallions, thinly sliced

8 ounces frozen spinach, thawed, squeezed, and chopped

12 large egg whites

6 large egg yolks

1 cup fat-free milk

½ teaspoon salt

½ teaspoon pepper

1. Preheat the oven to 375°F and lightly spray a 9" × 13" casserole dish with nonstick spray.

2. Heat 1 tablespoon of the olive oil over medium-high heat in a nonstick skillet and add half of the mushrooms. Cook them without moving until golden on one side, about 7 minutes, then stir. Continue cooking until softened, then add half the scallions. Remove the mixture to the prepared casserole dish. Repeat with remaining olive oil, mushrooms, and scallions.

3. Stir the spinach into the mushroom and scallion mixture.

4. Whisk the egg whites, yolks, milk, salt, and pepper together in a large bowl. Pour over the vegetables and stir gently to combine.

5. Bake the omelet, uncovered, on the middle rack until it is set in the center, 45–50 minutes.

PER SERVING Calories: 191 | Fat: 11g | Protein: 18g | Sodium: 383mg | Fiber: 2g | Carbohydrates: 5.8g | Sugar: 2g

Broccoli and Cheese Strata

Do not use regular whole-wheat sandwich bread in this recipe or the strata will lack flavor and be mushy. You may substitute a whole-wheat French baguette with the crust removed for the whole-grain artisan bread.

INGREDIENTS | SERVES 6

2 tablespoons olive oil

3 large shallots, minced

2 garlic cloves, minced

10 ounces frozen broccoli, thawed and chopped

6 large egg whites

3 large egg yolks

¾ cup fat-free milk

¼ teaspoon salt

¼ teaspoon pepper

4 cups lightly toasted whole-grain artisan bread, cubed

½ cup reduced-fat shredded Cheddar cheese

¼ cup grated Parmesan cheese

Whole Grains

Don't be misled into thinking all brown or tan breads are made from whole grains—often coloring is added to improve their appearance. Whole-grain flours are made from the entire grain seed: the bran, the endosperm, and the germ. Check the nutrition facts panel to make sure that the first ingredient on the list is a whole-grain flour.

1. Spray an 8" × 8" casserole dish with nonstick spray. Heat the olive oil in a large nonstick skillet over medium heat and sauté the shallot until it is translucent and softened, 7–10 minutes. Add the garlic and sauté until it just starts to turn golden, about 1 minute.

2. Remove the pan from the heat and stir in the broccoli. Allow the mixture to cool completely before proceeding with the next step.

3. Whisk together the egg whites, egg yolks, milk, salt, and pepper in a large bowl. Stir in the bread cubes, Cheddar and Parmesan cheeses, and cooled broccoli. Pour the mixture into the prepared casserole dish and cover tightly with plastic wrap.

4. Place a heavy weight on top of the strata so that the custard mixture can soak into the bread. Refrigerate for at least 1 hour and up to 1 day.

5. When ready to bake the strata, preheat the oven to 325°F. Place the strata on the middle rack and bake until the center is set and cooked through, about 1 hour.

PER SERVING Calories: 230 | Fat: 11g | Protein: 16g | Sodium: 479mg | Fiber: 2g | Carbohydrates: 18g | Sugar: 1g

Tomato, Basil, and Parmesan Strata

Breakfast stratas actually benefit from time spent in the refrigerator—the bread needs to soak up the custard, so they are an easy choice to make the night before a brunch. All you need to do is pop them in the oven the next morning, and you'll have your hands free for other tasks.

INGREDIENTS | SERVES 6

2 tablespoons olive oil

1 small onion, minced

2 garlic cloves

6 large egg whites

3 large egg yolks

¾ cup fat-free milk

½ teaspoon salt

¼ teaspoon pepper

4 cups cubed whole-wheat baguette

½ cup grated Parmesan cheese

½ cup chopped and reconstituted sun-dried tomatoes

¼ cup chopped basil

Reconstituting Sun-Dried Tomatoes

Sun-dried tomatoes are sunny and bright, and as close to pure concentrated tomato flavor as you can get. Before you use them (unless they are packed in oil), you must reconstitute them. Place them in a heat-proof bowl and pour boiling water over top. Allow them to soak for 10 minutes or until softened, then drain before proceeding with the recipe.

1. Spray an 8" × 8" casserole dish with nonstick spray. Heat the olive oil in a large nonstick skillet over medium heat and sauté the onion until it is translucent and softened, 7–10 minutes. Add the garlic and sauté until it just starts to turn golden, about 1 minute. Remove the pan from heat and allow to cool.

2. Whisk together the egg whites, egg yolks, milk, salt, and pepper in a large bowl. Stir in the bread cubes, Parmesan cheese, tomatoes, and basil. Pour the mixture into the prepared casserole dish and cover tightly with plastic wrap.

3. Place a heavy weight on top of the strata so that the custard mixture can soak into the bread. Refrigerate for at least 1 hour and up to 1 day.

4. When ready to bake the strata, preheat the oven to 325°F. Place the strata on the middle rack and bake until the center is set and cooked through, about 1 hour.

PER SERVING Calories: 214 | Fat: 11g | Protein: 13g | Sodium: 607mg | Fiber: 1.6g | Carbohydrates: 15g | Sugar: 2.9g

Savory Brown Rice Breakfast Pilaf

Serve this as an alternative to high-fat hash brown potatoes alongside egg dishes or tofu scrambles. For a different flavor, add chopped chives, cilantro, or chervil just before serving.

INGREDIENTS | SERVES 6

1 cup short-grain brown rice

¼ cup slivered almonds

2 cups chicken broth

1 cup water

1 tablespoon olive oil

¼ teaspoon salt

¼ cup grated Parmesan cheese

2 tablespoons parsley

1. Spray an 8" × 8" casserole dish with nonstick spray and preheat the oven to 375°F. Spread the rice and the almonds evenly over the bottom of the dish.

2. Bring the chicken broth, water, olive oil, and salt to a boil in a large saucepan. Pour the liquid carefully over the rice mixture and wrap the dish tightly with foil.

3. Bake the pilaf on the middle oven rack until the liquid is absorbed and the rice is tender, about 1 hour.

4. Sprinkle the Parmesan and parsley over the rice and fluff gently with a fork. Re-cover dish with foil and allow the rice to sit for 5 minutes before serving.

PER SERVING Calories: 178 | Fat: 5.7g | Protein: 4.2g | Sodium: 347g | Fiber: 1.1g | Carbohydrates: 8.8g | Sugar: 0.23g

Vegan Vanilla Breakfast Brown Rice Casserole

Serve this slightly sweet casserole with blueberries and sliced bananas for a hearty and warming breakfast. You may substitute soymilk or almond milk in this recipe for the rice milk with equally good results.

INGREDIENTS | SERVES 4

1 cup short-grain brown rice

¼ cup chopped hazelnuts, toasted

½ cup golden raisins

1½ teaspoons grated orange zest

½ teaspoon cinnamon

2 cups vanilla rice milk

1 cup water

¼ teaspoon salt

Rice Milk Nutrition

Rice milk works as a substitute for cow's milk in many cooking applications, but it has a slightly different nutritional makeup. Rice milk is lower in protein, fat, calcium, and calories, but has more carbohydrates. Look for fortified brands in either the dairy case or the boxed-milk aisle of your grocery store.

1. Spray an 8" × 8" casserole dish with nonstick spray and preheat the oven to 375°F. Spread the rice and hazelnuts evenly over the bottom of the dish. Sprinkle with the raisins, orange zest, and cinnamon.

2. Bring the rice milk, water, and salt to a boil in a large saucepan. Pour the liquid carefully over the rice mixture and wrap the dish tightly with foil.

3. Bake the pilaf on the middle oven rack until the liquid is absorbed and the rice is tender, about 1 hour.

4. Fluff the casserole with a fork, re-cover with foil, and allow the rice to sit for 5 minutes before serving.

PER SERVING Calories: 339 | Fat: 7.4g | Protein: 7.8g | Sodium: 217mg | Fiber: 3.8g | Carbohydrates: 35g | Sugar: 14g

Savory Fontina and Turkey Bacon Brown Rice Casserole

*Fontina is an intensely flavored Italian cheese with supreme melting capabilities.
Serve this casserole as a side to a main course oven omelet.*

INGREDIENTS | SERVES 6

1 teaspoon olive oil

¼ cup chopped turkey bacon

1 small onion, minced

1 cup short-grain brown rice

2 cups chicken broth

1 cup water

1 teaspoon crumbled dried thyme

¼ teaspoon salt

½ cup fontina cheese

1 tablespoon chopped parsley

1. Spray an 8" × 8" casserole dish with nonstick spray and preheat the oven to 375°F.

2. Heat olive oil over medium heat in a small nonstick skillet and add turkey bacon. Cook, stirring often, until bacon crisps and browns, 7–10 minutes. Remove bacon with slotted spoon to paper towels to drain.

3. Remove all but 1 teaspoon of fat from skillet and add the onion. Cook over medium heat, stirring frequently, until the onion is just translucent, about 5 minutes. Add rice and stir to coat with fat. Sauté for about 3 minutes more until rice begins to smell slightly toasty.

4. Spread the rice mixture in an even layer in prepared casserole dish. Sprinkle turkey bacon over the top.

5. Bring the chicken broth, water, thyme, and salt to a boil in a large saucepan. Pour the liquid carefully over the rice mixture and wrap the dish tightly with foil.

6. Bake the pilaf on the middle oven rack until the liquid is absorbed and the rice is tender, about 1 hour.

7. Sprinkle the fontina cheese and parsley over the rice and fluff gently with a fork. Re-cover dish with foil and allow the rice to sit for 5 minutes before serving.

PER SERVING Calories: 184 | Fat: 5.2g | Protein: 5.5g | Sodium: 430mg | Fiber: 0.67g | Carbohydrates: 8.3g | Sugar: 0.22g

Huevos Rancheros Breakfast Casserole

This is a quick and easy version of the classic dish.
Serve with warmed corn or whole-wheat tortillas and reduced-fat sour cream.

INGREDIENTS | SERVES 6

1 tablespoon safflower or sunflower oil

1 large onion

1 green bell pepper

1 (14.5-ounce) can black beans, rinsed and drained

½ cup mild or medium jarred salsa

12 large egg whites

6 large egg yolks

1 cup fat-free milk

3 tablespoons chopped cilantro

½ teaspoon salt

½ cup shredded extra-sharp reduced-fat Cheddar cheese

Tex-Mex

Tex-Mex food is a combination of Spanish and Mexican cuisine as adopted by Texans. It first became popularized in the 1970s, though recipes for Tex-Mex dishes were published in cookbooks as early as the 1940s.

1. Preheat the oven to 375°F and lightly spray a 9" × 13" casserole dish with nonstick spray.

2. Heat the oil over medium-high heat in a nonstick skillet and sauté the onion and pepper until softened, about 5 minutes. Spread the vegetable mixture on the bottom of the casserole dish in an even layer. Spread the beans, then the salsa, over the vegetables.

3. Whisk the egg whites, egg yolks, milk, cilantro, and salt together in a large bowl. Pour into the prepared casserole dish, then sprinkle cheese on top.

4. Bake the casserole, uncovered, on the middle rack until it is set in the center, 45–50 minutes.

PER SERVING Calories: 377 | Fat: 9.9g | Protein: 30g | Sodium: 502mg | Fiber: 9g | Carbohydrates: 40g | Sugar: 1.2g

Breakfast Quinoa with Maple, Walnuts, and Apples

*Chopped dried apples and crunchy walnuts give this breakfast porridge a toothsome bite.
Enjoy it with a fruit salad or a bowl of fresh blueberries.*

INGREDIENTS | SERVES 4

1 cup quinoa
½ cup dried apples, chopped
½ cup chopped walnuts
¼ cup maple syrup
½ teaspoon cinnamon
¼ teaspoon nutmeg
¼ teaspoon salt
2 cups fat-free milk

1. Preheat the oven to 350°F and spray a 9" × 9" casserole dish lightly with nonstick spray.

2. Place the quinoa in a dry skillet and stir it over medium heat until it smells toasty, about 2 minutes.

3. Pour the quinoa into the prepared casserole dish and stir in the apples, walnuts, maple syrup, cinnamon, nutmeg, and salt.

4. Heat the milk to a bare simmer on the stovetop or in the microwave, then stir into the quinoa mixture.

5. Cover the casserole tightly with aluminum foil and bake until the quinoa is cooked through, about 45 minutes. Let the casserole sit for about 5 minutes before serving.

PER SERVING Calories: 339 | Fat: 8.5g | Protein: 12g | Sodium: 223mg | Fiber: 4.6g | Carbohydrates: 56g | Sugar: 17g

Sweet Potato Hash

Sweet potatoes and savory sausage combine to make a wholesome breakfast meal.
For a variation, substitute zucchini, yellow squash, or even carrots and celery for the bell peppers.

INGREDIENTS | SERVES 4

3 medium sweet potatoes, diced into ½"
pieces
2 teaspoons olive oil
6 ounces bulk chicken breakfast sausage
1 red bell pepper, diced into ½" pieces
1 green bell pepper, diced into ½"
pieces
6 scallions, thinly sliced
2 cloves garlic, minced
½ teaspoon cumin
¼ teaspoon salt
⅛ teaspoon pepper

Knife Safety

Believe it or not, a sharp knife is safer than one that is dull. Sharp knives require less pressure to slice though food than dull knives, and using one reduces the chance that the food will slip out from under the knife. Have your knives sharpened professionally a few times a year or invest in a sharpening stone and keep the blades sharpened yourself.

1. Preheat the oven to 375°F and spray a 9" × 9" casserole dish lightly with nonstick spray.

2. Place the sweet potatoes in the prepared casserole dish and heat the oil in a large skillet over medium-high heat. When hot, add the sausage and cook, breaking up clumps with the back of a spoon, until the sausage is browned, 7–10 minutes.

3. Stir in the bell peppers, scallions, garlic, cumin, salt, and pepper. Cook, stirring frequently, until the vegetables just begin to soften, about 5 minutes.

4. Pour the skillet contents into the prepared casserole dish and toss with the sweet potatoes. Bake, stirring a few times during cooking, until the sweet potatoes are tender and beginning to brown, 25–30 minutes.

PER SERVING Calories: 212 | Fat: 8.2g | Protein: 8.4g | Sodium: 640mg | Fiber: 4g | Carbohydrates: 27g | Sugar: 4.7g

Appetizers and Snacks

Baked Feta Cheese

For a spicy variation, you can add a teaspoon of chili pepper flakes to this recipe.

INGREDIENTS | SERVES 4

2 tablespoons extra-virgin olive oil

1 medium onion, sliced

1 large green bell pepper, seeded and chopped

1 large red bell pepper, seeded and chopped

½ pound Greek feta cheese (1 thick slice)

1 teaspoon dried oregano

Fresh ground pepper, to taste

1. Preheat the oven to 350°F and spray a small casserole dish lightly with nonstick spray.

2. Heat the oil in a medium nonstick skillet over medium-high heat. When hot, add the onion and peppers and cook, stirring frequently, until soft.

3. Place feta in the prepared casserole dish. Add the onion and peppers and sprinkle with the oregano and pepper. Cover with foil and bake for 15 minutes. Serve hot with fresh crusty bread or warm pita bread.

PER SERVING Calories: 235 | Fat: 19g | Protein: 9g | Sodium: 640mg | Fiber: 1g | Carbohydrates: 8g | Sugar: 3g

Light Lemony Herb Shrimp

This recipe is a cinch to put together and can double as a main course if served over pasta or rice. Use the Basil Pesto recipe in Chapter 14 or save time by using a store-bought version.

INGREDIENTS | SERVES 6

1½ pounds medium shrimp, peeled and deveined

3 tablespoons lemon juice

2 tablespoons lemon zest

2 tablespoons pesto

¼ teaspoon chili flakes

1. Preheat the oven to 450°F and lightly spray a 9" × 13" casserole dish lightly with nonstick spray.

2. Toss the shrimp together with the lemon juice, zest, pesto, and chili flakes, then pour into the prepared casserole dish.

3. Bake the shrimp until they are cooked through and pink, about 15 minutes.

PER SERVING Calories: 105 | Fat: 2.9g | Protein: 18g | Sodium: 126mg | Fiber: 0g | Carbohydrates: 2g | Sugar: 0g

Sfogato (Aegean Omelet)

For Greeks, eggs are not limited to breakfast dishes; they often make an appearance at the lunch or dinner table as an appetizer or main course.

INGREDIENTS | SERVES 4

2 tablespoons extra-virgin olive oil

1 small onion, finely diced

4 large eggs

4 large egg whites

4 tablespoons all-purpose flour

¼ cup bread crumbs

2 tablespoons fresh mint, finely chopped

½ cup crumbled Greek feta cheese

¼ teaspoon salt

⅛ teaspoon pepper

1 tablespoon dried thyme

1. Preheat the oven to 350°F and spray an 8" × 8" casserole dish lightly with nonstick spray.

2. Heat the oil in a medium nonstick skillet over medium-high heat. When hot, add the onion and cook, stirring frequently, until translucent, about 5 minutes. Remove the pan from the heat and allow the onion to cool slightly.

3. Beat the eggs and egg whites together in a large bowl. Stir in the onion, flour, bread crumbs, mint, feta, salt, pepper, and thyme. Pour the mixture into the prepared casserole dish and bake until the omelet puffs and sets, about 25 minutes.

PER SERVING Calories: 285 | Fat: 19g | Protein: 13g | Sodium: 353mg | Fiber: 1g | Carbohydrates: 15g | Sugar: 2g

Vegan Hot Artichoke Spinach Dip

Serve this creamy dip hot with some baguette slices, crackers, pita bread, or sliced bell peppers and jicama. If you want to get fancy, you can carve out a bread bowl for an edible serving dish.

INGREDIENTS | SERVES 8

1 (12-ounce) package frozen spinach, thawed

1 (14-ounce) can artichoke hearts, drained

¼ cup vegan margarine

¼ cup flour

2 cups soymilk

½ cup nutritional yeast

1 teaspoon garlic powder

1½ teaspoons onion powder

¼ teaspoon salt

1. Preheat the oven to 350°F and spray a 1½-quart casserole dish lightly with nonstick spray. Pulse the spinach and artichokes together in a food processor until the vegetables are finely chopped, but not puréed.

2. In a medium saucepan, melt the vegan margarine over low heat. Slowly whisk in the flour, 1 tablespoon at a time, stirring constantly to avoid lumps. Whisk in the soymilk, nutritional yeast, garlic powder, onion powder, and salt.

3. Remove the saucepan from the heat and stir in the spinach and artichoke mixture.

4. Transfer the dip to the prepared casserole dish and bake until bubbly, about 20 minutes. Serve hot.

PER SERVING Calories: 134 | Fat: 7g | Protein: 7g | Sodium: 378mg | Fiber: 4g | Carbohydrates: 15g | Sugar: 1g

Traditional Artichoke Spinach Dip

For a slightly different flavor, try sprinkling a bit of low-fat mozzarella cheese on the dip instead of the bread crumbs.

INGREDIENTS | SERVES 4

1 tablespoon olive oil

2 cloves garlic, minced

1½ cups part-skim ricotta cheese

½ teaspoon thyme

1 teaspoon lemon zest

½ teaspoon cayenne pepper

1 (9-ounce) box frozen artichokes, thawed and drained

8 ounces frozen spinach, thawed and drained

¼ cup grated Parmesan cheese

½ teaspoon salt

¼ cup bread crumbs

1. Preheat the oven to 350°F and spray a 1½-quart casserole dish lightly with nonstick spray.

2. Heat the olive oil in a small nonstick skillet over medium heat. When hot, add the garlic and cook until fragrant and pale golden, about 1 minute. Remove the skillet from the heat and allow the garlic to cool.

3. Pulse the cooled garlic, ricotta cheese, thyme, lemon zest, and cayenne pepper in a food processor until creamy.

4. Add the artichokes, spinach, Parmesan, and salt; pulse again, but do not overblend.

5. Transfer the artichoke mixture into the prepared casserole dish and sprinkle with the bread crumbs.

6. Bake the dip until it is hot and bubbly and the bread crumbs are browned, about 20 minutes.

PER SERVING Calories: 255 | Fat: 14g | Protein: 18g | Sodium: 623mg | Fiber: 4.6g | Carbohydrates: 18g | Sugar: 1g

Feta and Roasted Red Pepper Piquante

*Serve this dip as part of an appetizer table with some warm pita bread,
marinated olives, and grilled vegetables.*

INGREDIENTS | SERVES 6

½ pound Greek feta cheese

1–1½ tablespoons dried chili pepper flakes

2 roasted red peppers

4 tablespoons extra-virgin olive oil

1 teaspoon fresh ground black pepper

Love of Olive Oil

The most characteristic aspect of the Mediterranean diet is the ubiquitous presence of the olive and its juice. It's used in the foods that comprise the traditional cuisines that evolved under its influence.

1. Preheat the oven to 350°F and spray a small casserole dish lightly with nonstick spray.

2. Crumble the feta into a food processor and add the chili pepper flakes. (This dip ought to be spicy but not red-hot, so adjust the amount of chili pepper flakes accordingly.)

3. Remove the seeds and skins from the roasted red peppers and add to the food processor along with the olive oil and 1 or 2 pinches of pepper. Purée until smooth, then pour mixture into prepared casserole dish.

4. Bake the cheese spread until just warm and beginning to bubble, 20–25 minutes.

PER SERVING Calories: 190 | Fat: 17g | Protein: 5g | Sodium: 510mg | Fiber: 0g | Carbohydrates: 4g | Sugar: 3g

Vegetarian Cranberry "Meatballs"

This appetizer makes a festive addition to the holiday table. The "meatballs" are already cooked, so it's just a matter of heating everything through. What could be easier?

INGREDIENTS | SERVES 12

¼ cup chili sauce

1 recipe Whole Berry Cranberry Sauce (see sidebar recipe)

1½ cups dark brown sugar

1 tablespoon ginger preserves

¾ cup orange juice

1 (28-ounce) package frozen vegetarian "meatballs" (about 24 meatballs)

Whole Berry Cranberry Sauce

Combine 12 ounces fresh cranberries, 1 cup freshly squeezed orange juice, 1 teaspoon orange zest, and ½ cup brown sugar in a medium saucepan. Cook over medium heat, stirring occasionally, until the cranberries start to pop, about 10 minutes.

1. Preheat the oven to 325°F.

2. Combine the chili sauce, Whole Berry Cranberry Sauce, dark brown sugar, ginger preserves, and orange juice in a 3-quart Dutch oven. Bring to a simmer over low heat and add the vegetarian "meatballs."

3. Stir to combine and cover. Bake until the meatballs are heated through and the sauce thickens slightly, about 30 minutes.

PER SERVING Calories: 280 | Fat: 6g | Protein: 14g | Sodium: 383mg | Fiber: 3.4g | Carbohydrates: 44g | Sugar: 38g

Bubbly Black Bean and Cheese Dip

Serve this dip with crispy tortilla chips. For an extra bit of richness, swirl in a spoonful of low-fat sour cream just before serving.

INGREDIENTS | SERVES 8

2 (14.5-ounce) cans black beans, drained and rinsed (about 3 cups)

¼ cup low-sodium chicken broth

¼ cup grated pepper jack cheese

2 cloves garlic, grated

1 tablespoon lime juice

1 tablespoon chopped oregano

¼ teaspoon salt

⅛ teaspoon pepper

½ cup chunky salsa

1. Preheat the oven to 350°F and spray a 1½-quart casserole dish lightly with nonstick spray.

2. Combine the beans, broth, cheese, garlic, lime juice, oregano, salt, and pepper in the bowl of a food processor. Process the mixture until it is very smooth, then stir in the salsa.

3. Pour the dip into the prepared casserole dish. Cover with aluminum foil and bake the dip on the middle oven rack until warmed through, about 25 minutes. Stir the dip just before serving.

PER SERVING Calories: 163 | Fat: 1g | Protein: 11g | Sodium: 163mg | Fiber: 6.8g | Carbohydrates: 28g | Sugar: 1g

Baked Tuscan White Bean Dip with Garlic and Rosemary

For extra flavor, stir seeded and chopped tomatoes, parsley, or a pinch of red pepper flakes into the dip before baking. Serve with toasted pita chips, crudités, or crostini.

INGREDIENTS | SERVES 8

2 (14.5-ounce) cans white beans, drained and rinsed (about 3 cups)

½ cup low-sodium chicken broth

¼ cup grated Parmesan cheese

3 tablespoons extra-virgin olive oil

2 cloves garlic, grated

1 tablespoon lemon juice

2 teaspoons minced rosemary

¼ teaspoon salt

⅛ teaspoon pepper

1. Preheat the oven to 350°F and spray a 1½-quart casserole dish lightly with nonstick spray.

2. Combine the white beans, broth, Parmesan, 2 tablespoons olive oil, garlic, lemon juice, rosemary, salt, and pepper in the bowl of a food processor. Process the mixture until it is very smooth.

3. Pour the dip into the prepared casserole dish and drizzle the remaining tablespoon of olive oil over the top. Cover with aluminum foil and bake the dip on the middle oven rack until warmed through, about 25 minutes. Stir the dip just before serving.

PER SERVING Calories: 194 | Fat: 6.4g | Protein: 9.4g | Sodium: 161mg | Fiber: 5.8g | Carbohydrates: 26g | Sugar: 0g

Hot Lemony Hummus

To make this dish vegetarian, simply substitute an equal amount of vegetable broth for the chicken broth. Sprinkle with fresh chopped parsley or chives for an elegant presentation.

INGREDIENTS | SERVES 8

2 (14.5-ounce) cans chickpeas, drained and rinsed (about 3 cups)

½ cup chicken broth

5 tablespoons extra-virgin olive oil

2 cloves garlic, grated

2 tablespoons lemon juice

1 tablespoon lemon zest

¼ teaspoon salt

⅛ teaspoon pepper

1. Preheat the oven to 350°F and spray a 1½-quart casserole dish lightly with nonstick spray.

2. Combine the chickpeas, broth, 4 tablespoons olive oil, garlic, lemon juice, lemon zest, salt, and pepper in the bowl of a food processor. Process the mixture until it is very smooth.

3. Pour the hummus into the prepared casserole dish and drizzle the remaining tablespoon of olive oil over the top. Cover with aluminum foil and bake the dip on the middle oven rack until warmed through, about 25 minutes. Stir the dip just before serving.

PER SERVING Calories: 200 | Fat: 9.6g | Protein: 5.4g | Sodium: 419mg | Fiber: 4.2g | Carbohydrates: 24g | Sugar: 0g

Spanish Garlic and Tomato Shrimp

This classic Spanish-style appetizer is usually served swimming in olive oil and garlic. This recipe is lightened with the addition of tomatoes and flavored with just a hint of olive oil and smoky Spanish paprika. Serve with crispy Melba toasts or pita chips.

INGREDIENTS | SERVES 6

1 (28-ounce) can diced tomatoes, drained

3 cloves garlic, minced

2 tablespoons extra-virgin olive oil

1 teaspoon smoked Spanish paprika

½ teaspoon salt

1 pound popcorn shrimp, peeled and deveined

¼ cup chopped fresh Italian parsley

1 tablespoon chopped fresh oregano

1. Preheat the oven to 450°F and lightly spray a 9" × 9" casserole dish with nonstick spray.

2. Add the tomatoes, garlic, olive oil, paprika, and salt to the prepared casserole dish and bake on the middle oven rack until the tomatoes are hot and begin to soften.

3. Stir in the shrimp, parsley, and oregano. Bake until the shrimp are fully cooked, about 20 minutes.

PER SERVING Calories: 144 | Fat: 6.1g | Protein: 14g | Sodium: 453mg | Fiber: 2.7g | Carbohydrates: 10g | Sugar: 0g

Roasted Tomatoes with Bright Herbs

The tomatoes in this recipe become so concentrated and sweet that even winter tomatoes end up tasting good! Serve on slices of toasted baguette.

INGREDIENTS | SERVES 8

5 medium tomatoes, cored and quartered

4 cloves garlic, minced

1 tablespoon minced oregano

1 tablespoon minced thyme

¼ cup olive oil

½ teaspoon kosher salt

3 tablespoons chopped fresh parsley

1. Preheat the oven to 450°F and lightly spray a 9" × 13" casserole dish with nonstick spray.

2. Toss the tomatoes, garlic, oregano, thyme, olive oil, and salt together in a large bowl. Pour the mixture into the prepared casserole dish and spread out evenly.

3. Bake, uncovered, until the tomatoes release their juices and become very soft, about 2 hours. Sprinkle with the parsley and serve.

PER SERVING Calories: 78 | Fat: 7g | Protein: 1g | Sodium: 150mg | Fiber: 1g | Carbohydrates: 4g | Sugar: 2.7g

Chicken Meatballs in a Tropical Sauce

This is a festive appetizer for a party! Serve leftovers with short-grain rice for a quick and easy meal.

INGREDIENTS | SERVES 15

MEATBALLS

2 pounds ground chicken breast

1 teaspoon ground ginger

½ cup bread crumbs

1 egg

¼ cup minced onion

2 cloves garlic, grated

SAUCE

1 tablespoon vegetable oil

1 onion, minced

1 tablespoon minced jalapeño pepper

1 tablespoon grated fresh ginger

1 cup pineapple juice

⅓ cup brown sugar

¼ cup teriyaki sauce

¼ cup ponzu sauce

3 tablespoons lime juice

1 tablespoon cornstarch

4 cups frozen pineapple chunks

1. Preheat the oven to 450°F. Line two rimmed baking sheets with foil and spray each lightly with nonstick spray.

2. Mix the chicken, ground ginger, bread crumbs, egg, minced onion, and garlic together in a large bowl. Form the mixture into 1" balls and divide balls evenly between the baking sheets. Bake the meatballs until they just begin to color, 10–15 minutes.

3. While the meatballs are cooking, heat the oil over medium-high heat in a 3-quart Dutch oven. When hot, add the onion, jalapeño, and ginger. Cook, stirring often, until the onion becomes translucent, about 5 minutes. Add the pineapple juice, brown sugar,, teriyaki sauce, and ponzu sauce. Mix the lime juice together with the cornstarch and whisk into the sauce. Stir in the pineapple chunks and bring the sauce to a boil.

4. Turn the oven down to 325°F. Add the meatballs to the sauce, stir gently to combine, and cover. Bake the meatballs until they are tender and flavorful, about 40 minutes, stirring to coat them with sauce once or twice during baking.

PER SERVING Calories: 128 | Fat: 2g | Protein: 15g | Sodium: 225mg | Fiber: 1g | Carbohydrates: 16g | Sugar: 12g

Italian Turkey Meatballs

Frozen Italian meatballs make this appetizer a snap to make.
Look for them near the meat products in your grocer's freezer.

INGREDIENTS | SERVES 6

1 tablespoon olive oil
1 small onion, diced
1 carrot, grated
3 cloves garlic, minced
2 tablespoons tomato paste
1 (28-ounce) can crushed tomatoes
¼ teaspoon salt
¼ teaspoon pepper
1 tablespoon chopped fresh basil
12 frozen Italian-style turkey meatballs

Using Tomato Paste

Tomato paste is a thick paste made from skinned, seeded tomatoes. Its concentrated taste enhances flavor without adding extra liquid. When combined with canned tomatoes, the result is a richer-tasting sauce.

1. Preheat the oven to 325°F.

2. Heat the olive oil over medium heat in a 3-quart Dutch oven. When hot, add the onion and carrot and cook, stirring occasionally, until the onion is translucent and the carrot is softened. Add the garlic and cook until fragrant, about 1 minute. Stir in the tomato paste, then add the crushed tomatoes, salt, pepper, and basil.

3. Bring the sauce to a simmer, then add the meatballs. Cover and bake until the meatballs are heated through and the sauce is slightly thickened, about 30 minutes.

PER SERVING Calories: 172 | Fat: 3.5g | Protein: 29g | Sodium: 292mg | Fiber: 3.6g | Carbohydrates: 13g | Sugar: 1.6g

Light and Creamy Swedish Meatballs

All of the flavor and none of the guilt! Serve leftover meatballs over yolk-free egg noodles.

INGREDIENTS | SERVES 20

MEATBALLS
2 thin slices white sandwich bread
½ cup 1% milk
2 pounds 93% lean ground beef
2 cloves garlic, minced
1 egg
¼ teaspoon salt
¼ teaspoon allspice
⅛ teaspoon nutmeg

SAUCE
1 tablespoon butter
⅓ cup all-purpose flour
3 cups low-sodium chicken broth
12 ounces fat-free evaporated milk
¼ teaspoon allspice
⅛ teaspoon nutmeg
¼ teaspoon salt
¼ teaspoon white pepper

Fat-Free Evaporated Milk
Use fat-free evaporated milk in place of cream to help cut calories and fat. Unlike regular milk, evaporated milk does not form a skin when cooked and adds body to a recipe much in the same way as heavy cream.

1. Preheat the oven to 450°F. Line two rimmed baking sheets with foil and spray each lightly with nonstick spray.

2. To make the meatballs, add the bread and milk to a shallow saucepan and cook on low until the milk is absorbed, about 1 minute. Place the bread into a large bowl and add the meat, garlic, egg, salt, allspice, and nutmeg.

3. Form the mixture into 1" balls and divide balls evenly between the baking sheets. Bake the meatballs until they just begin to color, 10–15 minutes. Drain the meatballs on paper towel–lined plates.

4. To make the sauce, while the meatballs are cooking, heat the butter over medium heat in a 3-quart Dutch oven. When melted, add the flour and stir to combine. Slowly stream in the chicken broth, whisking constantly to avoid lumps. Whisk in the evaporated milk, allspice, nutmeg, salt, and pepper. Simmer until the mixture thickens slightly, then remove from heat.

5. Turn the oven down to 325°F. Add the meatballs to the sauce, stir gently to combine, and cover. Bake the meatballs until they are tender and flavorful, about 40 minutes, stirring to coat them with sauce once or twice during baking.

PER SERVING Calories: 132 | Fat: 4.8g | Protein: 16g | Sodium: 196mg | Fiber: 0g | Carbohydrates: 5.7g | Sugar: 0g

Stuffed Grape Leaves

Although there are many versions of grape leaves served across the Mediterranean, these grape leaves are inspired by Greece.

INGREDIENTS | SERVES 30

1 tablespoon olive oil

¾ pound lean ground chicken

1 shallot, minced

¾ cup cooked brown rice

¼ cup minced dill

½ cup lemon juice

2 tablespoons chopped parsley

1 tablespoon chopped mint

1 tablespoon ground fennel

¼ teaspoon freshly ground black pepper

⅛ teaspoon salt

16 ounces jarred grape leaves (about 60 leaves)

2 cups water

Easy Greek-Style Dipping Sauce

In a medium bowl, stir together 1 cup fat-free yogurt and 1 teaspoon each dried oregano, mint, thyme, dill, and ¼ teaspoon white pepper. Stir in 3 tablespoons lemon juice. Refrigerate for 1 hour before serving to blend the flavors.

1. Heat the oil in a large nonstick skillet over medium heat. Add the chicken and shallot and cook, breaking up clumps with the back of a wooden spoon, until the chicken is thoroughly cooked. Drain off any excess fat and allow to cool slightly.

2. Combine the chicken, rice, dill, ¼ cup lemon juice, parsley, mint, fennel, pepper, and salt together in a large bowl.

3. Prepare the grape leaves according to the package instructions. Place a leaf, stem-side up, with the top of the leaf pointing away from you on a clean work surface. Place 1 teaspoon filling in the middle of the leaf. Fold the bottom toward the middle and then fold in the sides. Roll it toward the top to seal. Repeat with remaining leaves and filling.

4. Preheat the oven to 325°F. Place the rolled grape leaves in 2 or 3 layers in a 5-quart Dutch oven. Bring the water to a boil and pour over the grape leaves with the remaining lemon juice.

5. Cover Dutch oven and bake until the grape leaves are steamed and heated through, about 30 minutes. Drain any remaining water from the Dutch oven before serving.

PER SERVING Calories: 45 | Fat: 0.88g | Protein: 3.7g | Sodium: 12mg | Fiber: 1.8g | Carbohydrates: 4.1g | Sugar: 1g

Roasted Pear and Blue Cheese Spread

Serve this sweet and tangy spread on thin slices of toasted whole-grain bread or use it as a condiment to brighten up roast poultry or meat. If you can't find white balsamic vinegar, substitute cider vinegar.

INGREDIENTS | SERVES 10

4 large shallots, thinly sliced

3 tablespoons honey

2 tablespoons white balsamic vinegar

2 tablespoons extra-virgin olive oil

1 tablespoon fresh rosemary

½ teaspoon salt

¼ teaspoon pepper

3 large pears, peeled and cored

⅔ cup crumbled blue cheese

1. Preheat the oven to 350°F and lightly spray the inside of a 1-quart casserole with nonstick spray.

2. Combine the shallots, honey, vinegar, oil, rosemary, salt, and pepper in the casserole dish. Stir to coat the shallots evenly, cover with foil, and bake on the middle oven rack for 1 hour.

3. Chop the pears into small pieces, then add them to the roasted shallots. Stir to combine, replace cover, and bake on the middle rack for 1 hour longer.

4. Remove the casserole from the oven, remove foil, and mash the pears slightly with the back of a fork. Carefully taste and adjust seasoning if necessary.

5. Sprinkle with cheese and bake an additional 15–20 minutes until warmed and melted through.

PER SERVING Calories: 119 | Fat: 5.3g | Protein: 2g | Sodium: 238mg | Fiber: 2g | Carbohydrates: 17g | Sugar: 13g

CHAPTER 4

Vegetables

Eggplant Casserole

Jalapeño peppers add a touch of fire to an otherwise mellow dish.
For even more spice, add a dash or two of hot sauce.

INGREDIENTS | SERVES 6

1 medium eggplant
½ teaspoon garlic salt
½ cup canned jalapeño peppers
2 cups canned tomato sauce
½ cup low-fat sour cream
½ teaspoon ground cumin
1½ cups grated Cheddar cheese

1. Preheat the oven to 350°F.

2. Remove the stem from the eggplant and slice into ½"-thick rounds. Arrange the rounds in a 9" × 9" lightly greased baking pan. Sprinkle with the garlic salt.

3. Combine the jalapeños, tomato sauce, sour cream, and cumin; mix well. Pour over the eggplant rounds. Layer the cheese over the top.

4. Bake for 45–60 minutes or until the cheese is melted and the eggplant is tender.

PER SERVING Calories: 219 | Fat: 14g | Protein: 11g | Sodium: 302mg | Fiber: 4.1g | Carbohydrates: 12g | Sugar: 5.3g

Amish-Style Turnips

Turnips are wonderful autumn vegetables that are sadly often overlooked.
Serve this alongside a roast chicken and green salad for a cozy cool-weather meal.

INGREDIENTS | SERVES 6

1 slice whole-wheat bread
1 tablespoon butter, melted
½ cup low-fat milk
1 egg
3 cups turnips, cooked and mashed

1. Preheat the oven to 375°F and spray a 1-quart casserole dish with nonstick spray.

2. Place bread in food processor. Using the pulse setting, process until bread is the consistency of fine bread crumbs.

3. In a medium bowl, mix together bread crumbs, butter, milk, and egg. Add cooked turnip; mix well.

4. Turn mixture into prepared casserole dish. Bake, uncovered, until lightly browned, 30–35 minutes.

PER SERVING Calories: 71 | Fat: 3.3g | Protein: 3g | Sodium: 102mg | Fiber: 1.6g | Carbohydrates: 7.7g | Sugar: 2.8g

Vegan Green Bean Casserole

Shop for a vegan cream-of-mushroom soup to use in your traditional holiday recipe, or try this easy homemade vegan version. Delish!

INGREDIENTS | SERVES 4

1 (12-ounce) bag frozen green beans
¾ cup sliced mushrooms
2 tablespoons vegan margarine
2 tablespoons flour
1½ cups soymilk
1 tablespoon Dijon mustard
½ teaspoon garlic powder
½ teaspoon salt
¼ teaspoon sage
¼ teaspoon oregano
¼ teaspoon black pepper
1½ cups French-fried onions

1. Preheat the oven to 375°F. Place green beans and mushrooms in a large casserole dish.

2. Melt vegan margarine over low heat. Stir in flour until pasty and combined. Add soymilk, mustard, garlic powder, salt, sage, oregano, and pepper, stirring continuously to combine until thickened.

3. Pour sauce over mushrooms and green beans and top with French-fried onions.

4. Bake for 16–18 minutes until onions are lightly browned and toasted.

PER SERVING Calories: 279 | Fat: 18g | Protein: 5g | Sodium: 642mg | Fiber: 3g | Carbohydrates: 19g | Sugar: 1.8g

Corn Casserole

This corn casserole recipe is silky and creamy—without the cream! The natural starch from the corn, egg, and nonfat dry milk contains less fat and builds a luscious base that's just as satisfying as the cream traditionally used in corn casseroles.

INGREDIENTS | SERVES 2

1 tablespoon onion, finely chopped
1 tablespoon green or red bell pepper, finely chopped
1 cup frozen or fresh corn kernels
⅛ teaspoon ground mace
Dash ground white or black pepper
¾ cup skim milk
¼ cup nonfat dry milk
1 egg
1 teaspoon butter

1. Preheat the oven to 325°F and spray 3-cup casserole dish with nonstick spray. In a medium bowl, combine the onion, bell pepper, corn, mace, and pepper; toss to mix.

2. In a blender, combine the skim milk, dry milk, egg, and butter, and process until mixed. Pour over the corn mixture and toss to mix. Pour the entire mixture into the prepared casserole dish. Bake for 1 hour or until set.

PER SERVING Calories: 188 | Fat: 3g | Protein: 11g | Sodium: 133mg | Fiber: 2.5g | Carbohydrates: 32.5g | Sugar: 5.2g

Yams with Coconut Milk

This vegetable dish has an Afro-Caribbean flavor and is perfect with a fish or beef curry.
The nuts add healthy fat, fiber, and a bit of protein.

INGREDIENTS | SERVES 4; SERVING SIZE: 1 CUP

3 pounds sweet potatoes

1 cup coconut milk

¼ cup shredded coconut

½ cup chopped macadamia nuts

Yams Versus Sweet Potatoes

Yams and sweet potatoes are so close that they can be used interchangeably in cooking. Sweet potatoes are a rich orange inside and have a deeper brown skin. They're also by far the sweeter of the two. Both tubers are very high in soluble fiber. To add extra fiber, sprinkle them with nuts, cook them with apples, or mix them with sweet green peas.

1. Preheat the oven to 350°F and spray an 8" × 8" casserole dish with nonstick spray.

2. Peel sweet potatoes and slice them into ½"-thick rounds.

3. Overlap the sweet potato slices in prepared casserole dish.

4. Pour the coconut milk over the sweet potatoes, then sprinkle them with shredded coconut and macadamia nuts.

5. Bake, uncovered, for 1 hour.

PER SERVING Calories: 296 | Fat: 14g | Protein: 5.1g | Sodium: 106mg | Fiber: 6.5g | Carbohydrates: 40g | Sugar: 7.9g

Zucchini Onion Casserole

For added fiber and protein, sneak in ½ cup of ground walnuts and mix them into the bread crumbs.

INGREDIENTS | SERVES 8; SERVING SIZE: 1½ CUPS

2½ cups thinly sliced sweet onion

2½ cups sliced zucchini

2 medium-large sliced ripe red tomatoes

10 leaves fresh basil

1 tablespoon dried rosemary

Salt and pepper, to taste

2 cups whole-wheat croutons

1 cup shredded Cheddar cheese

1. Preheat the oven to 350°F and lightly spray a 3-quart casserole dish with nonstick spray.

2. Layer half of each of the sweet onion, zucchini, and tomatoes. Season the vegetables with herbs, salt, and pepper.

3. Scatter half of the croutons over the seasoned vegetables and half of the Cheddar cheese over the croutons.

4. Repeat the layering with the remaining vegetables, season with salt and pepper, and sprinkle the remaining croutons and Cheddar cheese on top.

5. Cover with lid or aluminum foil and bake for 1 hour. Serve hot.

PER SERVING Calories: 138 | Fat: 6.2g | Protein: 6.7g | Sodium: 167mg | Fiber: 3.5g | Sugar: 6.4g

Veggie-Stuffed Zucchini

Stuff the zucchini with any vegetables you like.
The vegetables in this recipe can easily be substituted with your favorites.

INGREDIENTS | SERVES 4

4 medium zucchini
1 teaspoon salt
2 teaspoons vegan margarine
2 teaspoons vegetable oil
1 onion, chopped
1 clove garlic, crushed
½ cup chickpeas
2 tablespoons flour
1 teaspoon ground coriander
1 potato, peeled, cooked, and diced
1 cup green peas
2 tablespoons chopped cilantro

1. Preheat the oven to 375°F.
2. Cut each zucchini in half lengthwise and scoop out the pulp. Place each half with the open side up on a shallow roasting pan and sprinkle with salt.
3. Heat margarine and oil in a skillet over medium heat. Add onion and garlic; sauté for 4 minutes, then stir in chickpeas, flour, coriander, potato, peas, and cilantro.
4. Spoon ¼ of potato mixture into each zucchini half and cover with foil.
5. Bake for 15 minutes or until zucchini is tender.

PER SERVING Calories: 205 | Fat: 5g | Protein: 8g | Sodium: 68mg | Fiber: 5g | Carbohydrates: 35g | Sugar: 6g

Carrot and Citrus Casserole

This slightly sweet casserole is colorful and nutritious. Serve as an appetizer or accompaniment to a roasted meat entrée.

INGREDIENTS | SERVES 10

2 tablespoons unsalted butter
Juice and zest of 3 large oranges
2 pounds fresh baby carrots
½ cup dried currants (or substitute raisins)
¼ cup brown sugar
½ cup long-cooking oats

1. Preheat the oven to 375°F. Lightly grease a casserole dish with ½ tablespoon of the butter.
2. Layer the remaining butter, orange juice, zest, carrots, currants, brown sugar, and oats in the prepared casserole dish.
3. Cover and bake for 1 hour. Uncover and bake for 15 minutes. Serve hot.

PER SERVING Calories: 155 | Fat: 3.1g | Protein: 3.1g | Sodium: 66mg | Fiber: 5.2g | Carbohydrates: 32g | Sugar: 20g

Oven-Roasted Ratatouille

This dish makes a great side to roasted fish, grilled poultry, or even baked tofu.
Serve with crusty bread to soak up the flavorful juices.

INGREDIENTS | SERVES 12

5 cups eggplant, peeled and cut into ½"
cubes
3 cups yellow squash, cut into ½" pieces
½ pound green beans
½ cup celery, chopped
1 cup red onion, chopped
4 cloves garlic, chopped
1 (28-ounce) can diced tomatoes
1 tablespoon fresh parsley, chopped
¼ teaspoon salt
½ teaspoon rosemary
½ teaspoon thyme
¼ cup olive oil
2 tablespoons balsamic vinegar

1. Preheat the oven to 375°F and lightly spray a 3-quart Dutch oven or 9" × 13" baking dish with nonstick spray. Add eggplant, yellow squash, green beans, celery, onion, garlic, tomatoes, parsley, salt, rosemary, thyme, and olive oil, and stir to combine.

2. Roast uncovered in oven. Stir after 30 minutes, then continue roasting for another 30 minutes or until vegetables are softened and lightly browned on top.

3. Remove from oven. Stir in balsamic vinegar and serve.

PER SERVING Calories: 85 | Fat: 5g | Protein: 2g | Sodium: 141mg | Fiber: 3.3g | Carbohydrates: 11g | Sugar: 1.3g

Baked Yellow and Green Squash

This dish is perfect for using up summer squash that overflows from everyone's garden at the end of the summer. Experiment with different combinations of herbs for a different twist.

INGREDIENTS | SERVES 4; SERVING SIZE: ⅔ CUP

1 teaspoon dried oregano leaves
1 teaspoon dried rosemary leaves
½ cup unsalted butter, melted
Juice of ½ lemon
1 teaspoon salt and freshly ground black pepper, to taste
1 sweet red onion, thinly sliced
1 large zucchini, ends removed, sliced crosswise into ¼"-thick rounds
1 large yellow squash, ends removed, sliced crosswise into ¼"-thick rounds
1 cup coarse whole-wheat bread crumbs

1. Preheat the oven to 350°F. Prepare an 8" × 8" casserole dish with nonstick spray.

2. Whisk the oregano and rosemary into the butter. Add lemon juice, salt, and pepper.

3. Layer the onion, zucchini, and yellow squash in the prepared baking dish. Sprinkle each layer with the melted butter and some bread crumbs.

4. When you get to the top, sprinkle with remaining bread crumbs and add the rest of the melted butter. Bake for 35 minutes.

PER SERVING Calories: 352 | Fat: 25g | Protein: 5.6g | Sodium: 210mg | Fiber: 3.1g | Carbohydrates: 29g | Sugar: 7.7g

Roasted Brussels Sprouts with Apples

Brussels sprouts are surprisingly delicious when prepared properly, so if you have bad memories of being force-fed soggy, limp baby cabbages as a child, don't let it stop you from trying this recipe!

INGREDIENTS | SERVES 4

2 cups Brussels sprouts, chopped into quarters
8 whole cloves garlic, peeled
2 tablespoons olive oil
2 tablespoons balsamic vinegar
¾ teaspoon salt
½ teaspoon black pepper
2 apples, chopped

1. Preheat the oven to 425°F and lightly spray a 9" × 13" casserole dish with nonstick spray.

2. Arrange the Brussels sprouts and garlic in a single layer in prepared dish. Drizzle with olive oil and balsamic vinegar and season with salt and pepper. Roast for 10–12 minutes, tossing once.

3. Remove dish from oven and add apples, tossing gently to combine. Roast for 10 more minutes or until apples are soft, tossing once.

PER SERVING Calories: 143 | Fat: 7g | Protein: 2g | Sodium: 451mg | Fiber: 4g | Carbohydrates: 19g | Sugar: 8.4g

Eggplant Rolls

The birthplace of the eggplant is thought to be India, though other Asian countries rival for that claim. The variety we most often see in our supermarkets today is deep purple and slightly bottom-heavy, though they range in color from brilliant white to marbled violet to dark red and come in all sorts of shapes and sizes.

INGREDIENTS | SERVES 6; SERVING SIZE: 2 ROLLS

1 cup low-fat ricotta cheese
1 egg
¼ cup Parmesan cheese
1 teaspoon dried oregano
¼ teaspoon or a good grinding of black pepper
2 medium eggplants, thinly sliced lengthwise
2 tablespoons olive oil in a spray container
1 cup sugar-free tomato sauce

1. Preheat the oven to 350°F and lightly spray a 9" × 13" casserole dish with nonstick spray. In a bowl, whisk together the first 5 ingredients. Set aside.

2. Place the eggplant slices on a piece of parchment paper. Spray both sides with olive oil. Bake for 5–8 minutes.

3. Cool slightly and spread a spoonful of the cheese mixture on each. Roll.

4. Place in prepared casserole dish, seam side down. Cover with tomato sauce and bake until baked through and bubbly, about 30 minutes.

PER SERVING Calories: 175 | Fat: 10g | Protein: 9g | Sodium: 133mg | Fiber: 5.4g | Carbohydrates: 14g | Sugar: 5.5g

Broccoli Crustless Quiche

Make this recipe any time you want the elegance of a quiche without all the calories and fat from a crust.

INGREDIENTS | SERVES 6

1½ cups (½") whole-wheat bread cubes

1 tablespoon olive oil

1 medium onion, diced

1 clove garlic, minced

2 cups chopped frozen broccoli

3 large eggs, beaten

3 large egg whites

1 cup Mock Cream (see Chapter 14)

¾ cup grated Emmentaler cheese

¼ teaspoon salt

1. Preheat the oven to 375°F and lightly spray a deep 9" pie plate with nonstick spray. Spread the bread cubes on a rimmed baking sheet and bake, stirring once or twice, until the bread is lightly toasted, 5–7 minutes.

2. While the bread is toasting, heat the olive oil in a small skillet over medium heat. When hot, add the onion and cook until it becomes soft and translucent, 7–10 minutes. Stir in the garlic and cook until fragrant, about 1 minute.

3. Place the toasted bread cubes, onion mixture, and broccoli in a large bowl and combine with the eggs, egg whites, Mock Cream, Emmentaler cheese, and salt.

4. Pour the mixture into the prepared pie plate and bake until the center of the quiche is set, about 40–50 minutes.

PER SERVING Calories: 137 | Fat: 6.4g | Protein: 11g | Sodium: 317mg | Fiber: 1.5g | Carbohydrates: 7.5g | Sugar: 1.7g

Baked Stuffed Tomatoes with Herbs and Cashews

This is a delicious new twist on baked stuffed tomatoes.
It's easy and is a very surprising combination of textures and flavors.

INGREDIENTS | SERVES 4; SERVING SIZE: 1 TOMATO PLUS NUTS AND HERBS

4 ripe medium tomatoes

4 teaspoons olive oil

1 small red onion, minced

½ cup cashews, toasted and chopped

1 cup fresh whole-wheat bread crumbs

1 teaspoon dried thyme leaves or 1 tablespoon fresh thyme

Salt and freshly ground pepper, to taste

2 tablespoons sugar-free tomato juice or freshly squeezed lemon juice

Stuffed Tomatoes

Try experimenting with different stuffing combinations. Vegetables, nuts, sausages, shrimp, scallops, and different herbs all make intensely flavored fillings. Also try cooked rice, meats, and shellfish for cold stuffed tomatoes.

1. Preheat the oven to 350°F. Prepare a baking sheet with parchment paper or nonstick spray. Cut the tops off the tomatoes and remove seeds and pulp with a melon scooper or grapefruit spoon.

2. Arrange the tomatoes on the baking sheet. Heat the olive oil in a large sauté pan over medium heat.

3. Add the remaining ingredients listed, one by one, into the sauté pan. Cook for 4–5 minutes and then pile into tomato shells.

4. Bake for 40 minutes.

PER SERVING Calories: 274 | Fat: 14g | Protein: 7.1g | Sodium: 208mg | Fiber: 2.9g | Carbohydrates: 29g | Sugar: 2.5g

Vegetable Potpie

This recipe can go vegetarian if you substitute the vegetable broth for chicken broth.
The vegetables give you plenty of fiber and flavor.

INGREDIENTS | SERVES 6

WHOLE-WHEAT BISCUITS
1½ cups all-purpose flour
1½ cups whole-wheat flour
4½ teaspoons baking powder
1½ teaspoons salt
1 tablespoon sugar
6 tablespoons chilled butter, cut into small pieces
1¼ cups buttermilk

VEGETABLE POTPIE
2 tablespoons butter
½ medium onion, diced
2 carrots, peeled and diced
2 celery stalks, diced
½ cup sliced leeks
¼ cup flour
3 cups low-sodium chicken broth
1 potato, peeled and cubed
½ cup cut green beans
1 bay leaf
½ cup frozen peas
½ cup Mock Cream (see Chapter 14)
Salt and pepper, to taste
¼ cup chopped chives

1. To make the biscuits, combine all-purpose flour, whole-wheat flour, baking powder, salt, and sugar in the bowl of a food processor. Add chilled butter pieces and pulse until the butter is the size of small peas. Pour in the buttermilk and pulse until the mixture just holds together (do not overmix). Pat the dough on a floured board to a thickness of 1". Cut circles out of the dough with a 2" or 3" cookie cutter and set aside.

2. To make the potpie, heat the butter in a 3-quart Dutch oven over medium heat; add the onion, carrots, celery, and leeks and cook, stirring occasionally until tender. Dust with flour, stir, and cook a few minutes. Add the chicken broth, potato, and green beans. Bring to a gentle simmer, add the bay leaf, and cook for 30–40 minutes until the vegetables are cooked and liquid is thickened.

3. Stir in the peas and Mock Cream and remove from the heat. Remove the bay leaf, season with salt and pepper, and stir in chopped chives. Preheat the oven to 400°F and spray a 9" × 13" casserole dish lightly with nonstick spray. Pour the filling into the prepared casserole dish and place on a rimmed baking sheet lined with foil.

4. Place the unbaked biscuits on top of the filling and bake for 25–30 minutes or until the biscuit top is golden and the casserole is bubbly.

PER SERVING Calories: 249 | Fat: 5.1g | Protein: 5g | Sodium: 469mg | Fiber: 4.2g | Carbohydrates: 30g | Sugar: 3.9g

Winter Vegetable Casserole

White and sweet potatoes add a pleasing visual contrast to this recipe.
Letting the casserole stand for a few minutes before serving will help you cut it into neat slices.

INGREDIENTS | SERVES 6

1½ russet potatoes, peeled and thinly sliced

1½ sweet potatoes, peeled and thinly sliced

1 cup parsnips, peeled and sliced

1 cup turnips, peeled and sliced

3 tablespoons butter

3 tablespoons all-purpose flour

½ teaspoon salt

¼ teaspoon white pepper

1½ cups low-fat milk

½ cup onions, chopped

Storing Potatoes

Don't store potatoes or sweet potatoes in the refrigerator or their starches will convert to sugar, which will make the potatoes taste too sweet. Instead, keep them in a cool, dark, well-ventilated place, such as a root cellar or cabinet.

1. Spray a 2-quart casserole dish with nonstick spray and preheat the oven to 350°F.

2. In a large bowl, combine russet potatoes, sweet potatoes, parsnips, and turnips.

3. In a small saucepan, melt butter; add flour, salt, and pepper to make a roux. Gradually stir in milk, cooking over low heat; stir well with a wire whisk.

4. Bring milk to a boil, stirring constantly, until milk has thickened into a sauce, about 10 minutes. Remove from heat.

5. Arrange half of sliced vegetables in casserole dish; top with half of chopped onion and white sauce; repeat to make second layer. Cover and cook for 45 minutes. Uncover and continue to cook until all vegetables are tender, about 60–70 minutes.

6. Let casserole stand for 10 minutes before serving.

PER SERVING Calories: 218 | Fat: 7g | Protein: 5g | Sodium: 392mg | Fiber: 5g | Carbohydrates: 36g | Sugar: 3.3g

Greek Stuffed Peppers

These beautiful stuffed peppers are delicious served hot or cold.
The combination of oregano, parsley, mint, and feta cheese evokes the cuisine of Greece.

INGREDIENTS | SERVES 6

½ cup brown rice

1 cup vegetable stock

2 tablespoons olive oil

1 onion, chopped

4 cloves garlic, minced

½ cup golden raisins

½ teaspoon salt

½ teaspoon dried oregano leaves

¼ cup parsley, minced

¼ cup fresh mint leaves, minced

3 tablespoons lemon juice

2 tomatoes, chopped

⅓ cup crumbled feta cheese

6 red bell peppers

1 cup dry white wine

¼ cup grated Parmesan cheese

1. In a small saucepan, combine rice and stock; bring to a simmer over medium-high heat. Cover, reduce heat to low, and simmer for 35–40 minutes until rice is tender. Set aside.

2. In a large skillet, heat olive oil over medium heat. Add onion and garlic; cook and stir for 5 minutes. Add raisins, salt, oregano, parsley, mint, lemon juice, and tomatoes; bring to a simmer. Cook for 5–6 minutes to blend flavors.

3. Preheat the oven to 375°F. Stir rice and feta cheese into tomato mixture and remove from heat. Cut the bell peppers in half lengthwise; remove stems, seeds, and membranes.

4. Arrange the peppers in a large casserole dish. Fill with the rice mixture. Pour the wine around the peppers. Cover with foil and bake for 30–35 minutes or until peppers are tender. Uncover, sprinkle with Parmesan cheese, and bake for 10 minutes longer until cheese melts. Serve immediately.

PER SERVING Calories: 259 | Fat: 8.5g | Protein: 9g | Sodium: 409mg | Fiber: 6g | Carbohydrates: 39g | Sugar: 10g

Vegetable Lasagna Rolls

These pretty little rolls are full of creamy cheese and spinach, topped with a rich artichoke-tomato sauce.

Rosemary: Fresh Versus Dried

Dried rosemary may be more readily available, but fresh rosemary has a more intense taste and tender leaf. Dried rosemary leaves can become very hard and brittle and can be difficult to eat. More and more grocery stores are stocking fresh rosemary; ask your grocer if you can't find it.

1. Preheat the oven to 350°F. Bring a large pot of water to a boil. In a large skillet, heat olive oil over medium heat. Add onion and garlic; cook and stir for 5 minutes. Add carrot and stir.

2. Finely chop the artichoke hearts and add to onion mixture along with rosemary and pepper; cook and stir for 3 minutes. Add pasta sauce and bring to a simmer.

3. Cook lasagna noodles according to package directions until al dente. Meanwhile, in a medium bowl, combine ricotta and cream cheese and mix well. Add mozzarella cheese. Drain spinach by squeezing in a kitchen towel and stir into cheese mixture.

4. Drain noodles and rinse with cold water; drain again. Spread on work surface. Spread about ⅓ cup of the ricotta mixture on each noodle and roll up.

5. Place half of artichoke sauce in a 9" × 13" baking pan. Top with filled noodles and rest of the artichoke sauce. Sprinkle with Parmesan cheese. Bake for 35–45 minutes until casserole bubbles and cheese browns.

PER SERVING Calories: 381 | Fat: 10g | Protein: 15g | Sodium: 539mg | Fiber: 4g | Carbohydrates: 57g | Sugar: 6g

Fluffy Corn Soufflé

*Soufflés will not wait for guests! Your guests must be ready and waiting for the soufflé.
It will still taste good if it falls, but half the drama is in the presentation.*

INGREDIENTS | SERVES 8

3 tablespoons butter

1 onion, chopped

2 cloves garlic, minced

3 tablespoons flour

⅛ teaspoon salt

⅛ teaspoon white pepper

1 teaspoon dried thyme leaves

1 cup skim milk

1 egg yolk

1 cup grated low-fat extra-sharp Cheddar cheese

2 cups frozen corn, thawed

2 (15-ounce) cans no-salt cream-style corn

4 egg whites

⅛ teaspoon cream of tartar

Nutritious Eggs—Even Better for you?

Eggs are naturally nutritious and are an excellent source of protein. Now, many companies market eggs and pasteurized egg products that have been enhanced with omega-3 fatty acids and additional vitamins. Read the labels and pick the eggs that fit your nutritional needs and budget.

1. Preheat the oven to 350°F and spray the bottom of a 2-quart soufflé dish with nonstick spray; set aside.

2. In a large saucepan, melt butter over medium heat. Add onion and garlic; cook and stir until tender, about 6 minutes. Add flour, salt, pepper, and thyme leaves; cook and stir until bubbling.

3. Add milk; cook and stir until mixture comes to a simmer. Stir in egg yolk and remove from heat. Add Cheddar cheese and both kinds of corn and set aside.

4. In a medium bowl, combine egg whites and cream of tartar; beat until stiff peaks form. Stir a dollop of the egg whites into the corn mixture, then gently fold in remaining egg whites.

5. Pour into prepared soufflé dish. Bake for 45–55 minutes or until soufflé is puffed, golden brown on top, and set. Serve immediately.

PER SERVING Calories: 218 | Fat: 6.5g | Protein: 15g | Sodium: 302mg | Fiber: 3g | Carbohydrates: 34g | Sugar: 3g

Pumpkin Soufflé

This beautiful little entrée is wonderful for entertaining.
Serve it with a crisp green salad and some whole-wheat pita triangles.

INGREDIENTS | SERVES 4

Peanut oil, as needed

1 tablespoon olive oil

1 onion, chopped

4 cloves garlic, minced

1 (13-ounce) can solid-pack pumpkin

1 egg yolk

2 teaspoons chopped fresh thyme

4 egg whites

¼ teaspoon salt

¼ teaspoon cream of tartar

2 tablespoons grated Parmesan cheese

Better than the Pumpkin Patch

Solid-pack pumpkin is a true, natural convenience product that will save you hours of work peeling, seeding, roasting, puréeing, and draining fresh pumpkin. It's packed with beta-carotene, vitamin C, and riboflavin.

1. Preheat the oven to 425°F. Grease the bottom of a 1-quart soufflé dish with peanut oil and set aside. In a small saucepan, heat olive oil over medium heat. Add onion and garlic; cook and stir until tender, about 5 minutes.

2. Place in a large bowl and let cool for 10 minutes. Blend in pumpkin, egg yolk, and thyme until smooth.

3. In a medium bowl, combine egg whites, salt, and cream of tartar and beat until stiff peaks form. Stir a spoonful of the beaten egg whites into pumpkin mixture, then fold in remaining egg whites along with the Parmesan cheese. Pour into prepared soufflé dish.

4. Bake for 15 minutes, then reduce heat to 350°F and bake for another 20–25 minutes or until soufflé is puffed and golden brown. Serve immediately.

PER SERVING Calories: 119 | Fat: 6g | Protein: 7.6g | Sodium: 183mg | Fiber: 3g | Carbohydrates: 4.7g | Sugar: 0.53g

Stuffed Onions

Onions can be turned into vessels for soufflés or stuffings. Onions are a good source of vitamin C and phytochemicals that may provide protection against certain types of cancer.

INGREDIENTS | SERVES 4; SERVING SIZE: ½ ONION

2 large sweet onions

1 tablespoon olive oil

2 ounces cooked and crumbled breakfast sausage

2 ounces shredded Monterey jack cheese

3 tablespoons bread crumbs

1 tablespoon chopped fresh herbs

2 tablespoons chopped green chilies

Salt and pepper, to taste

1 egg, beaten

1 cup enchilada or tomato sauce, warmed

Herbs and Crumbs

For toppings of broiled, grilled, or baked vegetables, herbs and crumbs are absolutely the most interesting and versatile ways to turn ho-hum into mouthwateringly delicious. Take some leftover whole-grain bread and put it in the food processor with seasoned salt, oregano, and Parmesan cheese, and let it grind away. Sprinkle over grilled vegetables.

1. Preheat the oven to 350°F and lightly spray a 9" × 13" casserole dish with nonstick spray. Peel the onions, then cut them in half horizontally.

2. Bring a pot of salted water to boil and cook the onions for 12 minutes. Drain and take out the center of each onion, creating four onion cups. Put the cups in the prepared casserole dish; set aside.

3. Chop the centers of the onions and sauté them in olive oil. Transfer them to a bowl and add the sausage, Monterey jack cheese, bread crumbs, herbs, green chilies, salt, and pepper. Mix well, add the egg, and mix again.

4. Make four balls out of the stuffing and put one in each onion cup.

5. Cover and bake for 20 minutes. Uncover and bake for 10 more minutes. Serve hot with enchilada or tomato sauce spooned on top.

PER SERVING Calories: 236 | Fat: 14g | Protein: 11g | Sodium: 507mg | Fiber: 3g | Carbohydrates: 18g | Sugar: 9g

Eggplant Soufflé

If you don't like eggplant, you've never had it prepared like this! The flavor combination is lovely and the texture very much like a soufflé. You can add various cheeses to the recipe in small quantities to give it a kick of added flavor.

INGREDIENTS | SERVES 4; SERVING SIZE: 3 TABLESPOONS

1 medium eggplant, peeled and cubed
1 teaspoon salt
1 tablespoon olive oil
1 clove garlic
½ cup sweet white onion, diced
1 teaspoon dried oregano
1 teaspoon dried basil
Juice of ½ lemon
½ teaspoon salt
Freshly ground black pepper, to taste
2 egg yolks
4 egg whites, beaten stiff
½ cup sugar-free tomato sauce

Eggplant

Soak or salt exceptionally large eggplants to reduce the bitterness. Larger eggplants tend to be more bitter than smaller ones and also have larger seeds. Long Japanese varieties have very few seeds and are exceptionally sweet.

1. In a large bowl, sprinkle the cubed eggplant with salt. Let rest for 20 minutes and then squeeze out the liquid using paper towels or linen kitchen towels.

2. Preheat the oven to 400°F. Lightly spray a 1-quart soufflé dish with nonstick spray. Heat the olive oil in a nonstick sauté pan over medium heat. Cook the eggplant with the garlic and onion until the eggplant is tender and the onion is translucent and no longer crunchy.

3. Remove from the heat and place in a food processor. Add the oregano, basil, and lemon juice, and pulse. Add the salt, pepper, and egg yolks. Pulse until smooth.

4. Fold in egg whites. Pour into the soufflé dish. Bake for 35–40 minutes or until puffed and golden. Serve with sugar-free tomato sauce on the side.

PER SERVING Calories: 149 | Fat: 6g | Protein: 8g | Sodium: 662mg | Fiber: 4.9g | Carbohydrates: 14g | Sugar: 7g

Roasted Scalloped Corn

Scalloped corn is an old-fashioned recipe that is excellent served with ham or pork. Add a green salad for a nice dinner.

INGREDIENTS | SERVES 6

1 (10-ounce) package frozen corn, thawed

2 tablespoons olive oil, divided

1 tablespoon butter

1 onion, finely chopped

2 cloves garlic, minced

2 slices oatmeal bread, toasted

1 (15-ounce) can creamed corn

2 eggs, beaten

½ teaspoon salt

⅛ teaspoon pepper

¾ cup shredded Cheddar cheese

¼ cup grated Parmesan cheese

Scalloped Vegetables

Scalloped means to cook in a cream sauce or a white sauce. You can achieve the same effect without making a white sauce; just beat together eggs and milk and stir that into cooked vegetables, then pour into a casserole and bake. This is a great way to turn leftover vegetables into another dish.

1. Preheat the oven to 425°F. Spray a 9" × 13" casserole dish with nonstick spray and set aside. Drain thawed corn and place on cookie sheet. Drizzle with 1 tablespoon olive oil and toss to coat. Roast for 10–20 minutes or until corn just starts to turn brown. Remove from oven and set aside. Reduce oven temperature to 350°F.

2. In a large saucepan, heat remaining 1 tablespoon olive oil with butter over medium heat. Add onion and garlic; cook and stir until tender, about 5 minutes. Remove from heat and set aside.

3. Crumble the toasted bread to make fine crumbs; reserve ¼ cup. Stir crumbs into onion mixture along with roasted corn and creamed corn; mix well. Add eggs, salt, and pepper, beating well to combine. Stir in Cheddar cheese.

4. Pour into prepared casserole dish. In a small bowl, combine reserved crumbs with the Parmesan cheese and sprinkle over the top of the corn mixture. Bake for 20–30 minutes or until casserole is set and beginning to brown.

PER SERVING Calories: 297 | Fat: 16g | Protein: 12g | Sodium: 446mg | Fiber: 2.2g | Carbohydrates: 29g | Sugar: 4g

Sun-Dried Tomato and Potato Crustless Quiche

This is a great way to use up leftover cooked potatoes. For a slightly different tomato flavor, try this recipe with the Roasted Tomatoes with Bright Herbs (see Chapter 3).

INGREDIENTS | SERVES 6

¼ cup chopped sun-dried tomatoes

1 cup boiling water

1 tablespoon olive oil

1 medium onion, diced

1 clove garlic, minced

1½ cups (½" diced) cooked potatoes, cooled

3 large eggs, beaten

3 large egg whites

1 cup Mock Cream (see Chapter 14)

¾ cup grated fontina cheese

¼ teaspoon salt

Individual Crustless Quiches

Make individual crustless quiches by dividing the quiche mixture among six small ramekins or baking dishes. The quiches can even be unmolded after baking. Serve with lightly dressed steamed vegetables or a small salad.

1. Preheat the oven to 375°F and lightly spray a deep 9" pie plate with nonstick spray. Place the sun-dried tomatoes in a small heatproof bowl and pour the boiling water over them.

2. While the tomatoes are rehydrating, heat the olive oil in a small skillet over medium heat. When hot, add the onion and cook until it becomes soft and translucent, 7–10 minutes. Stir in the garlic and cook until fragrant, about 1 minute.

3. Drain the tomatoes and combine them in a large bowl with the onion mixture, potatoes, eggs, egg whites, Mock Cream, fontina cheese, and salt.

4. Pour the mixture into the prepared pie plate and bake until the center of the quiche is set, about 40–50 minutes.

PER SERVING Calories: 214 | Fat: 12g | Protein: 12g | Sodium: 383mg | Fiber: 1g | Carbohydrates: 14g | Sugar: 1.7g

CHAPTER 5

Grains and Stuffings

Baked Barley Casserole

Barley is a great food to eat when you want to feel full because it absorbs more liquid during cooking than other grains. That's why it's such a favorite in soups. It's also a highly digestible fiber.

INGREDIENTS | SERVES 4

3 tablespoons olive oil

1 cup barley

2 tablespoons butter

1½ cups diced onion

½ teaspoon salt

¼ teaspoon pepper

6 cups beef broth

½ cup chopped Italian parsley

1. Preheat the oven to 350°F and spray a 3-quart casserole dish lightly with nonstick spray.

2. Heat the oil over medium heat in a large skillet. When hot, add the barley and cook, stirring often, until it begins to smell toasty, about 2 minutes. Transfer the barley to the casserole dish.

3. Heat the butter in the skillet over medium-high heat. When melted, add the onion and cook until it softens and begins to brown. Remove the onion to the prepared casserole dish and add the salt, pepper, and 3 cups beef broth.

4. Cover the casserole and bake for 1 hour.

5. Add the remaining beef broth, cover, and bake until the liquid is absorbed, about 40 minutes. Add parsley for garnish.

PER SERVING Calories: 394 | Fat: 21g | Protein: 16g | Sodium: 1,699mg | Fiber: 9g | Carbohydrates: 39g | Sugar: 0.46g

Almond Barley Casserole

The nutty flavor of barley is accented by two kinds of almonds, onions, and garlic in this recipe.

INGREDIENTS | SERVES 8

2 tablespoons butter

1 tablespoon olive oil

½ cup slivered almonds

1 onion, chopped

3 cloves garlic, minced

1 (8-ounce) package sliced mushrooms

1½ cups medium pearl barley

3 cups vegetable broth

½ cup sliced almonds

1. Preheat the oven to 350°F and spray a 2½-quart casserole dish lightly with nonstick spray. In a large skillet, melt the butter with the olive oil over medium heat. Add the slivered almonds and cook until toasted; remove with a slotted spoon.

2. Add the onion, garlic, and mushrooms to the skillet; sauté until crisp-tender, about 6–8 minutes. Add the barley and stir until coated.

3. Add the broth and toasted almonds to the pan; bring to a simmer. Transfer the mixture to the prepared casserole dish and top with sliced almonds. Bake for 65–75 minutes or until the barley is tender and the broth is absorbed.

PER SERVING Calories: 247 | Fat: 11g | Protein: 6.7g | Sodium: 34mg | Fiber: 7.5g | Carbohydrates: 32g | Sugar: 1.3g

Barley and Sage Casserole

Woodsy sage, walnuts, and shallots combine to bring the flavors of autumn to this casserole. If substituting dried sage for the fresh, use whole leaf sage, not powdered, or the casserole will taste dusty.

INGREDIENTS | SERVES 6

½ cup chopped walnuts

2 tablespoons olive oil

3 shallots, minced

3 cloves garlic, minced

2 stalks celery, minced

1 carrot, minced

1½ cups pearl barley

1 teaspoon salt

¼ teaspoon pepper

2 teaspoons fresh sage

3½ cups vegetable broth

½ cup grated Parmesan cheese

Toasting Nuts

No matter if you plan to use them to top salad or to fold into cookie dough, toasted nuts make a great addition to any dish. Toasting nuts helps to intensify their flavor and gives them a golden color and crisp texture. For the most even color, spread the nuts out on a rimmed baking sheet and toast, stirring occasionally, in a 325°F oven. Depending on the type and size of the nut, the toasting process can take as little as 5 minutes and up to 20.

1. Preheat the oven to 325°F and spray a 2½-quart casserole dish lightly with nonstick spray.

2. Spread the walnuts out on a rimmed baking sheet and toast on the middle oven rack, stirring occasionally, until the nuts are just golden, 7–10 minutes. Remove the baking sheet from the oven and increase the oven temperature to 350°F.

3. Heat the olive oil in a large skillet over medium heat. When hot, add the shallots, garlic, celery, and carrot. Cook the vegetables, stirring occasionally, until they are almost tender and fragrant, about 10 minutes. Add the barley, salt, pepper, and sage; stir to combine. Add the vegetable broth and bring to a simmer, then pour the mixture into the prepared casserole dish.

4. Bake the casserole until the barley is tender and the broth is absorbed, about 65–75 minutes. Stir in the Parmesan cheese and toasted walnuts just before serving.

PER SERVING Calories: 328 | Fat: 14g | Protein: 10g | Sodium: 548mg | Fiber: 9.6g | Carbohydrates: 43g | Sugar: 2g

Vegan Quinoa "Mac 'n Cheese" Casserole

Craving mac 'n cheese but don't want bland macaroni, or the cheese, for that matter?
Try this filling whole-grain substitute.

INGREDIENTS | SERVES 4

3 cups vegetable broth

1½ cups quinoa

2 tablespoons olive oil

1 onion, chopped

1 bunch broccoli, diced small

3 cloves garlic, minced

1 tablespoon flour

¾ cup soymilk

½ teaspoon sea salt

1 large tomato, diced

1 cup shredded vegan cheese

½ teaspoon dried parsley

1 cup seasoned bread crumbs

¼ teaspoon nutmeg

What Is Quinoa?

Pronounced "keen-wa," this is actually a seed disguised as a whole grain. Quinoa has been a staple food in South America since ancient times, as it's one of the few crops that thrives in the high altitudes of the Andes. Look for these tiny round seeds in the bulk food bin or baking aisle of a natural-foods store, or in the natural-foods section of a well-stocked supermarket.

1. Preheat the oven to 350°F and spray a 9" × 13" casserole dish lightly with nonstick spray.

2. Bring the vegetable broth to a simmer in a medium saucepan. Add the quinoa, cover, and cook until the broth is absorbed and the quinoa is tender, about 15 minutes.

3. In a large saucepan, heat the olive oil over medium heat. When hot, add the onion and broccoli, and cook, stirring occasionally until the vegetables begin to soften, 5–6 minutes. Add the garlic and cook until fragrant, about 1 minute.

4. Add the flour, stirring to coat, then stir in the soymilk and sea salt. Cook the mixture until the sauce thickens, about 3 minutes. Gently stir in the tomatoes.

5. Combine quinoa and broccoli sauce mixture with half of the vegan cheese in the prepared casserole. In a small bowl, toss the remaining vegan cheese with the parsley, bread crumbs, and nutmeg, then spread the topping evenly over the casserole.

6. Bake the casserole until the cheese is melted and the crumbs just begin to brown, 15–20 minutes.

PER SERVING Calories: 473 | Fat: 16g | Protein: 19g | Sodium: 1,269mg | Fiber: 10g | Carbohydrates: 41g | Sugar: 5g

Quinoa Pilaf

This grain is cooked the same way rice is cooked. Feel free to add other ingredients such as sun-dried tomatoes and shredded zucchini for more texture and flavor.

INGREDIENTS | SERVES 4

2 tablespoons olive oil

½ cup diced onion

¼ cup diced carrots

¼ cup diced celery

1 cup quinoa

1½ cups chicken broth

½ teaspoon salt

¼ teaspoon white pepper

1 bay leaf

One Tiny Seed's History

South American natives cultivated quinoa and thanked their creator for the miraculously sustaining food through ritual and celebration. The Spanish began to associate the grain with non-Christian beliefs, and so banned quinoa from being grown in the seventeenth and eighteenth centuries. Terraced mountain slopes covered with cultivated quinoa were burned, and people starved. Luckily, enough seeds were secretly stored so that quinoa—the grain prized for its ability to grow on the chilly slopes of the Andes—remains a staple to this day.

1. Preheat the oven to 350°F and spray a 9" × 9" casserole dish lightly with nonstick spray.

2. Heat the oil in a medium skillet over medium-high heat. When hot, add the onion, carrots, and celery; cook until the vegetables become tender, about 10 minutes.

3. Add the quinoa to the skillet and cook until it just begins to become translucent, 3–4 minutes.

4. Pour the quinoa mixture into a baking dish and stir in the chicken broth, salt, pepper, and bay leaf.

5. Cover and bake until the vegetables are tender and the quinoa cooked through, about 45 minutes. Remove the bay leaf before serving.

PER SERVING Calories: 229 | Fat: 9.3g | Protein: 6.8g | Sodium: 595 mg | Fiber: 2.9g | Carbohydrates: 31g | Sugar: 0.53g

Quinoa and Black Bean Casserole

Quinoa takes on the flavors of Mexico with the addition of black beans, tomatoes, jalapeño peppers, and cilantro in this high-protein casserole. Adjust the heat to your liking by adding more or less jalapeño.

INGREDIENTS | SERVES 6

2 tablespoons canola oil

1 medium onion, minced

1 tablespoon minced jalapeño pepper

2 garlic cloves, minced

¼ teaspoon salt

1 cup quinoa

1½ cups low-sodium chicken broth

1 (14.5-ounce) can diced tomatoes, drained

1 (14.5-ounce) can black beans, rinsed and drained

½ cup grated pepper jack cheese

¼ cup chopped cilantro

2 scallions, trimmed and thinly sliced

1. Preheat the oven to 350°F and spray a 9" × 9" casserole dish lightly with nonstick spray.

2. Heat the oil in a medium saucepan over medium-high heat. When hot, add the onion, jalapeño, garlic, and salt. Cook, stirring often, until the vegetables are slightly softened, about 4 minutes.

3. Stir in the quinoa and chicken broth, then bring the mixture to a boil. Gently stir in the tomatoes, black beans, and pepper jack cheese; pour the mixture into the prepared casserole dish.

4. Bake, covered, until the quinoa is cooked through and the vegetables are tender, about 45 minutes.

5. Stir the cilantro and scallions into the casserole just before serving.

PER SERVING Calories: 422 | Fat: 8.3g | Protein: 23g | Sodium: 402mg | Fiber: 13g | Carbohydrates: 66g | Sugar: 1.4g

Vegan "Cheesy" Broccoli and Rice Casserole

If you're substituting frozen broccoli, there's no need to cook it first;
just thaw and use about 1¼ cups. Serve with ketchup for kids.

INGREDIENTS | SERVES 4

1 head broccoli, chopped small
2 tablespoons olive oil
1 tablespoon vegan margarine
1 onion, chopped
4 cloves garlic, minced
2 tablespoons flour
2 cups unsweetened soymilk
½ cup vegetable broth
2 tablespoons nutritional yeast
¼ teaspoon nutmeg
¼ teaspoon mustard powder
½ teaspoon salt
3½ cups rice, cooked
⅔ cup bread crumbs or crushed vegan crackers

Nutritional Yeast

Known for its unique, cheesy flavor and yellow color, nutritional yeast is an inactive form of Saccharomyces cerevisiae, a type of yeast similar to brewer's yeast that has been grown on a molasses base for more flavor. Vegans love it because it adds a savory, umami quality to dishes and because it packs a good dose of vitamin B12, which is a key nutrient (found in animal foods) that is often missing from vegan diets.

1. Preheat the oven to 325°F and spray a 9" × 13" casserole dish with nonstick spray.

2. Steam or microwave broccoli until just barely tender. Do not overcook.

3. Heat the olive oil and margarine in a medium saucepan over medium-high heat. When hot, add the onion and garlic. Cook, stirring frequently, until the onion is tender and the garlic fragrant, about 5 minutes. Reduce the heat and add the flour, stirring continuously to combine.

4. Slowly whisk in the soymilk and vegetable broth to avoid lumps and simmer, whisking often, until the sauce thickens. Remove from heat and stir in nutritional yeast, nutmeg, mustard powder, and salt.

5. Combine sauce, steamed broccoli, and cooked rice and transfer to the prepared casserole dish. Sprinkle the top with bread crumbs or vegan crackers.

6. Cover and bake for 25 minutes, then uncover and cook until the crumbs crisp, about 10 more minutes.

PER SERVING Calories: 477 | Fat: 14g | Protein: 16g | Sodium: 401mg | Fiber: 7g | Carbohydrate: 52g | Sugar: 4g

Rice and Vegetable Casserole

Vegetables are layered with a rice and egg mixture in this easy and delicious vegetarian entrée.

INGREDIENTS | SERVES 8

1 tablespoon olive oil

2 onions, chopped

1 (8-ounce) package sliced mushrooms

2 red bell peppers, chopped

1 jalapeño pepper, minced

4 cups cooked brown rice

1½ cups milk

1 egg

2 egg whites

½ cup low-fat sour cream

1 cup shredded part-skim mozzarella cheese

½ cup shredded Colby cheese

1. Preheat the oven to 350°F and spray a 9" × 13" casserole dish lightly with nonstick spray.

2. Heat the olive oil in a large saucepan over medium-high heat. When hot, add the onions and mushrooms and cook, stirring occasionally, for 3 minutes. Add the bell peppers and jalapeño and cook for 3–4 minutes longer until vegetables are crisp-tender.

3. In a large bowl, combine the rice, milk, egg, egg whites, sour cream, mozzarella cheese, and Colby cheese. Layer half of this mixture in the prepared casserole dish. Top the rice mixture with the vegetables, then spread the remaining rice mixture over the top.

4. Bake the casserole until it bubbles and browns, 55–60 minutes. Let it stand for 5 minutes before serving.

PER SERVING Calories: 376 | Fat: 11g | Protein: 12g | Sodium: 175mg | Fiber: 3g | Carbohydrates: 32g | Sugar: 1g

Herbed Wild Rice Stuffing

Make sure the rice is completely tender before proceeding with the recipe—although the assembled casserole spends considerable time in the oven, the rice will remain hard if not thoroughly cooked through. Look in the fresh bakery section of your supermarket for the Italian bread.

INGREDIENTS | SERVES 12

2 cups wild rice

10 slices Italian bread

3 tablespoons olive oil

2 onions, minced

3 ribs celery, minced

4 cloves garlic, minced

2 teaspoons dried thyme

2 teaspoons dried sage

1½ cups fat-free evaporated milk

2 large eggs

1½ cups low-sodium chicken broth

½ teaspoon salt

½ teaspoon pepper

2 tablespoons melted butter

Wild Rice

Close cousin to Asian rice, wild rice is harvested from grasses that grow in shallow water in small lakes and sluggish streams. Historically, Native Americans harvested wild rice by canoe: They paddled into a stand of plants and beat the grain heads with wooden sticks into their boat. Today, production of this crop remains closely tied to many tribes in North America and Canada. Wild rice is high in protein and dietary fiber, and a good source of potassium, riboflavin, niacin, and thiamine.

1. Cook the wild rice according to the package directions until it is tender and cooked through. Preheat the oven to 350°F and spray a 9" × 13" casserole dish lightly with nonstick spray.

2. Tear the bread into small pieces and place on two rimmed baking sheets. Toast the bread, stirring once or twice, until it turns light golden, 20–25 minutes.

3. While the bread is toasting, heat the olive oil in a large skillet over medium heat. When hot, add the onion, celery, garlic, thyme, and sage. Cook until the vegetables are very tender, about 10 minutes.

4. Whisk the evaporated milk, eggs, chicken broth, salt, and pepper together in a large bowl. Stir in the rice and bread pieces and transfer to the prepared casserole dish. Brush the butter evenly over the top of the casserole.

5. Cover the casserole with foil and bake until it is set in the center, about 1 hour.

PER SERVING Calories: 252 | Fat: 7.5g | Protein: 10g | Sodium: 374mg | Fiber: 2.3g | Carbohydrates: 36g | Sugar: 1g

Hoppin' John

This dish, a type of pilaf, consists of black-eyed peas and long-grain rice and is traditionally served on New Year's Eve in the southern United States. The peas are considered a good-luck charm.

INGREDIENTS | SERVES 8

1¼ cups dried black-eyed peas

3 cups water

1½ cups diced onion

½ cup diced ham

½ teaspoon dried thyme

¼ teaspoon cayenne pepper

1 bay leaf

Salt and pepper, to taste

1 tablespoon butter

3 tablespoons bacon fat

1½ cups long-grain rice

2¾ cups chicken broth

1 teaspoon salt

2 tablespoons chopped parsley

Bean Cookery

Although many recipes work well with canned beans, others are better when you cook the beans from scratch. Begin by soaking the beans overnight with enough water to cover the beans by a few inches. Or, if you don't have time for an overnight soak, bring the beans up to a boil in a pot with enough water to cover the beans by a few inches, then turn off the heat and allow the beans to sit for 90 minutes. Once the beans have soaked, drain them, cover them with water or stock, and cook them gently until tender, but not falling apart.

1. Place the black-eyed peas in a large pot and cover them with water 1" above the peas. Bring to a boil and boil for 1 minute. Remove from heat and let sit for 90 minutes.

2. Drain and rinse the peas and return them to the pot along with 3 cups water, onion, ham, thyme, cayenne pepper, and bay leaf. Simmer, uncovered, for 25 minutes. Drain the liquid from the pot and remove the bay leaf. Season pea mixture with salt and pepper and set aside.

3. Preheat the oven to 325°F. Melt the butter and bacon fat in a 3-quart Dutch oven and sauté the rice for 1 minute. Add the chicken broth and 1 teaspoon salt and bring to a simmer.

4. Stir the simmering rice once, cover, and bake for 25 minutes. Uncover and add the pea mixture and parsley. Cover and return to the oven for 5 minutes. Remove from oven, fluff with a fork, and lightly toss to mix the ingredients together. Cover and let sit for 10 minutes, then serve.

PER SERVING Calories: 302 | Fat: 8g | Protein: 11g | Sodium: 639mg | Fiber: 5g | Carbohydrates: 46g | Sugar: 1g

Broccoli Cheddar Rice

If you prefer a creamier texture, use American cheese instead of Cheddar cheese.
If you want extra fiber and flavor, add ½ cup roasted walnuts or pecans or top with sesame seeds.

INGREDIENTS | SERVES 6

¼ cup olive oil

½ cup diced onion

1 cup long-grain white rice

2 cups chopped fresh broccoli

1¾ cups chicken broth

½ teaspoon salt

¼ teaspoon ground pepper

1 cup grated Cheddar cheese

1. Preheat the oven to 350°F and spray a 9" × 13" casserole dish lightly with nonstick spray.

2. Heat the olive oil in a medium saucepan over medium-high heat and cook the onion, stirring often, until it becomes tender, 7–10 minutes.

3. Add the rice and cook for 3–5 minutes with the onion. Stir the broccoli into the rice mixture.

4. Pour the rice mixture into the prepared casserole dish. Stir in the chicken broth, salt, pepper, and Cheddar cheese. Cover the casserole with foil and bake until the rice is cooked and the cheese bubbly, about 45 minutes.

PER SERVING Calories: 300 | Fat: 17g | Protein: 9.4g | Sodium: 503mg | Fiber: 1.2g | Carbohydrates: 27g | Sugar: 1g

Coconut Brown Rice

Slightly sweet, with the addictive chew of brown rice, this side makes a great accompaniment to curries and grilled dishes from across the tropical regions of the world.

INGREDIENTS | SERVES 4

1 tablespoon butter

2 cups long-grain brown basmati rice

2 cups light coconut milk

2½ cups water

½ teaspoon salt

¼ teaspoon pepper

2 tablespoons unsweetened shredded coconut, toasted

Coconut Conundrum

Coconut water, coconut milk, and cream of coconut all sound like they are pretty much the same product, but they are made differently and used in different ways. Coconut water is the liquid found naturally inside the coconut and is often marketed as a sports drink because of its high electrolyte content. Coconut milk is made by boiling equal parts of shredded coconut with water, then straining the mixture so that all the coconut solids are removed. It is used to make soups, curries, ice creams, and other dishes. Coconut cream is made the same way as coconut milk, but with a higher (4:1) proportion of coconut to water. It is used primarily in desserts or drinks where a higher fat content is desired.

1. Preheat the oven to 350°F and spray a 9" × 13" casserole dish lightly with nonstick spray.

2. Heat the butter in a large saucepan over medium heat. When melted, add the rice and toast, stirring often, until it is fragrant, 3 minutes.

3. Add the coconut milk, water, salt, and pepper; bring the mixture to a boil over high heat.

4. Remove the pan from the heat and pour the mixture into the prepared casserole dish. Cover the casserole tightly with aluminum foil and bake until the rice is tender and all the liquid is absorbed, about 45 minutes. Fluff with a fork before serving and sprinkle with toasted coconut.

PER SERVING Calories: 523 | Fat: 23g | Protein: 8g | Sodium: 339mg | Fiber: 2.8g | Carbohydrates: 61g | Sugar: 0.69g

Brown and Wild Rice Casserole

This hearty side makes a great accompaniment to grilled or roasted meats and braised winter vegetables.

INGREDIENTS | SERVES 6

1 cup wild rice
1½ cups medium-grain brown rice
½ teaspoon salt
2½ cups low-sodium chicken broth
2 teaspoons extra-virgin olive oil
1 teaspoon minced fresh rosemary

1. Cook the wild rice according to the package directions until it becomes tender. Preheat the oven to 350°F and spray a 9" × 9" casserole dish lightly with nonstick spray.

2. Stir the brown rice, salt, chicken broth, olive oil, and rosemary together with the cooked wild rice in the prepared casserole dish.

3. Cover the casserole tightly with foil and bake until the rice is tender and the chicken broth has absorbed, about 1 hour. Fluff the rice with a fork before serving.

PER SERVING Calories: 286 | Fat: 3.2g | Protein: 8.9g | Sodium: 430mg | Fiber: 3.4g | Carbohydrates: 56g | Sugar: 1.3g

Cranberry Pecan Savory Bread Pudding

This is a perfect solution to postholiday leftover turkey. It also freezes beautifully.
Serve with Whole Berry Cranberry Sauce (see Chapter 3).

INGREDIENTS | SERVES 8

1 tablespoon olive oil
½ cup diced celery
½ cup diced sweet onion
10 cups stale whole-wheat bread cubes
1½ cups diced cooked turkey
1 cup chopped toasted pecans
½ cup dried cranberries
5 egg yolks
7 whole eggs
2½ cups chicken broth
3½ cups fat-free evaporated milk
½ teaspoon sage
1 teaspoon thyme
¼ teaspoon ground black pepper
1 teaspoon kosher salt

Almond Apricot Savory Bread Pudding

For a mildly spiced variation of the Cranberry Pecan Savory Bread Pudding, try substituting 1 cup slivered almonds for the pecans, ½ cup chopped dried apricots for the cranberries, and 2 teaspoons curry powder for the sage.

1. Preheat the oven to 350°F and spray a 9" × 13" casserole dish lightly with nonstick spray.

2. Heat the oil in a medium skillet over medium-high heat. When hot, add the onion and celery and cook, stirring occasionally, until the vegetables are tender, 7–10 minutes. Put the bread cubes in the buttered dish. Sprinkle the celery, onion, turkey, pecans, and cranberries over the bread cubes and toss them together lightly with your hands.

3. Mix together the egg yolks, eggs, chicken broth, evaporated milk, sage, thyme, pepper, and salt. Pour evenly over the bread cubes. Press down the bread cubes to submerge them.

4. Bake the casserole until the center is set and the top begins to brown, about 1 hour.

PER SERVING Calories: 453 | Fat: 22g | Protein: 25g | Sodium: 822mg | Fiber: 3.6g | Carbohydrates: 41g | Sugar: 20g

Simple Corn Stuffing

*Serve this simple stuffing with your next holiday entrée.
The citrus notes of the juniper enhance the sweet flavor of the corn.*

INGREDIENTS | MAKES 4 CUPS

2 tablespoons butter

1 sweet medium onion, chopped

4 celery stalks with leaves, chopped

20 juniper berries, bruised

1 cup low-sodium chicken broth

1 teaspoon dried thyme

1 teaspoon dried savory

1 teaspoon dried sage

½ cup fresh parsley, chopped

2 cups packaged corn bread stuffing

2 cups frozen corn

1 cup 2% milk

1. Preheat the oven to 350°F and spray a 9" × 9" casserole dish lightly with nonstick spray.

2. Melt the butter in a skillet over medium heat. When hot, add the onions, celery, and juniper berries. Cook, stirring occasionally, until the vegetables are tender, about 10 minutes.

3. Transfer the vegetables to a large bowl and add the broth, thyme, savory, sage, and parsley. Mix well and add the corn bread stuffing, corn, and milk. Place the stuffing in the prepared casserole dish.

4. Bake the casserole until the stuffing has heated through and the top just begins to brown, about 30 minutes.

PER 1 CUP Calories: 460 | Fat: 26g | Protein: 8g | Sodium: 322mg | Fiber: 2.6g | Carbohydrates: 48g | Sugar: 12g

Tomato Tortilla Casserole

Use flour tortillas for a slightly different taste.

INGREDIENTS | SERVES 6

2 cups canned tomatoes, with juice

12 stale corn tortillas

2 tablespoons canola oil

1 large white onion, chopped into ¼"
pieces

2 garlic cloves, minced

1 teaspoon salt

½ teaspoon ground black pepper

½ teaspoon dried oregano

1 cup fat-free evaporated milk

1 cup grated Parmesan cheese

1 teaspoon paprika

1. Preheat the oven to 350°F and spray a 9" × 13" casserole dish lightly with nonstick spray.

2. Roughly chop the tomatoes, reserving the juice. Cut the tortillas into ½"-wide strips.

3. In a large saucepan, heat the oil over medium heat. When hot, add the onion and garlic; cook until the onion is soft but not brown. Add the tomatoes, salt, pepper, and oregano; stir until blended. Simmer the sauce for about 10 minutes.

4. While the sauce is simmering, place the tortilla strips in a single layer on two rimmed baking sheets. Bake the strips until they just begin to crisp, about 5–7 minutes.

5. Layer a little tomato sauce, a handful of tortilla strips, some evaporated milk, then Parmesan cheese in the prepared casserole dish. Repeat until all the ingredients are used, ending with cheese. Sprinkle the paprika on top.

6. Bake the casserole until it bubbles and the cheese begins to brown, about 25–30 minutes.

PER SERVING Calories: 316 | Fat: 12g | Protein: 19g | Sodium: 1,262mg | Fiber: 3g | Carbohydrates: 35g | Sugar: 8.4g

Mushroom Kasha Casserole

Serve this flavorful casserole in place of rice.
Do not skip the toasting of the kasha, or the casserole will be mushy.

INGREDIENTS | SERVES 8

3 tablespoons olive oil

1 medium onion, finely diced

3 cloves garlic, minced

8 ounces stemmed shiitake mushrooms, chopped

1 tablespoon chopped fresh thyme

1½ cups raw whole-grain buckwheat groats (kasha)

1 egg, beaten

1½ cups low-sodium chicken broth

¼ teaspoon salt

¼ teaspoon pepper

Kasha

In Slavic countries, kasha refers to any type of cereal grain commonly used to make porridge, though in the United States, it strictly means roasted buckwheat groats.

1. Preheat the oven to 350°F.

2. Heat the olive oil over medium-high heat in a 3-quart Dutch oven. When hot, add the onion, garlic, mushrooms, and thyme. Cook the vegetables, stirring occasionally, until they are softened and tender, about 10 minutes.

3. While the vegetables are cooking, stir the buckwheat groats and egg together in a large heavy nonstick skillet. Cook the mixture, stirring constantly, over medium-high heat until the groats separate and toast, about 10 minutes.

4. Stir the groats into the vegetable mixture and add the chicken broth, salt, and pepper. Turn up the heat to high and bring the casserole to a simmer.

5. Cover the Dutch oven and bake until the kasha is tender and has absorbed all of the chicken broth, about 25 minutes. Fluff with a fork before serving.

PER SERVING Calories: 185 | Fat: 6.7g | Protein: 5.6g | Sodium: 189mg | Fiber: 3.6g | Carbohydrates: 27g | Sugar: 1.1g

Cheesy Spiced Hominy Casserole

Look for hominy and chipotle chilies in the international foods aisle of your grocery store.
Either yellow or white hominy works well in this recipe. If you like a lot of spice, add more chipotle.

INGREDIENTS | SERVES 4

2 tablespoons butter

1 shallot, minced

4 tablespoons flour

2 cups fat-free milk

2 teaspoons minced chipotle chilies in adobo sauce

3 scallions, trimmed and thinly sliced

½ cup shredded Monterey jack cheese

2 (15-ounce) cans hominy

1. Preheat the oven to 350°F and spray a 9" × 13" casserole dish lightly with nonstick spray.

2. Melt the butter in a medium saucepan over medium heat. When melted, add the shallot and cook until just translucent, about 5 minutes. Whisk in the flour until blended, then slowly stream in the milk, whisking constantly to avoid lumps. Cook the sauce until it thickens slightly, about 5 minutes.

3. Remove the sauce from the heat and stir in the chilies, scallions, Monterey jack cheese, and hominy. Pour the mixture into the prepared casserole dish.

4. Bake the casserole until it bubbles and just begins to brown on top, about 35–40 minutes.

PER SERVING Calories: 304 | Fat: 9.1g | Protein: 11g | Sodium: 669mg | Fiber: 6.6g | Carbohydrates: 42g | Sugar: 4.4g

Spiced Millet with Cilantro

For an Italian version of this recipe, substitute fresh basil for the cilantro,
fontina for the Cheddar, and fresh parsley for the jalapeño pepper.

INGREDIENTS | SERVES 6

1 tablespoon oil
1 medium onion, chopped
1 jalapeño pepper, seeded and minced
2 cloves garlic, minced
¼ teaspoon salt
2 cups evaporated milk
2 large eggs
2 large egg whites
½ cup grated sharp Cheddar cheese
¼ cup grated Parmesan cheese
4 cups cooked millet
¼ cup cilantro

Cooked Millet

Bring 4 cups chicken broth and ½ teaspoon salt to a boil in a medium saucepan. Add 1½ cups millet, cover, and turn the heat to low. Cook until all of the broth is absorbed and the millet is tender, about 20 minutes.

1. Preheat the oven to 350°F and spray a 1½-quart casserole dish lightly with nonstick spray.

2. Heat the oil in a skillet over medium heat. When hot, add the onion, jalapeño, garlic, and salt. Cook the vegetables until they soften, about 10 minutes. Allow the vegetables to cool slightly.

3. Whisk together the evaporated milk, eggs, and egg whites in a large bowl. Stir in the Cheddar and Parmesan cheeses, millet, cilantro, and cooked vegetables.

4. Pour the mixture into the prepared casserole dish and bake, uncovered, until the casserole is set in the center and the top browns slightly, about 30 minutes.

PER SERVING Calories: 441 | Fat: 12g | Protein: 22g | Sodium: 373mg | Fiber: 6.1g | Carbohydrates: 59g | Sugar: 9.6g

Legumes and Pulses

Drunken Beans

Serve these beans with a tangy slaw and a steaming bowl of rice for a complete vegetarian meal. Adjust the heat to your liking by adding or omitting the jalapeño peppers. Serve with lime wedges.

INGREDIENTS | SERVES 4

1 tablespoon canola oil

1 medium onion, finely diced

3 garlic cloves, minced

1–2 jalapeño peppers, stemmed, seeded, and minced

¼ teaspoon salt

1 bottle lager beer

4 cups canned pinto beans, rinsed and drained

1. Preheat the oven to 350°F and spray a deep 2-quart casserole dish lightly with nonstick spray.

2. Heat the oil over medium-high heat in a medium saucepan. When hot, add the onion, garlic, jalapeños, and salt; cook until just softened, about 5 minutes.

3. Stir the onion mixture together with the beer and pinto beans in the prepared casserole dish. Cover tightly with aluminum foil and bake until the vegetables are tender, the beans flavorful, and the beer reduced, about 30 minutes.

PER SERVING Calories: 272 | Fat: 6 g | Protein: 12g | Sodium: 850mg | Fiber: 12g | Carbohydrates: 39g | Sugar: 0g

Maple Baked Beans

Tailor these saucy Boston-style baked beans to your liking by adding extra molasses, a bit of cayenne, or some TVP crumbles for a meaty texture.

INGREDIENTS | SERVES 8

3 cups navy or pinto beans

9 cups water

1 onion, chopped

⅔ cup maple syrup

¼ cup barbecue sauce

2 tablespoons molasses

1 tablespoon Dijon mustard

1 tablespoon chili powder

1 teaspoon paprika

1½ teaspoons salt

¾ teaspoon pepper

1. Cover the beans in water and soak at least 8 hours or overnight. Drain.

2. Preheat the oven to 350°F.

3. In a 3-quart Dutch oven or sturdy ovenproof pot, combine beans, onion, maple syrup, barbecue sauce, molasses, mustard, chili powder, paprika, salt, and pepper. Bring the beans to a simmer over medium-high heat.

4. Cover and bake the beans for 1½ hours, stirring once or twice. Uncover and cook for 1 more hour until the beans are tender and the sauce has thickened.

PER SERVING Calories: 214 | Fat: 0.51g | Protein: 7.5g | Sodium: 957mg | Fiber: 5g | Carbohydrates: 46g | Sugar: 22g

Spiced French Lentils with Swiss Chard

Find French lentils in the natural-foods aisle of your grocery store or in the bulk-foods section of most health food stores. If your store doesn't carry petite diced tomatoes, chop drained, diced tomatoes by hand until the pieces are about ¼" in size.

INGREDIENTS | SERVES 4

2 tablespoons olive oil

3 garlic cloves, minced

2 teaspoons smoked Spanish paprika

1 (14.5-ounce) can petite diced tomatoes, drained

3 scallions, trimmed and thinly sliced

1 cup French green lentils

3 cups low-sodium chicken broth

¼ teaspoon salt

2 cups chopped Swiss chard

1. Preheat the oven to 350°F.

2. Heat the oil over medium heat in a 3-quart Dutch oven. When hot, add the garlic and cook until fragrant, about 1 minute. Stir in the paprika, tomatoes, scallions, lentils, chicken broth, and salt; bring to a boil over high heat.

3. Cover and bake until the lentils are almost tender, but still a little crunchy, about 40 minutes. Stir in the Swiss chard and return the pot to the oven. Cook until the lentils are tender and the Swiss chard is cooked, about 15–20 minutes more.

PER SERVING Calories: 278 | Fat: 7.7g | Protein: 17g | Sodium: 738mg | Fiber: 17g | Carbohydrates: 38g | Sugar: 1.1g

Chickpea Curry

Serve this curry with brown rice and your favorite vegetables for a complete vegetarian meal.

INGREDIENTS | SERVES 6

1 tablespoon canola oil

1 medium onion, diced

3 cloves garlic, minced

1 tablespoon fresh grated ginger

1 tablespoon curry powder

¼ teaspoon salt

1 (14.5-ounce) can light coconut milk

2 (14.5-ounce) cans chickpeas, drained and rinsed

1 (14.5-ounce) can diced tomatoes, drained

¼ cup brown sugar

¼ cup cilantro leaves

1. Preheat the oven to 350°F.

2. Heat the oil over medium-high heat in a 3-quart Dutch oven. When hot, add the onion, garlic, ginger, curry powder, and salt. Cook, stirring occasionally, until the vegetables are tender and beginning to brown, about 10 minutes.

3. Stir in the coconut milk, chickpeas, tomatoes, and brown sugar and bring to a simmer. Cover and bake until the flavors have blended and the chickpeas are tender, about 30 minutes.

4. Stir in the cilantro just before serving.

PER SERVING Calories: 304 | Fat: 13g | Protein: 6.2g | Sodium: 307mg | Fiber: 4g | Carbohydrates: 34g | Sugar: 8.7g

Curried Lentils

Serve these lentils with whole-wheat pita or naan bread.
Yellow lentils may be substituted for the red lentils.

INGREDIENTS | SERVES 8

1 tablespoon canola oil

1 medium onion, diced

3 cloves garlic, minced

1 tablespoon fresh grated ginger

1½ tablespoons curry powder

2 cups water

2 cups light coconut milk

1¼ cups red lentils

1 (14.5-ounce) can diced tomatoes, drained

¼ cup cilantro leaves

1. Preheat the oven to 350°F.

2. Heat the oil over medium heat in a 3-quart Dutch oven. When hot, add the onion, garlic, and ginger and cook until the onion is softened and the vegetables fragrant, about 5 minutes. Stir in the curry powder, water, coconut milk, lentils, and tomatoes.

3. Bring the lentils to a simmer over high heat, cover, and bake until the lentils are very tender and resemble a thickened lentil soup, about 25–30 minutes. Stir in the cilantro just before serving.

PER SERVING Calories: 262 | Fat: 15g | Protein: 9.7g | Sodium: 77mg | Fiber: 4.3g | Carbohydrates: 25g | Sugar: 0g

Bean Stew with Three-Herb Pesto

This classic white bean stew is enlivened with a swirl of Three-Herb Pesto (see Chapter 14).
Serve with toasted whole-wheat pita chips or a crusty French baguette.

INGREDIENTS | SERVES 8

3 tablespoons olive oil

1 large onion, finely diced

1 head fennel, finely diced

2 stalks celery, finely diced

3 garlic cloves, minced

1 quart low-sodium chicken broth

½ teaspoon salt

2 (14.5-ounce) cans white beans, drained and rinsed

¼ cup Three-Herb Pesto (see Chapter 14)

1. Preheat the oven to 350°F.

2. Heat the oil in a 3-quart Dutch oven over medium-high heat. When hot, add the onion, fennel, celery, and garlic. Cook, stirring occasionally, until the vegetables begin to soften, about 7 minutes.

3. Add the chicken broth, salt, and white beans; bring the stew to a simmer over high heat. Cover and bake the stew until the vegetables are tender and the broth is slightly thickened, about 35–40 minutes.

4. Swirl in the Three-Herb Pesto just before serving.

PER SERVING Calories: 208 | Fat: 7.2g | Protein: 10g | Sodium: 450mg | Fiber: 6.2g | Carbohydrates: 26g | Sugar: 0.25g

Rich Baked Beans

*On the coldest day of winter, simmer these beans in the oven
to fill your home with warmth and a fabulous aroma.*

INGREDIENTS | SERVES 8

1 pound navy beans
1 onion, finely chopped
1 teaspoon salt
3 tablespoons mustard
½ cup brown sugar
½ cup ketchup
3 tablespoons tomato paste
½ cup molasses
¼ teaspoon pepper

1. Sort the beans and rinse well. Cover them with cold water and soak overnight. The next day, drain the beans well and rinse again. Place the beans in a large soup pot and cover with more cold water; bring to a boil over medium heat.

2. Simmer the beans uncovered for 1½ hours, then drain, reserving the cooking liquid.

3. Preheat the oven to 325°F. Pour the beans into a 3-quart Dutch oven and mix in the onion, salt, mustard, brown sugar, ketchup, tomato paste, molasses, and pepper.

4. Add enough reserved bean liquid to just cover the beans. Cover and bake until the mixture is thick and the beans are tender, 3½–4 hours. Check the pot a few times during baking to make sure that the beans do not dry out; add reserved cooking liquid as necessary.

PER SERVING Calories: 196 | Fat: 0.36g | Protein: 4.8g |
Sodium: 1,019mg | Fiber: 3.3g | Carbohydrates: 45g | Sugar: 29g

Barbecued Baked Beans

If you can't find canned pinto beans, kidney beans are a good substitute.
Add a dash of hot sauce or cayenne pepper if you want more heat.

INGREDIENTS | SERVES 6

2 tablespoons canola oil

1 large sweet onion, chopped

3 garlic cloves, minced

½ cup bottled barbecue sauce

¼ cup brown sugar

1 tablespoon dried mustard

1 teaspoon cumin

¼ teaspoon salt

1 cup canned tomato purée

4 cups canned pinto beans, drained and rinsed

1 tablespoon cider vinegar

1. Preheat the oven to 350F.

2. Heat the oil over medium-high heat in a 3-quart Dutch oven. Add the onion and cook until just tender, about 5 minutes. Add the garlic and cook until fragrant, 1 minute more.

3. Stir in the barbecue sauce, brown sugar, mustard, cumin, salt, and tomato purée. Bring the sauce to a simmer and add the pinto beans.

4. Cover the Dutch oven and bake until the beans are tender and flavorful, and the sauce has thickened slightly, about 30 minutes.

5. If the sauce is still too thin (it should cling to the back of a spoon), uncover the Dutch oven and bake until some of the liquid evaporates, about 10 minutes more. Gently stir in the cider vinegar just before serving.

PER SERVING Calories: 342 | Fat: 2.8g | Protein: 14g | Sodium: 596mg | Fiber: 9g | Carbohydrates: 62g | Sugar: 18g

Black Beans, Plantains, and Rice

Ripe plantains are black on the outside.
They look like big bananas and are featured in Caribbean and South American cuisine.

INGREDIENTS | SERVES 6

2 ripe plantains

¼ cup olive oil

3 tablespoons butter

2 garlic cloves, minced

½ cup sweet onion, sliced

1½ cups long-grain rice

2¾ cups chicken broth

1 teaspoon salt

2 cups cooked black beans, drained

2 tablespoons chopped cilantro

Juice of 1 lime

Going South!

Plantains, sweet potatoes, yams, mangoes, papayas, and wonderful spices will perk up tired recipes. Plantain chips add fiber and make a fine garnish for soups and stews. Break them into beef stew or sprinkle them over a pork roast. Shredded coconut is a delicious garnish for shrimp. Fresh pineapple will go a long way to perk up a chicken dish.

1. Peel the plantains and cut them into 1"-thick slices.

2. Heat the olive oil in a heavy skillet and brown the plantains on each side. Drain on paper towels and set aside.

3. Melt the butter in a 3-quart Dutch oven and add the garlic, onions, and rice. Cook, stirring occasionally, for 3 minutes. Add the chicken broth and salt and bring to a simmer.

4. Preheat the oven to 325°F.

5. Stir the simmering rice once. Cover the Dutch oven and bake for 25 minutes. Add the black beans, plantains, and cilantro. Cover and return the Dutch oven to the oven until the beans are heated through and the rice has absorbed all of the liquid, 5–10 minutes. Pour lime juice over the casserole just before serving.

PER SERVING Calories: 436 | Fat: 16g | Protein: 12g | Sodium: 706mg | Fiber: 7.3g | Carbohydrates: 64g | Sugar: 9.9g

Simple Spiced Black Beans and Tomatoes

Baking this dish in the oven allows the spices to gently infuse throughout the beans. Serve them as a side dish, or with rice and vegetables for a hearty vegetarian meal.

INGREDIENTS | SERVES 4

1 tablespoon canola oil

1 large red onion, diced

3 cloves garlic, minced

1 teaspoon dried oregano

1 tablespoon chili powder

1 tablespoon chili sauce

½ cup vegetable broth

1 (14.5-ounce) can diced tomatoes, drained

4 cups black beans, drained and rinsed

¼ cup chopped cilantro

1. Preheat the oven to 325°F and spray a 2-quart casserole dish lightly with nonstick spray.

2. Heat the oil over medium heat in a medium saucepan. When hot, add the onion and cook, stirring occasionally, until the onion begins to soften, about 7 minutes. Add the garlic and cook until fragrant, about 1 minute. Stir in the oregano, chili powder, chili sauce, broth, and tomatoes. Bring the sauce to a simmer, then remove from the heat.

3. Stir the beans and tomato sauce mixture together gently in the prepared casserole dish. Cover tightly with foil and bake until the beans are heated through and the flavors have combined, about 30 minutes. Stir in the cilantro just before serving.

PER SERVING Calories: 553 | Fat: 5.7g | Protein: 33g | Sodium: 208.4mg | Fiber: 22g | Carbohydrates: 74g | Sugar: 3g

Lentils Braised in Red Wine

These lentils are festive and delicious served as a side with baked fish or as part of a salad course. If you choose not to cook with the wine, add an equivalent amount of broth or tomato juice.

INGREDIENTS | SERVES 8

2 tablespoons olive oil

1 carrot, minced

1 stalk celery, minced

1 large sweet onion, minced

2 cloves garlic, minced

1 tablespoon dried thyme

2 bay leaves

1¼ cups red wine

3 cups low-sodium chicken broth

2⅓ cups small lentils such as beluga or French green

3 tablespoons chopped parsley

Lentils

Lentils are a type of quick-cooking pulse (the edible seeds of legumes) and are high in protein, vitamins, and dietary fiber. Choose lentils according to the type of recipe you plan on making. Small lentils, such as beluga or French green lentils (lentils du Puy), tend to hold their shape during cooking and are excellent for use in salads and in braised side dishes. Brown, yellow, and red lentils fall apart easily after cooking and are better for use in soups or traditional Indian dishes.

1. Preheat the oven to 350°F.

2. Heat the oil over medium-high heat in a 3-quart Dutch oven. When hot, add the carrot, celery, and onion; cook, stirring occasionally, until the vegetables are tender, about 7 minutes. Add the garlic and cook for 1 minute more.

3. Stir in the thyme, bay leaves, wine, broth, and lentils. Bring the mixture to a boil over high heat; cover and bake until the lentils have absorbed most of the liquid and are tender, about 45 minutes. Check the lentils every so often, adding water as necessary, to make sure that the Dutch oven does not become dry before the lentils are cooked.

4. Remove the lentils from the oven and stir in the parsley just before serving.

PER SERVING Calories: 233 | Fat: 4g | Protein: 14g | Sodium: 230mg | Fiber: 16g | Carbohydrates: 35g | Sugar: 4g

Black-Eyed Peas Curry

This dish is unusual and quite delicious. Serve with hot whole-wheat naan bread or over brown rice for a satisfying vegetarian main course.

INGREDIENTS | SERVES 6

2 tablespoons canola oil

1 tablespoon minced fresh ginger

2 cloves garlic, minced

1 large red onion, minced

2 small tomatoes, finely chopped

½ teaspoon turmeric powder

1 teaspoon red chili powder

2 teaspoons coriander powder

¼ teaspoon salt

1 teaspoon tamarind pulp concentrate

1 cup water

2 (14.5-ounce) cans black-eyed peas, rinsed and drained

⅛ cup cilantro, chopped

1. Preheat the oven to 350°F.

2. In a 3-quart Dutch oven, heat the oil over medium-high heat. When hot, add the ginger and garlic and cook until fragrant, about 1 minute. Add the onion and cook for 7–8 minutes or until well browned.

3. Add the tomatoes, turmeric powder, chili powder, coriander powder, salt, tamarind, water, and black-eyed peas. Bring to a boil over high heat, then cover.

4. Bake until the flavors have mingled, the beans are hot, and the sauce has thickened slightly, about 30 minutes. Stir in the chopped cilantro just before serving.

PER SERVING Calories: 164 | Fat: 6.9g | Protein: 4g | Sodium: 562mg | Fiber: 4.7g | Carbohydrates: 23g | Sugar: 1g

Tamarind

The tamarind is the fruit of a tree native to Asia that is used to add a sweet and sour taste to foods. Tamarind can be found in the international foods aisle of some grocery stores or in most East Indian and some Asian markets. It is sold as a concentrate or in a concentrated dried form.

Lima Beans with Smoky Ham

Smoky ham brings out the sweet flavor of the lima beans. If you prefer not to use smoked ham, substitute an equal amount of diced smoked turkey breast.

INGREDIENTS | SERVES 8

1 tablespoon olive oil

1 small onion, minced

2 garlic cloves, minced

½ cup chopped celery

¼ cup diced smoked ham

1 recipe Condensed Cream-of-Mushroom Soup (Mock Mushroom Sauce) (see Chapter 14)

½ cup fat-free milk

4 ounces reduced-fat shredded Cheddar cheese

4 cups frozen lima beans

¼ cup seasoned bread crumbs

1. Preheat the oven to 350°F and spray a 2-quart casserole dish lightly with nonstick spray.

2. Heat the olive oil over medium-high heat in a medium saucepan. When hot, add the onion, garlic, celery, and smoked ham. Cook, stirring occasionally, until the vegetables are tender, about 10 minutes. Stir in the Condensed Cream-of-Mushroom Soup (Mock Mushroom Sauce) and milk and bring to a bare simmer. Remove from heat and stir in the cheese.

3. Place the lima beans in the prepared casserole dish and mix with the cheese sauce.

4. Scatter the bread crumbs over the casserole and cover tightly with foil. Bake for 25 minutes, then remove the foil and bake for an additional 10 minutes until the bread crumbs are lightly browned and the casserole is bubbly.

PER SERVING Calories: 228 | Fat: 8g | Protein: 14g | Sodium: 246mg | Fiber: 5.2g | Carbohydrates: 24g | Sugar: 0.5g

Moroccan Chickpeas

Serve these chickpeas with whole-wheat couscous or brown rice.

2 tablespoons olive oil

1 red onion, diced

3 cloves garlic, minced

1 tablespoon minced fresh ginger

1 teaspoon ground coriander

1 teaspoon ground cumin

½ teaspoon ground cinnamon

¼ teaspoon salt

1 cup vegetable or low-sodium chicken broth

1 (14.5-ounce) can chickpeas, drained and rinsed

¼ cup chopped parsley

1. Preheat the oven to 350°F and spray a 2-quart casserole dish lightly with nonstick spray.

2. Heat the oil in a medium saucepan over medium-high heat. When hot, add the onion, garlic, and ginger. Cook the vegetables, stirring often, until the onion has softened, about 5 minutes. Add the coriander, cumin, cinnamon, salt, broth, and chickpeas. Bring to a simmer, then pour into the prepared casserole dish.

3. Cover the casserole tightly with foil and bake until the flavors have blended and the liquid is reduced slightly, 30–35 minutes. Stir in the parsley just before serving.

PER SERVING Calories: 338 | Fat: 11g | Protein: 15g | Sodium: 302mg | Fiber: 13g | Carbohydrates: 46g | Sugar: 8.3g

The Flavors of Morocco

Morocco is an ethnically diverse country in North Africa, and its cuisine reflects its people. Saffron, turmeric, mint, parsley, citrus fruit, and olives are featured prominently in its dishes.

The Five-Lentil Delight

Also called "Panchratan" or "The Five Jewels," this creamy dal (dahl) is a gourmet's delight. Serve with naan bread. The lentils may be found in the international grocery section of some supermarkets or are readily available in Indian grocery stores.

INGREDIENTS | SERVES 4

¼ cup chana dal or yellow split peas, rinsed

¼ cup red split lentils, rinsed

¼ cup pigeon peas, rinsed

¼ cup green split mung beans, rinsed

Water, as needed, plus 6 cups

1 teaspoon turmeric powder

½ teaspoon salt

2 tablespoons canola oil

1 teaspoon cumin seeds

2 cloves garlic, minced

½ tablespoon minced ginger

1 medium red onion, minced

1 teaspoon red chili powder

½ teaspoon curry powder

Cleaning Dals

No matter what type of dal you are cooking, rinse it well in 4–5 changes of water. This will get rid of any husks that might be in the dal.

1. Soak all the dals together in a deep pot with enough water to cover them well. Soak for about 2 hours, then drain and set aside.

2. Preheat the oven to 350°F. Combine the dals with 6 cups water, the turmeric powder, and salt in a 3-quart Dutch oven. Bring to a full boil over high heat, cover, and bake until the dals are soft. If the water begins to dry out, add up to 1 cup more. (The consistency should be like a creamy soup.)

3. While the dals are cooking, heat the oil in a medium skillet. When hot, add the cumin seeds, garlic, and ginger. Cook for 30 seconds and add the onions. Cook, stirring occasionally, until the onions are well browned, 7–8 minutes.

4. Add the red chili powder and curry powder; mix well. Stir the onion mixture into the dals and mix well.

PER SERVING Calories: 182 | Fat: 1g | Protein: 12g | Sodium: 297mg | Fiber: 8.5g | Carbohydrates: 31g | Sugar: 2g

Mediterranean Chickpea Casserole

Bright lemon, fresh thyme, and a crispy bread crumb topping make this dish just as inviting for a meatless supper as for a vegetarian side.

INGREDIENTS | SERVES 8

4 tablespoons olive oil

3 shallots, minced

3 cloves garlic, minced

3 tablespoons flour

1½ cups low-sodium chicken broth

1 tablespoon chopped fresh thyme

¾ cup grated Parmesan cheese

3 (14.5-ounce) cans chickpeas, drained and rinsed

1 tablespoon lemon juice

1 tablespoon lemon zest

½ cup coarse bread crumbs

1. Preheat the oven to 375°F and spray a 9" × 13" casserole dish lightly with nonstick spray.

2. Heat 3 tablespoons oil in a medium saucepan over medium-high heat. When hot, add the shallots, stirring occasionally, until tender, about 5 minutes. Add the garlic and cook for 1 minute more. Slowly whisk in the flour and chicken broth to avoid lumps and simmer until the sauce thickens slightly, about 3 minutes. Remove the sauce from the heat and stir in the thyme, ½ cup Parmesan cheese, chickpeas, lemon juice, and lemon zest. Pour the chickpea mixture into the prepared casserole dish.

3. Toss the bread crumbs with the remaining ¼ cup Parmesan cheese and 1 tablespoon olive oil in a small bowl and scatter over the casserole.

4. Bake until the casserole bubbles and the topping browns, about 45 minutes.

PER SERVING Calories: 202 | Fat: 10g | Protein: 8g | Sodium: 450mg | Fiber: 2.5g | Carbohydrates: 19g | Sugar: 0.5g

Chickpea and Quinoa Pilaf

This hearty pilaf can be served as a side dish to braised or stewed meats,
or as a vegetarian course all its own.

INGREDIENTS | SERVES 6

2 tablespoons canola oil

1 medium onion, minced

2 garlic cloves, minced

¼ teaspoon salt

1 cup quinoa

1½ cups vegetable broth

2 (14.5-ounce) cans chickpeas, rinsed and drained

¼ cup chopped parsley

2 scallions, trimmed and thinly sliced

Pilafs

A pilaf is technically a rice dish where the rice is browned in butter or oil before cooking it in flavorful stock. However, other grains may be cooked in the pilaf style or with the flavors of traditional pilafs, which often include aromatic vegetables, herbs, and spices.

1. Preheat the oven to 350°F and spray a 9" × 9" casserole dish lightly with nonstick spray.

2. Heat the oil in a medium saucepan over medium-high heat. When hot, add the onion, garlic, and salt. Cook, stirring often, until the vegetables are slightly softened, about 4 minutes.

3. Stir in the quinoa and broth, then bring the mixture to a boil. Gently stir in the chickpeas and pour the mixture into the prepared casserole dish.

4. Bake the casserole, covered tightly with foil, until the quinoa is cooked through and the vegetables are tender, about 45 minutes.

5. Stir the parsley and scallions into the casserole just before serving.

PER SERVING Calories: 229 | Fat: 7.2g | Protein: 7.1g | Sodium: 308mg | Fiber: 4.4g | Carbohydrates: 35g | Sugar: 0g

Three-Bean Casserole with Crunchy Crumb Topping

This dish makes a welcome addition to any potluck or supper party.
Increase the spice by adding more chipotle.

INGREDIENTS | SERVES 8

3 tablespoons extra-virgin olive oil

3 garlic cloves, minced

1 (28-ounce) can crushed tomatoes

1½ tablespoons chopped oregano leaves

½ cup chopped fresh parsley

1½ tablespoons adobo sauce from a can of chipotle chili peppers

1 (14.5-ounce) can cannellini beans, drained and rinsed

1 (14.5-ounce) can butter beans, drained and rinsed

1 (14.5-ounce) can navy beans, drained and rinsed

¾ cup coarse whole-wheat bread crumbs

¼ cup Parmesan cheese

1. Preheat the oven to 400°F and spray a 9" × 13" casserole dish lightly with nonstick spray.

2. Heat 2 tablespoons oil in a large saucepan over medium heat. When hot, add the garlic and cook until fragrant, about 30 seconds. Add the tomatoes, oregano, parsley, and adobo sauce. Bring the sauce to a simmer, then remove from heat.

3. Add all beans to the prepared casserole dish. Spoon the tomato sauce over the top of the beans and stir gently to combine.

4. Toss the bread crumbs with the Parmesan cheese and remaining 1 tablespoon olive oil in a small bowl, and sprinkle the crumbs over the top of the beans.

5. Bake until the casserole bubbles and the topping browns, about 35–40 minutes.

PER SERVING Calories: 308 | Fat: 7.4g | Protein: 16g | Sodium: 488mg | Fiber: 10g | Carbohydrates: 47g | Sugar: 1g

Removing Sodium from Canned Beans

Many manufacturers process canned foods with salt, which can improve the texture and flavor of the product, but may be problematic for people looking to reduce their sodium intake. To remove almost half of the sodium from canned beans, simply rinse them under cool running water and drain.

White Beans Baked with Salsa Verde

Salsa Verde (see Chapter 14) gives canned beans zippy flavor. Serve them as a side to grilled meats or fish. Make a vegetarian version of the dish by swapping vegetable broth for the chicken broth.

INGREDIENTS | SERVES 6

2 tablespoons olive oil

1 large sweet onion, diced

2 cloves garlic, minced

1 tablespoon flour

1 tablespoon low-sodium chicken broth

¼ teaspoon pepper

2 (14.5-ounce) cans cannellini beans

¼ cup Salsa Verde (see Chapter 14)

½ cup whole-wheat bread crumbs

3 tablespoons grated Parmesan cheese

1. Preheat the oven to 400°F and spray a 9" × 9" casserole dish lightly with nonstick spray.

2. Heat 1½ tablespoons oil in a medium saucepan over medium heat. When hot, add the onion and garlic and cook until tender, about 7 minutes. Whisk in the flour and slowly stream in the chicken broth. Add the pepper and simmer the mixture, whisking occasionally until slightly thickened, about 5 minutes.

3. Add the cannellini beans to the prepared casserole dish. Swirl in the Salsa Verde and stir gently to combine.

4. Toss the bread crumbs with the Parmesan cheese and remaining 1½ teaspoons olive oil in a small bowl and sprinkle the crumbs over the top of the beans.

5. Bake until the casserole bubbles and the topping browns, about 35–40 minutes.

PER SERVING Calories: 239 | Fat: 5.2g | Protein: 11g | Sodium: 100mg | Fiber: 7.6g | Carbohydrates: 38g | Sugar: 3.2g

Savory Succotash

This version of succotash may not be traditional, but the extra flavor gained by roasting the vegetables coupled with the addition of fresh herbs make for a delicious side.

INGREDIENTS | SERVES 6

1 (10-ounce) package frozen corn kernels
1 (10-ounce) package frozen lima beans
2 tablespoons extra-virgin olive oil
1 small onion, minced
1 tablespoon chopped fresh thyme
½ teaspoon kosher salt
¼ cup chopped fresh parsley

Succotash

Succotash was popular during the Depression era because the ingredients—beans and corn—were relatively inexpensive, but its roots date back to the Native Americans who introduced it to the first colonists.

1. Preheat the oven to 400°F and spray a 9" × 13" casserole dish lightly with nonstick spray.

2. Combine the corn, lima beans, and 1 tablespoon of the olive oil together in the prepared casserole dish.

3. Roast, stirring occasionally, until the vegetables heat through and begin to color, about 30 minutes.

4. While the vegetables are roasting, heat the remaining tablespoon of oil in a medium skillet over medium-high heat. When hot, add the onion, thyme, and salt; cook until the onion softens and just begins to caramelize, about 10–15 minutes.

5. Remove the casserole from the oven and stir in the onions and parsley just before serving.

PER SERVING Calories: 144 | Fat: 5.2g | Protein: 5.2g | Sodium: 220mg | Fiber: 3.8g | Carbohydrates: 22g | Sugar: 1.4g

Three-Bean Vegan Chili

This hearty vegan dish is sure to satisfy any meat lover. Increase the amount of jalapeño peppers to ramp up the heat. Serve with vegan (or regular) shredded Cheddar cheese, vegan (or regular) sour cream, lime wedges, and chopped cilantro.

INGREDIENTS | SERVES 8

2 tablespoons canola oil

1 large yellow onion, diced

1 green bell pepper, diced

3 cloves garlic, minced

1 jalapeño pepper, stemmed, seeded, and minced

2 cups frozen corn kernels

2 tablespoons chili powder

2 teaspoons ground cumin

1 (28-ounce) can diced tomatoes

1 cup vegetable broth

1 (14.5-ounce) can black beans, drained and rinsed

1 (14.5-ounce) can kidney beans, drained and rinsed

1 (14.5-ounce) can pinto beans, drained and rinsed

1. Preheat the oven to 350°F.

2. Heat the oil in a 3-quart Dutch oven over medium-high heat. When hot, add the onion, green pepper, garlic, and jalapeño. Cook, stirring occasionally, until the vegetables begin to soften, about 7 minutes.

3. Add the corn, chili powder, cumin, tomatoes, vegetable broth, and all beans to the pot. Stir, bring to a simmer, and cover.

4. Bake the chili until the flavors have combined and the vegetables have softened, about 35–40 minutes.

PER SERVING Calories: 320 | Fat: 5.8g | Protein: 17g | Sodium: 437mg | Fiber: 13g | Carbohydrates: 55g | Sugar: 3g

Flageolet Bean Gratin

These delicate beans are delicious served with lamb or halibut,
or on their own with a green salad for a simple vegetarian lunch.

INGREDIENTS | SERVES 8

2 cups flageolet beans that have been soaked overnight, drained

4 cups water

1 carrot, peeled

1 stalk celery, trimmed

2 onions: 1 whole, peeled; 1 finely diced

2 tablespoons olive oil

4 cloves garlic, minced

2 tablespoons thyme

1 (14.5-ounce) can diced tomatoes

½ teaspoon salt

½ cup chopped parsley

1 cup coarse whole-wheat bread crumbs

¼ cup Parmesan cheese

1. Bring the flageolet beans, water, carrot, celery, and 1 whole onion to a simmer in a large heavy-bottomed pot. Cook, uncovered, until the beans are tender, about 1½ hours, adding more water if the beans become dry. Discard the carrot, celery, and onion; drain the beans, reserving the cooking liquid

2. Preheat the oven to 350°F and spray a 9" × 13" casserole dish lightly with nonstick spray.

3. Heat the oil in a medium saucepan over medium heat. When hot, add the diced onion and cook until tender, about 10 minutes. Add the garlic and cook for 30 seconds. Stir in the thyme, tomatoes, salt, and parsley and bring the sauce to a gentle simmer.

4. Combine the beans and tomato sauce in the prepared casserole dish. If the mixture seems too dry, add a little of the reserved cooking liquid. Toss the bread crumbs and cheese together in a small bowl and sprinkle on top of the casserole.

5. Bake, uncovered, until the casserole is bubbly and the crumb topping golden, 35–40 minutes.

PER SERVING Calories: 294 | Fat: 5.6g | Protein: 15g | Sodium: 427mg | Fiber: 9.3g | Carbohydrates: 45g | Sugar: 4.8g

Meatless Mains

Sweet Orange Tofu Bake

This glazed tofu becomes slightly chewy and almost "meaty" when baked.
Enjoy it alongside roasted or steamed vegetables.

INGREDIENTS | SERVES 6

3 tablespoons orange juice

1 tablespoon soy sauce

1 tablespoon lime juice

1 tablespoon Dijon mustard

1 teaspoon brown sugar

3 tablespoons olive oil

2 blocks extra-firm tofu

2 tablespoons chopped cilantro

Tender Stems

Don't bother removing the stems from cilantro. They are tender and can be chopped finely along with the leaves for a slightly stronger cilantro flavor.

1. Whisk the orange juice, soy sauce, lime juice, Dijon mustard, brown sugar, and olive oil together. Spray a 9" × 13" baking dish lightly with nonstick spray. Arrange the tofu in the dish and pour the marinade over, turning the tofu in the sauce. Marinate for at least 1 hour and up to overnight.

2. Preheat the oven to 350°F.

3. Bake the tofu in the marinade for 15 minutes, turn over, then bake for another 10–12 minutes until cooked and slightly springy to the touch. Garnish with cilantro.

PER SERVING Calories: 226 | Fat: 16g | Protein: 18g | Sodium: 184mg | Fiber: 2.2g | Carbohydrates: 6g | Sugar: 1.4g

Curried Tofu with Sweet Potatoes

This Thai-inspired dish is delicious served over brown rice or with a crisp veggie slaw.

INGREDIENTS | SERVES 6

2 tablespoons vegetable oil

1 medium onion, diced

1 tablespoon Thai curry paste

1 red bell pepper, seeded and diced

1 yellow bell pepper, seeded and diced

1 (14-ounce) can light coconut milk

¼ cup brown sugar

¼ cup vegetable broth

1 (14.5-ounce) can diced tomatoes

2 medium sweet potatoes, cut into 1" chunks

1 pound firm tofu, well drained and cut into 1" chunks

¼ cup chopped basil

1 tablespoon lime juice

1. Preheat the oven to 350°F.

2. In a 3-quart Dutch oven, heat the vegetable oil. When hot, add the onion and curry paste. Cook until the onion is tender, about 10 minutes. Add the bell peppers, coconut milk, brown sugar, vegetable broth, tomatoes, sweet potatoes, and tofu. Bring the curry to a simmer and cover.

3. Bake the curry, stirring once or twice, until the vegetables are tender, the tofu cooked through, and the sauce somewhat thickened, 30–35 minutes

4. Stir in the basil and lime juice just before serving.

PER SERVING Calories: 393 | Fat: 26g | Protein: 15g | Sodium: 195mg | Fiber: 4g | Carbohydrates: 30g | Sugar: 13g

Tofu Oven Stew with Pinto Beans and Tomatoes

This hearty main dish is chock-full of ripe tomato and herb flavor. Enjoy with baked pita chips and a crisp green salad. For extra flavor, swirl in a little of the Three-Herb Pesto (see Chapter 14) before serving.

INGREDIENTS | SERVES 6

16 ounces firm or extra-firm tofu, drained

3 tablespoons fresh thyme, chopped

2 tablespoons reduced-sodium soy sauce

3 tablespoons olive oil

2 leeks, whites and pale green parts, washed, halved, and sliced into rings

4 cloves garlic, minced

1 stalk celery, chopped

1 carrot, chopped

¼ cup flour

1½ cups vegetable broth

1 (14.5-ounce) can diced tomatoes, drained

1 (14.5-ounce) can pinto beans

½ teaspoon salt

¼ teaspoon pepper

½ cup whole-wheat bread crumbs

3 tablespoons grated Parmesan cheese

1. Chop the tofu into ¼" pieces and stir it gently together with the thyme and soy sauce in a bowl. Preheat the oven to 350°F and spray a 9" × 13" casserole dish lightly with nonstick spray.

2. Heat the oil in a large saucepan over medium heat. When hot, add the leeks, garlic, celery, and carrot. Cook, stirring occasionally, until the vegetables soften, about 10–13 minutes. Stir in the flour and slowly stream in the vegetable broth, stirring constantly to avoid lumps. Add the tomatoes, beans, salt, pepper, tofu, and marinade. Bring the mixture to a gentle simmer, then pour in the prepared casserole dish. Toss together the bread crumbs and Parmesan cheese in a small bowl: sprinkle over the casserole.

3. Bake the casserole, uncovered, until it bubbles, the vegetables become tender, and the crumbs brown, 40–45 minutes.

PER SERVING Calories: 345 | Fat: 16g | Protein: 21g | Sodium: 1,021mg | Fiber: 7.5g | Carbohydrates: 35g | Sugar: 5.7g

Tofu

Tofu stands out for its ability to absorb just about any flavor that you add to it. To prepare it for cooking, you must drain it first. Remove the tofu from the water that it is packed in, place it between two plates or rimmed baking sheets, then weigh it down with a can or two. Allow the tofu to drain for 10–20 minutes, then cut it to the desired shape, and use in your favorite recipes.

Tofu, Orzo, and Pesto Bake

This baked dish is bursting with the taste of summer.
Enjoy with a simple salad and crusty whole-grain rolls.

INGREDIENTS | SERVES 6

16 ounces firm or extra-firm tofu, drained

¼ teaspoon salt-free lemon pepper

2 tablespoons reduced-sodium soy sauce

1 pound orzo

1 tablespoon olive oil

1 medium onion, diced

3 cloves garlic, minced

1 red bell pepper, seeded and diced

1 (14.5-ounce) can diced tomatoes

½ cup Basil Pesto (see Chapter 14)

½ cup shredded fontina cheese

1. Chop the tofu into ¼" pieces and stir it gently together with the lemon pepper and soy sauce in a bowl. Preheat the oven to 350°F and spray a 9" × 13" casserole dish lightly with nonstick spray.

2. While the tofu is marinating, cook the orzo according to package directions until just barely al dente.

3. Heat the oil in a skillet over medium-high heat. When hot, add the onion and cook until just tender, about 5 minutes. Add the garlic and cook for 1 minute. Stir in the bell pepper and cook for another 3 minutes, then remove the vegetables from the heat.

4. Stir together the orzo, tofu, marinade, vegetables, tomatoes, Basil Pesto, and fontina cheese in the prepared casserole dish.

5. Bake, uncovered, until the orzo is al dente and the cheese is melted, 25–30 minutes.

PER SERVING Calories: 492 | Fat: 16g | Protein: 27g | Sodium: 580mg | Fiber: 5.4g | Carbohydrates: 66g | Sugar: 4.4g

Satisfying Summer Garden Baked Tofu

Serve this flavorful tofu dish with rice pilaf or baked quinoa,
with the extra sauce spooned over the top.

INGREDIENTS | SERVES 6

1 teaspoon garlic powder

1 shallot, minced

1 tablespoon Dijon mustard

2 teaspoons rice vinegar

1 tablespoon grated lemon zest

1 tablespoon lemon juice

¾ teaspoon sugar

2 tablespoons soy sauce

3 tablespoons olive oil

2 blocks firm tofu, well pressed

1 small zucchini, julienned

1 small yellow squash, julienned

¼ cup chopped fresh basil

Freezing Tofu

Freezing tofu alters its texture, causing it to become slightly more dense and chewy. However, it also enables the tofu to soak up more marinade, thereby enhancing its flavor.

1. Whisk the garlic powder, shallot, Dijon mustard, vinegar, lemon zest, lemon juice, sugar, soy sauce, and 2 tablespoons olive oil together in a bowl. Spray a 9" × 13" casserole dish lightly with nonstick spray.

2. Slice the tofu into ½"-thick strips and arrange in the baking dish. Spoon the marinade over the tofu, turning the pieces to coat with the marinade; marinate for at least 1 hour and up to overnight.

3. Preheat the oven to 350°F.

4. Toss the zucchini and squash with the remaining tablespoon of olive oil and sprinkle around the tofu.

5. Bake for 15 minutes, turn the tofu over, and bake for another 10–12 minutes until the vegetables are tender and the tofu lightly browned. Garnish with the basil.

PER SERVING Calories: 234 | Fat: 17g | Protein: 19g | Sodium: 352mg | Fiber: 3g | Carbohydrates: 7.1g | Sugar: 1.9g

Shells Stuffed with Tofu and White Beans

The beans add a slightly unusual flavor and a creamy texture to the filling. These shells will please any carnivore, but are much lighter than traditional ricotta-stuffed shells and are completely vegan.

INGREDIENTS | SERVES 6

1 pound jumbo shells

2 tablespoons extra-virgin olive oil

2 cloves garlic, minced

1 (16-ounce) bag frozen spinach, thawed and well drained

1 cup fresh vegan bread crumbs

1 (14.5-ounce) can cannellini beans, well drained

8 ounces firm tofu, well drained

1 teaspoon salt

1 teaspoon chili powder

3 tablespoons chopped fresh basil

1 tablespoon chopped oregano

1 recipe Basic Tomato Sauce (see Chapter 14)

2 tablespoons chopped parsley

1. Cook the shells according to the package directions, then spread out on a clean rimmed baking sheet to cool.

2. Heat the olive oil in a large skillet. When hot, add the garlic and cook until it is fragrant and almost pale straw yellow. Add the spinach and toss in the skillet to remove any excess moisture. Remove to a large bowl to cool.

3. Combine the bread crumbs, cannellini beans, and tofu in the bowl of a food processor. Pulse until the mixture is creamy and smooth, 10–15 pulses. Remove the mixture to the bowl with the spinach and stir in the salt, chili powder, basil, and oregano.

4. Preheat the oven to 350°F and spray a 9" × 13" casserole dish lightly with nonstick spray.

5. Spread 1½ cups of the sauce on the bottom of the prepared casserole dish. Divide the filling among the cooked shells and place seam side up in the baking dish. When all the shells are filled, pour the remaining sauce over the shells and wrap tightly with foil.

6. Bake until the casserole bubbles and the pasta and filling are cooked through, about 45 minutes. Sprinkle with parsley before serving.

PER SERVING Calories: 566 | Fat: 11g | Protein: 26g | Sodium: 592mg | Fiber: 12g | Carbohydrates: 94g | Sugar: 6.4g

Portobello, Tofu, and Spinach Bake

This tofu is tender and luscious. Serve over brown rice or baked barley.

INGREDIENTS | SERVES 6

¼ cup reduced-sodium soy sauce

1 tablespoon rice vinegar

1 tablespoon sesame oil

1 pound firm tofu, well drained

3 tablespoons vegetable oil

3 portobello mushroom caps, cleaned and sliced into ½" pieces

3 shallots, minced

2 cloves garlic, minced

1 tablespoon ginger, minced

3 scallions, cleaned and thinly sliced

3 tablespoons flour

2 cups mushroom broth

¼ teaspoon salt

8 ounces chopped frozen spinach, thawed

Cleaning Portobellos

The portobello has a large thick cap with dark feathery gills. While perfectly edible, the gills can turn the rest of a cooked dish murky if they aren't removed first. Scrape them off the mushroom cap gently with a spoon before cooking with the mushroom.

1. Preheat the oven to 350°F and spray a 9" × 13" casserole dish lightly with nonstick spray. Stir 2 tablespoons of the soy sauce, vinegar, and sesame oil in the prepared casserole dish. Cut the tofu into ¾" cubes and toss in the marinade.

2. While the tofu is marinating, heat 1½ tablespoons of the vegetable oil in a large nonstick skillet over medium-high heat. When hot, add the mushrooms and cook without moving them for 5 minutes. Stir the mushrooms and cook until browned and reduced in volume, about 5 minutes longer.

3. Push the mushrooms to the sides of the pan and add the remaining oil. When hot, add the shallots, garlic, ginger, and scallions. Cook until fragrant, about 1 minute. Stir in the flour, then slowly stream in the mushroom broth, stirring constantly to avoid lumps. Add the salt and remaining soy sauce and bring the sauce to a simmer; cook until the liquid is slightly thickened, about 3 minutes.

4. Remove the skillet from the heat, stir in the spinach, and pour over the tofu in the prepared casserole dish.

5. Bake until the casserole bubbles and the tofu and mushrooms are cooked, about 25 minutes.

PER SERVING Calories: 241 | Fat: 17g | Protein: 17g | Sodium: 804mg | Fiber: 4g | Carbohydrates: 11g | Sugar: 1.8g

Udon Noodle, Shiitake, and Tofu Casserole

Chewy udon noodles and eggy custard combine with silky tofu to make a savory vegetarian meal with Asian flavors.

INGREDIENTS | SERVES 8

1 pound udon noodles

1 tablespoon canola oil

1 cup scallions, thinly sliced

1 tablespoon fresh ginger, minced

3 cloves garlic, minced

8 ounces shiitake mushrooms, sliced

8 ounces (½ package) frozen stir-fry vegetables

1 pound firm tofu, well drained and cut into ½" pieces

1 teaspoon toasted sesame oil

3 tablespoons reduced-sodium soy sauce

½ cup mushroom broth

2 eggs

2 egg whites

Vegetable Variation

Instead of the mixed stir-fry vegetables, try using just broccoli, spinach, or tender young asparagus to give the casserole a singular focus. Change the flavors slightly by adding some orange zest and orange juice concentrate, or a little chili garlic sauce for some extra heat.

1. Preheat the oven to 350°F and spray a 9" × 13" casserole dish with nonstick spray. Cook the udon noodles according to package directions until just al dente, then rinse under cool running water.

2. Heat the oil in a large skillet over medium-high heat. When hot, add the scallions, ginger, and garlic. Cook until fragrant, about 1 minute.

3. Push the aromatics to the side of the skillet and add the mushrooms. Cook, stirring occasionally, until the mushrooms are tender, about 7 minutes. Stir in the frozen stir-fry vegetables and tofu, then remove the skillet from the heat.

4. Whisk the sesame oil, soy sauce, mushroom broth, eggs, and egg whites together in a large bowl. Stir in the udon and vegetable mixture, then pour into the prepared casserole dish.

5. Bake the casserole until it is set in the center, 25–30 minutes.

PER SERVING Calories: 211 | Fat: 9g | Protein: 16g | Sodium: 183mg | Fiber: 2.4g | Carbohydrates: 21g | Sugar: 1.1g

Lemon Basil Tofu

Moist and chewy, this zesty baked tofu is reminiscent of lemon chicken.
Serve over steamed rice with extra marinade.

INGREDIENTS | SERVES 6

3 tablespoons lemon juice

1 tablespoon soy sauce

2 teaspoons apple cider vinegar

1 tablespoon Dijon mustard

¾ teaspoon sugar

3 tablespoons olive oil

2 tablespoons chopped basil, plus extra for garnish

2 blocks firm or extra-firm tofu, well pressed

1. Spray a 9" × 13" casserole dish lightly with nonstick spray. Whisk together the lemon juice, soy sauce, cider vinegar, Dijon mustard, sugar, olive oil, and basil. Pour into prepared casserole dish.

2. Slice the tofu into ½"-thick strips or triangles.

3. Place the tofu in the marinade and coat well. Allow to marinate for at least 1 hour or overnight, being sure tofu is well coated in the marinade.

4. Preheat the oven to 350°F.

5. Bake the tofu for 15 minutes, turn over, then bake for another 10–12 minutes or until done. Garnish with a few extra bits of chopped basil.

PER SERVING Calories: 222 | Fat: 16g | Protein: 18g | Sodium: 184mg | Fiber: 2.2g | Carbohydrates: 5g | Sugar: 0.58g

Braised Tofu and Veggie Cacciatore

If you'd like a more grown-up Italian dish, use ½ cup white wine in place of ½ cup broth. Serve over pasta or try it with rice, whole-grain pilaf, or even baked potatoes or polenta.

INGREDIENTS | SERVES 4

2 tablespoons olive oil

½ yellow onion, diced

½ cup mushrooms, sliced

1 carrot, peeled and diced

3 cloves garlic, minced

2 blocks firm tofu, well drained and cubed

1½ cups vegetable broth

1 (14.5-ounce) can diced tomatoes

1 (6-ounce) can tomato paste

1 bay leaf

½ teaspoon salt

1 teaspoon parsley

1 teaspoon basil

1 teaspoon oregano

1. Preheat the oven to 350°F and heat the oil in a 3-quart Dutch oven. When hot, add the onion, mushrooms, carrot, and garlic. Cook the vegetables until they are just tender, about 5 minutes. Add the tofu and cook another 2 minutes.

2. Add the vegetable broth, tomatoes, tomato paste, bay leaf, and salt. Bring the mixture to a simmer, then cover.

3. Bake until the tofu is slightly firmed and the sauce reduced, about 20–25 minutes. Stir in the parsley, basil, and oregano just before serving.

PER SERVING Calories: 376 | Fat: 22g | Protein: 29g | Sodium: 601mg | Fiber: 7.4g | Carbohydrates: 24g | Sugar: 10g

Cajun-Spiced Cornmeal-Breaded Tofu

Reminiscent of oven-breaded catfish, this is a Southern-inspired breaded tofu that can be baked or fried. Serve with barbecue sauce or a squeeze of lemon.

INGREDIENTS | SERVES 3

⅔ cup soymilk

2 tablespoons lime juice

¼ cup flour

⅓ cup cornmeal

1 tablespoon Cajun seasoning

1 teaspoon onion powder

½ teaspoon cayenne pepper, or to taste

½ teaspoon salt

½ teaspoon black pepper

1 block extra-firm tofu, well pressed

Quick Barbecue Sauce

Combine 1 cup ketchup, ¼ cup cider vinegar, ½ teaspoon chili powder, 2 tablespoons brown sugar, 1 tablespoon Dijon mustard, ¼ teaspoon salt, and ½ teaspoon black pepper in a small saucepan. Simmer over low heat for 3 minutes, then cool.

1. Preheat the oven to 375° and spray a 9" × 13" casserole dish with nonstick spray.

2. Combine the soymilk and lime juice in a wide shallow bowl. In a separate bowl, combine the flour, cornmeal, Cajun seasoning, onion powder, cayenne, salt, and pepper.

3. Slice the tofu into triangles and dip in the soymilk mixture. Next, coat each piece well with the cornmeal and flour.

4. Transfer tofu to the prepared casserole dish and bake for 8–10 minutes on each side.

PER SERVING Calories: 277 | Fat: 11g | Protein: 22g | Sodium: 433mg | Fiber: 4.1g | Carbohydrates: 27g | Sugar: 0.7g

Mexican Spice-Crusted Tofu

These little bites are packed with spices, so no dipping sauce is needed.
Eat with rice or enjoy as a snack.

INGREDIENTS | SERVES 3

3 tablespoons soy sauce

3 tablespoons hot chili sauce

1 teaspoon sugar

1 block firm or extra-firm tofu, well pressed and sliced into ¾" strips

1 teaspoon garlic powder

1 teaspoon onion powder

1 tablespoon chili powder

¾ teaspoon cumin

¾ teaspoon oregano

2 tablespoons flour

1. Whisk together the soy sauce, chili sauce, and sugar in a shallow pan; add the tofu. Marinate the tofu for at least 1 hour and up to 8 hours.

2. Preheat the oven to 350°F and spray a 9" × 13" casserole dish with nonstick spray.

3. In a shallow baking dish, combine the garlic powder, onion powder, chili powder, cumin, oregano, and flour. Carefully dip each piece of tofu in the spice mixture and place in the prepared casserole dish.

4. Bake, turning once, for 7–9 minutes until the tofu is sizzling and slightly springy to the touch.

PER SERVING Calories: 179 | Fat: 9.8g | Protein: 19g | Sodium: 1,016mg | Fiber: 2.5g | Carbohydrates: 7.4g | Sugar: 2.2g

Vegan TVP-Stuffed Peppers

This is a great way to use up any leftover rice.
Top with a bit of grated vegan cheese, if you'd like.

INGREDIENTS | SERVES 6

6 bell peppers, any color

¾ cup TVP

¾ cup hot vegetable broth

2 tablespoons olive oil

1 onion, chopped

2 ribs celery, diced

⅔ cup mushrooms, chopped small

1½ cups rice, cooked

1 teaspoon parsley

½ teaspoon oregano

½ teaspoon salt

2 cups tomato or marinara sauce

TVP Tips

TVP is shelf-stable and can be stored for up to a year if sealed in an airtight container. Keep in a cool, dry place until ready to use.

1. Preheat the oven to 325°F and spray a 9" × 13" casserole dish lightly with nonstick spray.

2. Slice the tops off the bell peppers and remove their inner seeds and membranes. Reserve the tops.

3. Combine the TVP and vegetable broth and allow to sit for 6–7 minutes to rehydrate. Drain.

4. In a large skillet, heat the olive oil over medium heat. When hot, add the onion, celery, and mushrooms; cook until the onions are soft and mushrooms are browned, about 10 minutes. Reduce the heat to medium-low and add cooked rice, TVP, parsley, oregano, salt, and tomato sauce, reserving about ½ cup. Heat just until combined.

5. Stuff mixture into bell peppers, place in the prepared casserole dish, and spoon a bit of the remaining sauce on top of each pepper. Place the "lids" back on the bell peppers (optional).

6. Bake, uncovered, for 30 minutes or until peppers are cooked.

PER SERVING Calories: 145 | Protein: 10g | Fat: 1g | Sodium: 757mg | Fiber: 6g | Carbohydrates: 28g | Sugar: 3.7g

Southwestern TVP and Black Bean Casserole

Creamy and mildly spiced sweet potatoes crown this delectable vegan pie.
Serve with a chopped salad and corn bread.

INGREDIENTS | SERVES 8

FILLING

1½ cups TVP
1½ cups hot vegetable broth
1 tablespoon olive oil
1 onion, chopped
3 cloves garlic, minced
2 red bell peppers, seeded and diced
1 yellow bell pepper, seeded and diced
½ teaspoon salt
1 tablespoon chili powder
1 tablespoon chopped fresh oregano
1 tablespoon flour
1 cup vegetable broth
1 (14.5-ounce) can black beans, rinsed and drained
¼ cup cilantro

TOPPING

3 large sweet potatoes, cooked
2 tablespoons vegan margarine
3 tablespoons soymilk
1 teaspoon cumin
½ teaspoon salt
¼ teaspoon pepper

1. Preheat the oven to 350°F and spray a 9" × 13" casserole dish lightly with nonstick spray.

2. Combine the TVP with the vegetable broth and allow to sit for 6–7 minutes. Gently drain any excess moisture.

3. Heat the oil in a large skillet. When hot, add the onion, garlic, bell peppers, salt, chili powder, and oregano. Cook the mixture until the vegetables are tender, about 10 minutes. Stir in the flour and slowly stream in the vegetable broth, stirring continuously to avoid lumps. Bring to a simmer, add the TVP, and pour into the prepared casserole dish.

4. Stir the black beans together with the cilantro in a bowl, then spread over the TVP mixture.

5. Mash the sweet potatoes, margarine, soymilk, cumin, salt, and pepper together in a bowl. Spread the mixture over the black beans.

6. Bake until the sweet potatoes start to lightly brown and the casserole bubbles, 30–35 minutes.

PER SERVING Calories: 338 | Fat: 8g | Protein: 22g | Sodium: 532mg | Fiber: 12g | Carbohydrates: 48g | Sugar: 3g

Vegan No Shepherd, No Sheep Pie

This sheep- and shepherdless pie is a hearty vegan entrée for big appetites!

INGREDIENTS | SERVES 6

1½ cups TVP
1½ cups hot vegetable broth
2 tablespoons olive oil
½ onion, chopped
2 cloves garlic, minced
1 large carrot, thinly sliced
¾ cup sliced mushrooms
½ cup green peas
1 tablespoon flour
½ cup vegetable broth
½ cup plus 3 tablespoons soymilk
5 medium potatoes, cooked
2 tablespoons vegan margarine
½ teaspoon fresh chopped rosemary
¼ teaspoon dried sage
½ teaspoon paprika
½ teaspoon salt
¼ teaspoon black pepper

1. Preheat the oven to 350°F and spray a 9" × 13" casserole dish lightly with nonstick spray.

2. Combine the TVP with the hot vegetable broth and allow to sit for 6–7 minutes. Gently drain any excess moisture.

3. In a large skillet, heat the oil over medium-high heat. When hot, add the onions, garlic, and carrots until the vegetables are softened, about 10 minutes. Add the mushrooms and green peas. Stir in the flour and slowly stream in the vegetable broth and ½ cup soymilk, stirring constantly to avoid lumps. Add the TVP and cook until the sauce thickens, about 5 minutes. Transfer the mixture to a casserole dish.

4. Mash together the potatoes, margarine, and 3 tablespoons soymilk with the rosemary, sage, paprika, salt, and pepper, and spread over the vegetables.

5. Bake the casserole for 30–35 minutes or until lightly browned on top.

PER SERVING Calories: 345 | Fat: 7.4g | Protein: 18g | Sodium: 553mg | Fiber: 9g | Carbohydrates: 53g | Sugar: 2g

Lump-Free Gravy and Sauces

When adding liquid to a roux (flour and fat) or another type of flour-thickened sauce, slowly stream in the liquid component, whisking constantly to avoid lumps. The hot flour and fat mixture will immediately swell and sputter, but don't let that slow you down—keep whisking and the sauce will become velvety smooth in no time.

TVP Tomato Sauce and Polenta Layered Casserole

This tasty baked casserole is chock-full of vegetables and ripe tomato flavor.
Serve with a simple green salad.

INGREDIENTS | SERVES 6

3 cups vegetable broth

1 teaspoon salt

1 cup polenta meal

1 tablespoon olive oil

1 small onion, minced

1 zucchini, diced

2 tablespoons fresh chopped basil

3 cups prepared TVP Tomato Sauce (see Chapter 14)

1 cup shredded part-skim mozzarella

½ cup grated Parmesan cheese

Polenta

Don't let the fancy name fool you. Polenta is really just cornmeal that is cooked with a flavorful liquid and sometimes cheese. If your store doesn't carry polenta meal, simply substitute coarse cornmeal.

1. Preheat the oven to 400°F and spray two 8" × 8" square casserole dishes with nonstick spray. If you don't own two 8" × 8" pans, use a disposable metal pan.

2. Bring the vegetable broth and salt to a simmer in a medium saucepan over medium heat. Whisk in the polenta meal and stir constantly for about 8 minutes, until the mixture is very thick. Immediately divide the mixture between the two pans, spreading the polenta into an even layer. Allow to cool.

3. While the polenta is cooling, heat the olive oil in a skillet over medium heat. When hot, add the onion and cook until just tender, about 7 minutes. Add the zucchini and cook until just cooked through, 4 minutes longer. Stir in the basil and remove from the heat.

4. Layer the zucchini mixture over one of the polenta layers and top with half the sauce, then half of the cheeses. Loosen the second polenta layer from the bottom of the pan and flip into the first casserole dish. Layer with the remaining sauce and cheese.

5. Bake until the sauce is bubbly and the cheeses are melted, about 40 minutes.

PER SERVING Calories: 434 | Fat: 16g | Protein: 36g | Sodium: 1,190mg | Fiber: 11g | Carbohydrates: 37g | Sugar: 5.6g

Pineapple TVP Baked Beans

Add a kick to these saucy homemade vegetarian baked beans with a bit of cayenne pepper if you'd like.

INGREDIENTS | SERVES 4

1 cup TVP

1 cup hot water

1 tablespoon vegetable oil

1 large sweet onion, diced

2 cloves garlic, minced

1 (8-ounce) can crushed pineapple

⅔ cup barbecue sauce

2 tablespoons prepared mustard

2 tablespoons brown sugar

¾ teaspoon salt

½ teaspoon pepper

2 (15-ounce) cans pinto beans, partially drained

1. Preheat the oven to 350°F. Combine the TVP with the hot water and allow to sit for 6–8 minutes, then drain.

2. Heat the oil in a 3-quart Dutch oven over medium-high heat. When hot, add the onion and cook until translucent, 5 minutes. Add the garlic and cook for 1 minute. Stir in the pineapple, barbecue sauce, mustard, brown sugar, salt, and pepper; bring to a simmer.

3. Stir in the beans and TVP; cover and bake until the liquid has reduced slightly and the casserole is bubbling, 20–25 minutes.

PER SERVING Calories: 332 | Fat: 7.7g | Protein: 18g | Sodium: 1,059mg | Fiber: 11g | Carbohydrates: 50g | Sugar: 25g

Canadian Baked Beans

Why not omit the brown sugar and use pure maple syrup for sweetened Canadian-style baked beans, eh?

Ginger-Soy Tempeh Bake

Baked tempeh is a simple entrée, or use as a patty to make veggie burgers or sandwiches. Slice your tempeh into cubes to add to fried rice, noodles, or stir-fry dishes.

INGREDIENTS | SERVES 2

1 (8-ounce) package tempeh

1 cup vegetable broth

3 tablespoons soy sauce

2 tablespoons apple cider vinegar

3 cloves garlic, minced

1 tablespoon fresh grated ginger

2 teaspoons sesame oil

What Is Tempeh?

Long a staple food in the Indonesian islands, tempeh sounds a bit odd when it's described: It's made from cultured (that is, fermented) cooked soybeans. Don't let that turn you off, though, as tempeh is chewy, textured, meaty, and super tasty! Look for tempeh in the refrigerated section of natural foods stores. Several different kinds are usually available, but they're all interchangeable, so try them all.

1. If your tempeh is thicker than ¾" thick, slice it in half through the center to make two thinner pieces, then slice into the desired shape.

2. Bring the vegetable broth up to a simmer in a saucepan and add the tempeh. Simmer until it plumps slightly, about 10 minutes. Drain the tempeh.

3. Whisk the soy sauce, vinegar, garlic, ginger, and sesame oil together and marinate the tempeh for at least 1 hour and up to 8 hours.

4. Preheat the oven to 375°F and spray a 9" × 13" casserole dish lightly with nonstick spray.

5. Transfer the tempeh to the prepared casserole dish and bake for 10–12 minutes per side.

PER SERVING Calories: 278 | Fat: 17g | Protein: 25g | Sodium: 1,307mg | Fiber: 0.5g | Carbohydrates: 12g | Sugar: 0.5g

Tempeh and Bean Cassoulet with Winter Vegetables

*Don't be tempted to use canned beans for this recipe;
the long cooking time will turn them to mush.*

INGREDIENTS | SERVES 10

BEANS

1 pound dried great northern beans,
soaked overnight, drained

1 onion, peeled

1 carrot, peeled

1 stalk celery, trimmed

TEMPEH

2 cups water

2 (8-ounce) packages tempeh, cut into
½" strips

2 tablespoons olive oil

1 large onion, diced

1 carrot, minced

1 stalk celery, minced

3 cloves garlic, minced

½ teaspoon kosher salt

2 cups peeled and diced butternut
squash

2 tablespoons tomato paste

1 tablespoon fresh minced thyme

1 quart vegetable broth

1 cup dry white wine

½ cup coarse bread crumbs

1. Place the beans in a large pot with enough water to cover by 2". Add the onion, carrot, and celery; cook at a gentle simmer until the beans are just tender but still slightly underdone, 1¼–1½ hours. Drain the beans and discard the vegetables.

2. Preheat the oven to 350°F and bring 2 cups water to a simmer in a medium saucepan. Add the tempeh to the simmering water and cook until slightly plumped, about 10 minutes. Drain the tempeh and blot with paper towels.

3. Heat the oil over medium-high heat in a 3-quart Dutch oven. When hot, add the tempeh and brown on both sides; remove to a plate.

4. Add the onion, carrot, celery, garlic, and salt to the Dutch oven. Cook until the vegetables are just beginning to soften, about 5 minutes. Add the squash and stir in the tomato paste, thyme, vegetable broth, and wine.

5. Add the beans and tempeh back to the pot; cover and cook until the beans, squash, and tempeh are all tender, about 1 hour.

6. Uncover the Dutch oven and scatter the bread crumbs over the top of the casserole. Bake until the crumbs are browned and crisp, about 15 minutes more.

PER SERVING Calories: 315 | Fat: 8.5g | Protein: 20g | Sodium: 180mg |
Fiber: 10g | Carbohydrates: 42g | Sugar: 2.9g

Baked Mexican Tempeh Cakes

Like tofu, tempeh can be baked in a flavorful sauce, but it does need to be simmered first, just to soften it up a bit. Serve with salsa or a red sauce.

INGREDIENTS | SERVES 4

2 (8-ounce) packages tempeh

1 cup water

⅓ cup tomato paste

3 cloves garlic, minced

2 tablespoons soy sauce

2 tablespoons apple cider vinegar

3 tablespoons water

1½ teaspoons chili powder

½ teaspoon oregano

¼ teaspoon cayenne

Chili Powder

Commercially sold chili powder is usually a mix of dried powdered chilies and occasionally other spices, such as garlic powder and salt. If you prefer a more pure chili flavor, substitute ground ancho chili powder.

1. If your tempeh is thicker than ¾", slice it in half through the middle to create two thinner halves. Slice each block of tempeh in fourths and simmer in water for 10 minutes, then drain.

2. Whisk together the tomato paste, garlic, soy sauce, apple cider vinegar, water, chili powder, oregano, and cayenne. Add the tempeh and allow to marinate for at least 1 hour or overnight.

3. Preheat the oven to 375°F and spray a 9" × 13" baking dish with nonstick spray.

4. Transfer the tempeh to the prepared casserole dish and reserve marinade. Bake for 15 minutes, then turn the tempeh over and baste with a bit of the marinade. Bake for 15–17 minutes until lightly browned.

PER SERVING Calories: 242 | Fat: 13g | Protein: 23g | Sodium: 530mg | Fiber: 1.2g | Carbohydrates: 15g | Sugar: 2.3g

Massaman Curried Seitan

With its Indian influences and popularity among Muslim communities in southern Thailand, massaman curry is truly a global dish. This version is simplified but still has a distinct kick. Diced tomatoes, baby corn, or green peas would work well in this recipe if you wanted to add veggies.

INGREDIENTS | SERVES 4

1 tablespoon vegetable oil

1 tablespoon Chinese five-spice powder

½ teaspoon fresh grated ginger

½ teaspoon turmeric

¼ teaspoon cayenne pepper

1½ cups coconut milk

1 cup vegetable broth

2 potatoes

1½ cups seitan, chopped small

2 whole cloves

1 teaspoon salt

1 tablespoon peanut butter

¼ teaspoon cinnamon

2 teaspoons brown sugar

⅓ cup peanuts

1. Preheat the oven to 350°F and heat the oil in a 3-quart Dutch oven over medium heat. When hot, add the five-spice powder, ginger, turmeric, and cayenne; cook until fragrant, about 1 minute.

2. Reduce the heat to medium-low and add the coconut milk and vegetable broth, stirring to combine. Add the potatoes, seitan, cloves, and salt. Cover and bake for 20 minutes.

3. Uncover the Dutch oven and add the peanut butter, cinnamon, sugar, and peanuts. Return to the oven, covered, for 10 more minutes until the flavors have melded and the sauce thickened slightly.

PER SERVING Calories: 432 | Fat: 37g | Protein: 18g | Sodium: 619mg | Fiber: 1.3g | Carbohydrates: 16g | Sugar: 3g

Seitan, Mushroom, and Dijon Stroganoff

Serve this stroganoff over noodles, rice, pasta, or baked potatoes.

INGREDIENTS | SERVES 4

2 tablespoons vegan margarine

1 onion, minced

2 cups sliced mushrooms

½ teaspoon dried sage

½ teaspoon garlic powder

1 tablespoon flour

2 cups soymilk

¼ teaspoon salt

⅛ teaspoon pepper

1½ cups seitan pieces, sliced ¼" thick

½ cup nondairy sour cream

2 teaspoons Dijon mustard

1 tablespoon parsley

Mushroom Mashup

Substitute your favorite kind of mushroom for the white buttons in this recipe or use a combination for a slightly different flavor.

1. Preheat the oven to 350°F and melt the margarine in a 3-quart Dutch oven. When hot, add the onion and cook until just tender, 7 minutes.

2. Add the mushrooms, sage, and garlic powder; cook the mixture until the mushrooms have released most of their liquid, about 10 minutes.

3. Stir in the flour, then stream in the soymilk, stirring constantly to avoid lumps. Stir in the salt, pepper, and seitan; bring to a bare simmer.

4. Cover and bake until the vegetables are tender and the sauce is somewhat reduced, about 20 minutes. Stir in the sour cream, Dijon mustard, and parsley just before serving.

PER SERVING Calories: 306 | Fat: 21g | Protein: 19g | Sodium: 319mg | Fiber: 1.6g | Carbohydrates: 15g | Sugar: 3.8g

CHAPTER 8

Seafood

Miso Baked Cod

This cod bakes up browned and sweet with deep flavor. You can find the mirin and miso paste in the international and refrigerated aisles of your grocery store.

INGREDIENTS | SERVES 4

1½ pounds cod, cut into 4 even pieces
¼ cup sake
¼ cup mirin
¼ cup white miso paste

Cooking with Sake

Sake is a type of alcohol from Japan that is made out of rice in a process much like brewing beer. If you choose not to cook with alcohol, you might substitute a nonalcoholic sake, fruit juice, clam juice, chicken broth, or vinegar, depending on the recipe.

1. Place the cod, sake, mirin, and miso paste in a large zip-top bag and gently shake so that the cod is evenly coated with the marinade. Refrigerate the cod overnight.

2. Preheat the oven to 400°F and spray a 9" × 13" casserole dish lightly with nonstick spray. Gently shake the excess marinade off of the fish and place it in the prepared casserole dish.

3. Bake the cod until it is browned and flakes easily with a fork, 10–15 minutes.

PER SERVING Calories: 214 | Fat: 3.5g | Protein: 32g | Sodium: 680mg | Fiber: 1.9g | Carbohydrates: 9.8g | Sugar: 2.1g

Salmon with Asian Flavors

Garnish this beautiful salmon with sliced scallions and serve with brown rice and steamed vegetables.

INGREDIENTS | SERVES 4

4 (6-ounce) skinned salmon pieces
¼ cup soy sauce
2 tablespoons oyster sauce
2 tablespoons rice vinegar
2 teaspoons chili garlic paste
1 teaspoon dark sesame oil
1 teaspoon minced ginger

1. Place the salmon, soy sauce, oyster sauce, rice vinegar, chili garlic paste, sesame oil, and ginger in a large zip-top bag. Marinate the salmon for at least 30 minutes and up to 2 hours.

2. Preheat the oven to 400°F and spray a 9" × 13" casserole dish lightly with nonstick spray. Gently shake the excess marinade off of the fish and place it in the prepared casserole dish.

3. Bake the salmon until it is browned and flakes easily with a fork, about 20 minutes.

PER SERVING Calories: 254 | Fat: 9.4g | Protein: 40g | Sodium: 1,256mg | Fiber: 1.5g | Carbohydrates: 2.3g | Sugar: 0.27g

Soy-Ginger Tilapia

This zippy fish dish would go well with baked brown rice and a tangy cabbage slaw made with a lime juice vinaigrette. You can find chili garlic paste and toasted sesame oil in the international foods section of most grocery stores.

INGREDIENTS | SERVES 6

6 (4-ounce) tilapia fillets (1.5 pounds total)

1 tablespoon chili garlic paste

2 teaspoons toasted sesame oil

3 scallions, chopped

1 tablespoon minced fresh ginger

⅓ cup dry sherry

¼ cup low-sodium soy sauce

1. Preheat the oven to 450°F and spray a 9" × 13" casserole dish lightly with nonstick spray. Arrange the tilapia in a single layer on the bottom of the baking dish.

2. Whisk together the chili garlic paste, sesame oil, scallions, ginger, sherry, and soy sauce; pour over the fish.

3. Bake until the fish flakes easily with a fork and is opaque in the center, about 10 minutes.

PER SERVING Calories: 223 | Fat: 5.6g | Protein: 40g | Sodium: 440mg | Fiber: 0.17g | Carbohydrates: 2.6g | Sugar: 0.78g

Spotlight on Tilapia

Tilapia is a freshwater fish with mild and sweet white flesh. It is native to the Middle East and Africa, but is now farmed in commercial aquaculture systems across the world. Tilapia is an excellent source of lean protein and easily adopts the flavor of any seasonings you add to it.

Oven-Seared Tuna Steaks with Olives and Lemon

Serve with lemon wedges and an extra grind or two of black pepper at the table.

INGREDIENTS | SERVES 4

4 (6-ounce) tuna steaks

¼ teaspoon cumin

¼ teaspoon black pepper

½ cup pitted and chopped green olives

2 small shallots, minced

¼ cup chopped parsley

3 tablespoons lemon juice

1 tablespoon capers, rinsed and chopped

1 tablespoon extra-virgin olive oil

1. Preheat the oven to 375°F and spray a 9" × 13" casserole dish lightly with nonstick spray. Pat the tuna dry, place it in the prepared dish, and sprinkle it with the cumin and pepper.

2. Stir the olives, shallots, parsley, lemon juice, capers, and olive oil together in a bowl. Spread the mixture over the tuna steaks and place on the top oven rack to bake.

3. Bake the tuna to the desired degree of doneness, about 15–20 minutes.

PER SERVING Calories: 224 | Fat: 11g | Protein: 30g | Sodium: 224mg | Fiber: 0.3g | Carbohydrates: 0.38g | Sugar: 0g

Fantastic Fish Pie

This dish captures the flavors of Spain: briny cod, smoky paprika, and garden-ripe tomatoes. Enjoy with some roasted asparagus and a crisp, leafy salad.

INGREDIENTS | SERVES 6

1 pound cod fillets, cut into bite-sized pieces

1 (14.5-ounce) can stewed tomatoes

¼ teaspoon dried minced onion

½ teaspoon dried minced garlic

¼ teaspoon dried basil

¼ teaspoon dried parsley

⅛ teaspoon dried oregano

⅛ teaspoon granulated sugar

1 tablespoon freshly grated Parmigiano-Reggiano cheese

1 recipe Yukon Gold Mashed Potatoes (see sidebar recipe)

¼ teaspoon paprika

1. Preheat the oven to 375°F and spray a 9½" deep-dish pie pan lightly with nonstick spray.

2. Arrange the fish pieces evenly across the bottom of the pan.

3. In a bowl, mix together the stewed tomatoes, onion, garlic, basil, parsley, oregano, sugar, and Parmigiano-Reggiano cheese. Pour over the fish. Pipe or spread the mashed potatoes evenly over the top of the sauce. Sprinkle generously with paprika. Bake for 45 minutes or until the potatoes are lightly browned and the sauce is bubbly.

PER SERVING Calories: 199 | Fat: 1.9g | Protein: 17g | Sodium: 578mg | Fiber: 3.4g | Carbohydrates: 30g | Sugar: 2.1g

Cod and Potatoes

Thinly sliced potatoes are layered with olive oil and herbs and baked until crisp, then topped with cod and lemon juice. Yum!

INGREDIENTS | SERVES 4

3 Yukon Gold potatoes

¼ cup olive oil

⅛ teaspoon white pepper

1½ teaspoons dried herbs de Provence, divided

4 (4-ounce) cod steaks

1 tablespoon butter or margarine

2 tablespoons lemon juice

1. Preheat the oven to 350°F and spray a 9" × 13" casserole dish lightly with nonstick spray. Thinly slice the potatoes and layer them in the baking dish, drizzling each layer with a tablespoon of olive oil, a sprinkle of pepper, and some of the herbs de Provence.

2. Bake for 35–45 minutes or until potatoes are browned on top and tender when pierced with a fork. Arrange cod steaks on top of potatoes. Dot with butter and sprinkle with lemon juice and remaining herbs de Provence.

3. Bake for 15–25 minutes longer or until fish flakes when tested with fork.

Yukon Gold Mashed Potatoes

Peel and cube 5 large Yukon Gold potatoes. Boil until tender, then drain and mash with 2 tablespoons butter, salt and pepper to taste, and ½ cup skim milk.

PER SERVING Calories: 363 | Fat: 17g | Protein: 23g | Sodium: 92mg | Fiber: 3.5g | Carbohydrates: 38g | Sugar: 0g

Creamy Shrimp Pie with Rice Crust

Cream-of-mushroom soup gives this pie its delicate earthy flavor and silky texture. Use the Condensed Cream-of-Mushroom Soup (Mock Mushroom Sauce, Chapter 14), which has all the flavor of traditional mushroom soup with fewer calories and less fat.

INGREDIENTS | SERVES 4

1⅓ cups cooked white rice

2 teaspoons dried parsley

2 tablespoons grated onion

1 teaspoon olive oil

1 tablespoon butter

1 clove garlic, crushed

1 pound shrimp, peeled and deveined

1 recipe Condensed Cream-of-Mushroom Soup (Mock Mushroom Sauce, see Chapter 14)

1 teaspoon lemon juice

1 cup sliced mushrooms, steamed

Fat-Free Flavor

To add the flavor of sautéed mushrooms or onions without the added fat of butter or oil, roast or grill them first. Simply spread them on a baking sheet treated with non-stick spray. Roasting them for 5 minutes in a 350°F oven will be sufficient if the vegetables are sliced and will not add additional cooking time to the recipe.

1. Preheat the oven to 350°F. Combine the cooked rice, parsley, and onion in a large bowl; mix well. Use the olive oil to coat a 10" pie plate. Press the rice mixture evenly around the sides and bottom. This works best if the rice is moist; if necessary, add 1 teaspoon water.

2. Melt the butter in a deep, nonstick skillet over medium heat and sauté the garlic. Add the shrimp and cook, stirring frequently, until pink, about 5 minutes. Add the soup and lemon juice to the skillet. Stir until smooth and thoroughly heated. (If the soup seems too thick, add some water, 1 teaspoon at a time.) Stir the mushrooms into the soup mixture, then pour it over the rice "crust." Bake for 30 minutes or until lightly browned on top. Serve hot.

PER SERVING Calories: 273 | Fat: 6g | Protein: 26g | Sodium: 172mg | Fiber: 2g | Carbohydrates: 27g | Sugar: 1g

Shrimp Microwave Casserole

Make this casserole when you are squeezed for time.
Microwave cooking will help you get dinner on the table in minutes!

INGREDIENTS | SERVES 4

½ cup chopped celery
Water, as needed
⅛ cup Ener-G potato flour
1⅓ cups uncooked egg noodles
1 cup chopped green onion
1 cup chopped green pepper
1 cup sliced mushrooms
1 teaspoon Worcestershire sauce
4 drops Tabasco sauce
¼ cup diced canned pimientos
½ cup pitted, chopped ripe olives
½ cup skim milk
½ pound (8 ounces) cooked shrimp, peeled and deveined

1. In a covered microwave-safe container, microwave celery for 2 minutes or until tender. Do not drain any resulting liquid. Add enough water to bring celery and liquid to 1 cup total. Blend together with Ener-G potato flour. Set aside.

2. Cook the egg noodles according to package directions and keep warm. Place the green onion and green pepper in a covered microwave-safe dish and microwave on high for 1 minute. Add the mushroom slices and microwave for 1 minute or until all the vegetables are tender.

3. Add the celery mixture, Worcestershire sauce, Tabasco sauce, pimientos, olives, and milk; stir well. Microwave covered for 1–2 minutes until the mixture is hot and bubbly.

4. Add the cooked shrimp and noodles and stir to mix; microwave for another 30 seconds to 1 minute or until the mixture is hot.

PER SERVING Calories: 196 | Fat: 2g | Protein: 17g | Sodium: 290mg | Fiber: 2g | Carbohydrates: 27g | Sugar: 2.7g

Baked Stuffed Shrimp

This recipe is lower in fat and calories than most traditional recipes, but still has plenty of big shrimp flavor and decadent crabmeat stuffing—even the most die-hard seafood lover will be satisfied.

INGREDIENTS | SERVES 6

4 tablespoons butter

2 shallots, minced

4 cloves garlic, minced

1 cup diced carrot

¼ cup dry white wine

½ teaspoon salt

⅛ teaspoon cayenne pepper

1 cup diced crabmeat

1 cup soft whole-wheat bread crumbs

1 teaspoon dried marjoram leaves

½ cup shredded low-fat Swiss cheese

24 jumbo shrimp, peeled and deveined

1. Preheat the oven to 375°F and spray a 9" × 13" casserole dish lightly with nonstick spray.

2. Heat 2 tablespoons of the butter in a large nonstick skillet over medium heat. When the butter melts, add the shallots, garlic, and carrots. Cook until tender, stirring occasionally, about 6 minutes. Add the wine, salt, and cayenne pepper; cook for 2 minutes longer. Remove from the heat.

3. Add the crab, bread crumbs, marjoram, and Swiss cheese; mix gently.

4. Pat the shrimp dry, then slit them down the back without cutting all the way through. Stuff the shrimp with the crab mixture and place them stuffing side up in the prepared dish. Melt the remaining butter and drizzle over the shrimp.

5. Bake until the shrimp are cooked and the stuffing heats through and begins to brown, 20–23 minutes. Serve immediately.

PER SERVING Calories: 227 | Fat: 12g | Protein: | Sodium: 472mg | Fiber: 1g | Carbohydrates: 9g | Sugar: 2.7g

Shrimp and Wild Rice Pilaf

Bacon and shrimp are natural partners. This recipe is a bit healthier because it's made with turkey bacon and a lower-fat version of creamy white sauce.

INGREDIENTS | SERVES 8

4 slices turkey bacon, chopped

2 tablespoons olive oil

1 onion, chopped

1 leek, chopped

3 cloves garlic, minced

2 cups uncooked wild rice

4 cups low-sodium chicken broth

1 recipe Mock White Sauce (see Chapter 14)

2 cups frozen baby peas

2 pounds frozen cooked medium shrimp, thawed

¼ cup grated Parmesan cheese

Transport Tips

To transport and serve, pack the baking dish with the rice mixture into a casserole holder or wrap it in newspaper. Keep the thawed shrimp in the original packaging and package along with the bacon and cheese in a cooler. Then combine everything in the dish and bake when you arrive.

1. Preheat the oven to 400°F and spray a 9" × 13" casserole dish with nonstick spray. In a medium saucepan, fry the bacon until crisp, then drain on paper towels. Drain the bacon fat from the saucepan, but do not wipe out.

2. Heat the olive oil in the saucepan over medium heat. Add the onion, leek, and garlic. Cook and stir until the vegetables are tender, about 6 minutes. Add the rice and chicken broth; bring to a boil. Turn heat down, cover, and simmer until the rice is almost tender, about 30 minutes.

3. Stir the Mock White Sauce and peas into the rice mixture, then transfer the mixture to the prepared casserole dish. At this point, you can take the dish to the party or continue with the recipe.

4. Stir the shrimp and bacon into the casserole and sprinkle the Parmesan cheese on top. Bake until the casserole is bubbly and the cheese is melted, 20–25 minutes.

PER SERVING Calories: 330 | Fat: 8g | Protein: 28g | Sodium: 297mg | Fiber: 4.5g | Carbohydrates: 36g | Sugar: 3.4g

Shrimp Creole Casserole

Choose a smaller-sized shrimp for this recipe. Either 21:25s or 26:30s will do.
Turn the heat up on this casserole with a pinch of cayenne or a dash of salt-free hot sauce.

INGREDIENTS | SERVES 8

1 tablespoon olive oil

1 medium sweet onion, minced

1 medium green bell pepper, minced

2 teaspoons salt-free Creole seasoning

½ teaspoon salt

1½ cups short-grain white rice

1 (28-ounce) can chopped tomatoes, drained

3 cups low-sodium chicken broth

1½ pounds shrimp, peeled and deveined

Sizing Shrimp 101

The terms popcorn, jumbo, and colossal all mean different things depending on where you live. A better way to size shrimp lists the average number of shrimp you can expect to find per pound. For example, if you bought a bag of 16:20s, you could expect to find about 16 to 20 shrimp per pound.

1. Preheat the oven to 350°F.

2. Heat the olive oil in a 3-quart Dutch oven over medium-high heat. Add the onion, pepper, Creole seasoning, and salt. Cook, stirring often, until the onion is translucent and the pepper is soft, about 7 minutes.

3. Add the rice and stir to coat with the seasonings and oil. Add the tomatoes and chicken broth and bring to a simmer. Stir in the shrimp and cover.

4. Bake on the middle rack in the oven until the rice is cooked through and the shrimp are pink and cooked, about 25 minutes.

PER SERVING Calories: 167 | Fat: 3.2g | Protein: 16g | Sodium: 666mg | Fiber: 1.4g | Carbohydrates: 19g | Sugar: 6.1g

Healthy Fish Enchiladas

Use any type of firm and meaty white fish in this recipe. Halibut works especially well.
Substitute your favorite jarred salsa for the fresh if you are running short on time.

INGREDIENTS | SERVES 8

2 tablespoons olive oil

1 onion, chopped

3 garlic cloves, minced

1 jalapeño pepper, minced

1 red bell pepper, chopped

1 green bell pepper, chopped

6 (6-ounce) white fish fillets

½ teaspoon salt

⅛ teaspoon pepper

1 cup Citrus Salsa (see Chapter 14)

1½ cups shredded low-fat pepper jack cheese

12 (6") corn tortillas

1 (8-ounce) can enchilada sauce

Canned Sauces

You can certainly make your own enchilada or tomato sauce, but there are some good-quality canned products available. Get in the habit of reading labels and choose the products with the lowest sodium content and fewest artificial ingredients. Keep a good supply of these products on hand for quick and easy meals.

1. Preheat the oven to 400°F and spray a 9" × 13" casserole dish with nonstick spray. In a large skillet, heat the olive oil over medium heat and sauté the onion, garlic, and jalapeño until crisp-tender, about 5 minutes. Add the red and green bell pepper. Cook, stirring often, for 4 minutes longer.

2. Place the fish on top of vegetables; season with salt and pepper. Cover and cook for 6–8 minutes or until fish flakes when tested with fork. Add the salsa and ½ cup cheese and stir gently to combine.

3. Divide the fish mixture among the tortillas and roll up. Place the enchiladas seam side down in the prepared casserole dish, cover with enchilada sauce, and sprinkle with 1 cup cheese. Bake for 15–25 minutes or until thoroughly heated through.

PER SERVING Calories: 329 | Fat: 11g | Protein: 31g | Sodium: 503mg | Fiber: 3g | Carbohydrates: 19g | Sugar: 1.1g

Baked Cod with Tomato Sauce, Capers, and Olives

The briny capers and olives bring out the sweet ocean flavor of the cod.
Serve with whole-grain pasta or slices of crusty whole-wheat baguette and a green salad.

INGREDIENTS | SERVES 4

2 tablespoons extra-virgin olive oil

1 medium onion, minced

2 garlic cloves, minced

1 (28-ounce) can chunky tomato sauce

2 tablespoons capers, rinsed

⅓ cup pitted black olives, halved

½ teaspoon salt

4 (6-ounce) cod fillets

3 tablespoons fresh chopped basil

Frozen or Fresh Seafood

You might think that the fresh seafood you buy at the fish counter in your grocery store is of better quality than frozen brands, but think again. Unless you live on the coast, the "fresh" seafood you are buying was likely frozen at sea, then defrosted before it was sold to you. Before you buy, ask your fishmonger about where your seafood was caught or raised.

1. Heat the olive oil in a large saucepan over medium heat. When hot, add the onion and cook until it becomes tender and translucent, about 7 minutes. Add the garlic and cook for 1 minute.

2. Add the tomato sauce, capers, olives, and salt to the pan and bring the sauce to a simmer, stirring once or twice. Turn the heat to low while maintaining a simmer and cook until the flavors blend and the sauce thickens slightly, about 15 minutes.

3. Preheat the oven to 400°F and spray a 9" × 13" casserole dish lightly with nonstick spray. Spoon ¾ of the sauce in the prepared dish, nestle the fish fillets in the sauce, and spoon the remaining sauce over the top of the fish.

4. Bake, uncovered, until the fish turns opaque and easily flakes when pierced with a fork, about 20–25 minutes. Sprinkle with basil before serving.

PER SERVING Calories: 277 | Fat: 11g | Protein: 32g | Sodium: 868mg | Fiber: 4.1g | Carbohydrates: 15g | Sugar: 0g

Sea Bass Wrapped in Savoy Cabbage

*Serve this luscious fish over cooked brown rice that you've spiked with nuts,
fresh ginger, fresh herbs, and a bit of minced green onion.*

INGREDIENTS | SERVES 4

4 large leaves Savoy cabbage

4 tablespoons unsalted butter, softened

1 tablespoon grated fresh gingerroot

1 teaspoon grated orange zest

1 minced shallot

4 (1"-thick) sea bass fillets

¼ teaspoon salt, plus more to taste

¼ teaspoon pepper, plus more to taste

½ cup coconut milk

¼ cup fresh lemon juice

3" piece lemongrass, thinly chopped

½ cup Mock Cream (see Chapter 14)

1 tablespoon grated lemon zest

Wrapping Food Before Cooking

Sea bass wrapped in Savoy cabbage produces the same moist results as wrapping it in pastry or a paper bag! However, the cabbage retains its nutritional and fiber value. The paper bag wrapping for food must be discarded, and the puff pastry will get soggy and retain its fattening properties. Try wrapping chicken or duck breasts in cabbage and enjoy a healthy, super-succulent dinner.

1. Preheat the oven to 375°F and spray a 9" × 13" baking dish lightly with nonstick spray.

2. Blanch the Savoy cabbage leaves in boiling water to soften and make them flexible, then plunge them into ice water to cool. Lay them out on paper towels to drain.

3. Combine the butter, gingerroot, orange zest, and shallot to make a compound butter.

4. Divide the compound butter among the blanched cabbage leaves. Season the sea bass fillets with ¼ teaspoon each salt and pepper and place one on each cabbage leaf. Wrap the cabbage leaves around the fish fillets to make packages.

5. Place packages seam side down in the prepared casserole dish. Pour the coconut milk and lemon juice over the packages. Top with lemongrass.

6. Cover casserole dish tightly with foil and bake for 20 minutes. Remove the packages from the baking dish, place on a serving platter, and tent with foil. Strain the baking liquid into a saucepan and bring to a boil. Add the Mock Cream and simmer to reduce into a slightly thickened sauce. Pour sauce over the packages on the platter. Sprinkle with lemon zest and serve hot.

PER SERVING Calories: 313 | Fat: 22g | Protein: 25g | Sodium: 256mg | Fiber: 1.1g | Carbohydrates: 4.7g | Sugar: 1.2g

Baja-Style Crab

Serve with Fresh Peach-Mango Salsa (see Chapter 14) and a side of grilled vegetables when you want a refreshing meal that reminds you of summer.

INGREDIENTS | SERVES 4

1 cup white rice
1 pound crabmeat
1 medium white onion
2 garlic cloves
2 fresh pimientos
2 medium tomatoes
2 medium carrots
¼ cup olive oil
1 teaspoon ground annatto seeds
2½ cups low-sodium chicken broth
1 teaspoon salt
½ teaspoon ground white pepper
¼ cup dry sherry

1. Soak the rice in hot water for 30 minutes. Break the crabmeat into 1" pieces. Peel the onion and garlic and chop into quarters. Chop the pimientos into quarters. Remove the stems and skin from the tomatoes; chop into quarters. Peel the carrots and slice into ¼" rounds.

2. Preheat the oven to 350°F.

3. Drain the rice and place on paper towels to dry. Heat the olive oil to medium temperature in a medium frying pan; sauté the rice until it is golden brown.

4. Put the onion, garlic, tomatoes, annatto, and ½ cup of the chicken broth in a blender or food processor; blend on medium setting until smooth. Pour the mixture into a mixing bowl.

5. Add the remaining broth, salt, pepper, crabmeat, pimientos, and carrots. Mix well and pour into a 3-quart Dutch oven. Cover and bake for 30 minutes. Gently stir in the sherry and cover. Heat in the oven for an additional 5 minutes.

PER SERVING Calories: 301 | Fat: 15g | Protein: 20g | Sodium: 1,188mg | Fiber: 3g | Carbohydrates: 21g | Sugar: 4.4g

Salmon Cream Enchiladas

*This mild dish is suitable for any crowd. If your crowd likes it spicy,
add chili powder and cayenne pepper to the tomato mixture.*

INGREDIENTS | SERVES 6

2 tablespoons olive oil

1 onion, chopped

2 cloves garlic, minced

1 (4-ounce) can chopped green chilies, undrained

1 cup salsa

1 (8-ounce) can tomato sauce

1 (12-ounce) pouch salmon, drained

1½ cups sour cream

1½ cups shredded Monterey jack cheese

8 (10") flour tortillas

¼ cup grated Cotija cheese

Salmon

Salmon is a cold-water fish that lives along the coasts of the North Atlantic and the Pacific. It has a deep pinkish flesh and is high in omega-3 fatty acids. Atlantic salmon is typically produced by aquaculture (sea farming), whereas Pacific salmon is mostly caught in the wild.

1. Preheat the oven to 350°F and spray a 9" × 13" casserole dish lightly with nonstick spray. In a large saucepan, heat the olive oil over medium heat. Add the onion and garlic and cook, stirring often, until the onion is translucent, about 5 minutes. Add the chilies, salsa, and tomato sauce; bring to a simmer.

2. Meanwhile, in a medium bowl, combine the salmon, sour cream, and Monterey jack cheese.

3. Dip the tortillas, one at a time, into tomato sauce and place on the work surface. Top with a spoonful of the salmon mixture and roll up; place in baking dish, seam side down.

4. Repeat with remaining sauce, tortillas, and filling. Pour the sauce over the filled tortillas and sprinkle with Cotija cheese. Bake until the sauce bubbles and the cheese melts, about 20–25 minutes.

PER SERVING Calories: 535 | Fat: 35g | Protein: 28g | Sodium: 1,056mg | Fiber: 2.2g | Carbohydrates: 27g | Sugar: 4.1g

Mustard Dill Salmon Bake

This is a quick and easy dish perfect for a weeknight. It works great with frozen salmon, too—just move the fish from the freezer to the fridge in the morning, and by evening you can pop it right into the casserole dish to bake.

INGREDIENTS | SERVES 4

4 (6-ounce) salmon fillets, skinned

¼ teaspoon black pepper

1 tablespoon extra-virgin olive oil

2 cloves garlic, minced

¾ cup clam juice

¼ cup dry white wine

1½ tablespoons Dijon mustard

3 tablespoons fresh chopped dill

1 tablespoon butter

1. Preheat the oven to 375°F and spray a 9" × 13" casserole dish lightly with nonstick spray. Pat the salmon dry, place in prepared dish, and sprinkle it with pepper.

2. Heat the olive oil in a small saucepan over medium heat. When hot, add garlic and cook, stirring often, until fragrant and just beginning to turn golden.

3. Immediately whisk in clam juice, white wine, and Dijon mustard. Bring to a simmer and cook until slightly reduced and thickened, about 2 minutes. Whisk in dill and butter and pour over salmon.

4. Bake salmon, uncovered, on the middle oven rack until it flakes easily with a fork, 12–15 minutes.

PER SERVING Calories: 295 | Fat: 14g | Protein: 39g | Sodium: 787mg | Fiber: 1.4g | Carbohydrates: 0.23g | Sugar: 0g

Lighter Tuna Noodle Casserole

Made with a creamy, cream-free sauce and lots of fresh flavors, this recipe is a healthier take on the classic tuna noodle casserole from childhood.

INGREDIENTS | SERVES 4

8 ounces yolk-free egg noodles

1 tablespoon olive oil

1 (8-ounce) carton sliced button mushrooms

3 tablespoons unsalted butter

⅓ cup all-purpose flour

2 cups fat-free milk

2 tablespoons cornstarch

¼ cup dry white wine

1 cup low-sodium chicken broth

½ teaspoon salt

1½ cups frozen peas

2 (6-ounce) cans chunk light tuna, drained and flaked

2 tablespoons chopped parsley

¼ cup grated Parmesan cheese

Tuna Safety and Mercury

Seafood contaminated with mercury is a health concern, especially for pregnant and nursing mothers and young children because it disrupts normal growth and development. Current FDA guidelines for tuna say that it is safe for everyone to eat up to 12 ounces a week of canned light tuna. Albacore tuna has more mercury than canned light tuna, so guidelines suggest limiting the amount of albacore tuna to 6 ounces per week.

1. Preheat the oven to 375°F and spray a 8" × 8" casserole dish lightly with nonstick spray. Cook the noodles according to package directions and place in a large bowl.

2. Heat the olive oil over medium-high heat. When hot, add the mushrooms and cook until browned, stirring occasionally, about 10 minutes. Remove the mushrooms to the bowl with the noodles.

3. Melt the butter in a medium saucepan over medium heat and add the flour. Add the milk gradually, whisking constantly to avoid lumps. Turn the heat to low and bring the milk sauce to a gentle simmer. In a medium bowl, whisk the cornstarch, wine, chicken broth, and salt together. Add the cornstarch mixture to the milk sauce and whisk to combine. Simmer, whisking often, until the sauce is thickened, 2–3 minutes.

4. Pour the sauce over the noodles and mushrooms; add the peas, tuna, and parsley. Mix gently to combine and pour into the prepared casserole dish. Sprinkle Parmesan cheese over the top of the casserole, and bake on the middle oven rack until browned and bubbly, 25–30 minutes.

PER SERVING Calories: 461 | Fat: 16g | Protein: 35g | Sodium: 943mg | Fiber: 4.6g | Carbohydrates: 43g | Sugar: 3.4g

Tuna, Leek, and Fennel Casserole with Fresh Chives

Leeks and fennel have bright flavors that bring to mind the coming of spring and marry well with a lightened cream sauce. Make sure to wash the leeks in several changes of water to rid them of grit.

INGREDIENTS | SERVES 4

8 ounces whole-wheat penne

1 tablespoon olive oil

1 fennel bulb, chopped

2 leeks, white and light green parts only, chopped

3 tablespoons unsalted butter

⅓ cup all-purpose flour

2 cups fat-free milk

2 tablespoons cornstarch

1 teaspoon dry mustard powder

¼ cup dry white wine

1 cup low-sodium chicken broth

½ teaspoon salt

2 (6-ounce) cans chunk light tuna, drained and flaked

2 tablespoons chopped fresh chives

1. Preheat the oven to 375°F and spray an 8" × 8" casserole dish lightly with nonstick spray. Cook the pasta according to package directions and place in a large bowl.

2. Heat the olive oil over low heat in a medium saucepan and add the fennel and leeks. Cook, covered, stirring occasionally until tender, about 20 minutes. Remove the vegetables to the bowl with the noodles.

3. Melt the butter in a medium saucepan over medium heat and add the flour. Add the milk, gradually, whisking constantly to avoid lumps. Turn the heat to low and bring the milk sauce to a gentle simmer. In a medium bowl, whisk the cornstarch, mustard powder, wine, chicken broth, and salt together. Add the cornstarch mixture to the milk sauce and whisk to combine. Simmer, whisking often, until the sauce is thickened, 2–3 minutes.

4. Pour the sauce over the noodles, add the tuna and chives, and mix gently to combine. Pour into the prepared casserole dish. Bake on the middle oven rack until browned and bubbly, 25–30 minutes.

PER SERVING Calories: 522 | Fat: 14g | Protein: 33g | Sodium: 570mg | Fiber: 4.9g | Carbohydrates: 67g | Sugar: 2.7g

Sicilian-Style Baked Shrimp

Serve this zesty and mildly sweet baked shrimp recipe over whole-wheat pasta or whole-wheat couscous. You won't want to waste a drop of this delicious sauce!

INGREDIENTS | SERVES 4

1½ pounds large shrimp, peeled and deveined
1 tablespoon extra-virgin olive oil
1 rib celery, sliced into paper-thin slices
2 shallots, minced
3 plum tomatoes, seeded and diced
2 tablespoons currants
1 tablespoon capers, rinsed and drained
½ cup Marsala wine

1. Preheat the oven to 375°F and spray a 9" × 13" casserole dish lightly with nonstick spray. Place the shrimp in the prepared casserole dish.

2. Heat the olive oil over medium-high heat in a medium skillet. When hot, add the celery and shallots; cook until fragrant and just tender, about 2 minutes.

3. Add the tomatoes, currants, capers, and Marsala wine to the pan; simmer until the liquid in the mixture is slightly reduced, about 2 minutes more.

4. Pour the vegetable mixture and juices over the shrimp and bake until the shrimp is cooked through and pink, about 10–15 minutes.

PER SERVING Calories: 197 | Fat: 5.8g | Protein: 27g | Sodium: 272mg | Fiber: 1g | Carbohydrates: 6g | Sugar: 2.9g

Arctic Char with Scandinavian Flavors

This fish bakes up flaky and moist. Serve it with braised fennel or a tossed green salad.

INGREDIENTS | SERVES 4

4 (6-ounce) arctic char pieces, skinned

¼ teaspoon black pepper

1 tablespoon olive oil

2 shallots, minced

¾ cup clam juice

¼ cup dry white wine

1½ tablespoons Dijon mustard

3 tablespoons fresh chopped dill

3 tablespoons fresh chopped parsley

1 tablespoon butter

Arctic Char

Pale pink and moist, it's no wonder that arctic char is a close cousin of salmon. This fish is often farmed and raised in a sustainable manner and can be used in any recipe calling for salmon.

1. Preheat the oven to 375°F and spray a 9" × 13" casserole dish lightly with nonstick spray. Pat the arctic char dry, place it in the prepared dish, and sprinkle it with pepper.

2. Heat the olive oil in a small saucepan over medium heat. When hot, add shallots and cook, stirring often, until fragrant and just beginning to soften.

3. Immediately whisk in the clam juice, white wine, and Dijon mustard. Bring to a simmer and cook until slightly reduced and thickened, about 2 minutes. Whisk in the dill, parsley, and butter; pour over the arctic char.

4. Bake the arctic char, uncovered, on the middle oven rack until it flakes easily with a fork, 12–15 minutes.

PER SERVING Calories: 295 | Fat: 14g | Protein: 39g | Sodium: 787mg | Fiber: 1.4g | Carbohydrates: 0.23g | Sugar: 0g

CHAPTER 9

Chicken and Turkey

Chicken and Mushroom Rice Casserole

Herbs de Provence add a delightful fresh flavor to this savory and satisfying casserole.

INGREDIENTS | SERVES 6

1 recipe Condensed Cream-of-Chicken Soup (see Chapter 14)

1 cup diced chicken breast

1 large onion, chopped

½ cup chopped celery

1 cup uncooked white rice

¼ teaspoon pepper

1 teaspoon dried herbes de Provence

2 cups boiling water

2½ cups chopped broccoli florets

1 cup sliced fresh mushrooms

1. Preheat the oven to 350°F and spray a deep 4-quart casserole dish (large enough to prevent boilovers in the oven) lightly with nonstick spray.

2. Combine the condensed soup, chicken breast, onion, celery, rice, pepper, and herbes de Provence in the prepared dish and mix well. Pour the boiling water over the top of the mixture and bake, covered, for 30 minutes.

3. Stir the casserole, adding the broccoli and mushrooms; replace the cover and return to the oven to bake for an additional 20–30 minutes, or until the celery is tender and the rice has absorbed all the liquid.

PER SERVING Calories: 204 | Fat: 5.5g | Protein: 14g | Sodium: 569mg | Fiber: 1.6g | Carbohydrates: 24g | Sugar: 1.6g

Chicken and Broccoli Casserole

This is a great way to use up leftover cooked chicken. The lemon perks up the creamy sauce, and the bread crumbs give the top a pleasing crunch.

INGREDIENTS | SERVES 4

2 cups broccoli

½ pound (8 ounces) cooked, chopped chicken

½ cup skim milk

⅛ cup (2 tablespoons) Hellmann's or Best Foods Real Mayonnaise

¼ teaspoon curry powder

1 recipe Condensed Cream-of-Chicken Soup (see Chapter 14)

1 tablespoon lemon juice

½ cup grated Cheddar cheese

½ cup bread crumbs

1 teaspoon melted butter

1 teaspoon olive oil

1. Preheat the oven to 350°F and spray a 9" × 13" casserole dish with nonstick spray. Steam the broccoli until tender; drain.

2. Spread the chicken on the bottom of the dish and cover it with the broccoli. Combine the milk, mayonnaise, curry powder, chicken soup, and lemon juice; pour over broccoli.

3. Mix together the Cheddar cheese, bread crumbs, butter, and oil; sprinkle mixture over the top of the casserole. Bake until browned and bubbling around the edges, about 30 minutes.

PER SERVING Calories: 328 | Fat: 17g | Protein: 26g | Sodium: 254mg | Fiber: 3g | Carbohydrates: 19.5g | Sugar: 2.1g

Mexican Chicken Oven Bake

Garnish with fresh chopped cilantro and wedges of lime.

INGREDIENTS | SERVES 6

1½ pounds boneless, skinless chicken breasts, cut into ½" cubes

2 medium white onions, cut into ¼" pieces

2 garlic cloves, peeled and minced

2 celery ribs, cut into ¼" pieces

1 tablespoon olive oil

4 cups low-sodium chicken broth

1 envelope dry chicken gravy mix

2 cups fat-free milk

½ cup canned, chopped jalapeño peppers, or 3 fresh jalapeño peppers, cut into ⅛" pieces

8 ounces reduced-fat Monterey jack cheese, cut into ½" cubes

2 cups salsa

1 (32-ounce) bag frozen hash brown potatoes

1. Preheat the oven to 300°F and spray a 9" × 13" casserole dish lightly with nonstick spray.

2. Combine the chicken, onions, garlic, celery, oil, and broth in a large mixing bowl; stir until well blended. Pour into the prepared casserole dish, cover with foil, and bake for 1 hour.

3. Dissolve the gravy mix in the milk in a medium mixing bowl. Stir into the cooked chicken mixture. Add the jalapeños, cheese, salsa, and potatoes; mix well. Cover and cook for an additional hour.

PER SERVING Calories: 655 | Fat: 33g | Protein: 40g | Sodium: 1,231mg | Fiber: 3.5g | Carbohydrates: 53g | Sugar: 5.2g

Stovetop Moroccan Turkey Casserole

Warm spices and sweet and savory flavors will fool your guests into thinking that this dish was difficult to make, when in fact it's deceptively simple!

INGREDIENTS | SERVES 6

1 tablespoon vegetable oil

2 cups chopped carrots

6 scallions, diced

3 cloves garlic, minced

1 teaspoon ground cumin

1 teaspoon paprika

½ teaspoon turmeric

¼ teaspoon ground cinnamon

⅛ teaspoon cayenne pepper

2 cups low-sodium chicken broth

⅔ cup quick-cooking couscous

6 pitted dates, quartered

3 cups cooked turkey, cubed

2 cups fresh spinach, torn

1. Heat the oil over medium heat in a 3-quart Dutch oven. When hot, add the carrots and scallions and sauté for 3 minutes. Stir in the garlic, cumin, paprika, turmeric, cinnamon, and cayenne pepper; cook for another 30 seconds. Stir in 1 cup of the broth and bring to a boil. Stir in the couscous and dates. Remove from heat, cover, and let stand for 5 minutes or until the liquid is absorbed.

2. Stir the remaining 1 cup of broth into the couscous mixture. Return to the heat and bring to a boil. Stir in the turkey and spinach. Reduce the heat, cover, and simmer for 3 minutes or until the turkey is heated through.

PER SERVING Calories: 217 | Fat: 3.8g | Protein: 17g | Sodium: 944mg | Fiber: 3.7g | Carbohydrates: 29g | Sugar: 9.9g

Country Captain Chicken

This oven stew is a southern favorite. The bone in the chicken breasts helps to keep the meat moist during cooking. Garnish with thinly sliced scallions, toasted almond slivers, or unsweetened toasted coconut.

INGREDIENTS | SERVES 6

4 pounds split bone-in chicken breasts

1 tablespoon olive oil

1 large sweet onion, diced

2 green bell peppers, diced

3 garlic cloves, minced

1½ tablespoons curry powder

1 teaspoon salt

2 tablespoons flour

1 (28-ounce) can crushed tomatoes

¼ cup raisins

½ cup finely diced frozen pineapple

1 Granny Smith apple, cored and diced

1. Preheat the oven to 350°F. Remove the chicken skin and halve the chicken breasts crosswise so that each split breast yields 2 pieces.

2. Heat the oil over medium-high heat in a 3-quart Dutch oven. When hot, add the onion, peppers, and garlic. Cook, stirring often, until the onion is translucent and the peppers begin to lose their crunch, about 7 minutes.

3. Add the curry powder, salt, and flour; stir to coat the vegetables. Stir in the tomatoes, raisins, pineapple, and apple. Bring the sauce to a gentle simmer, then add the chicken breasts, making sure that they are covered with sauce.

4. Cover the pot with a lid and bake on the center rack in the oven until the chicken is cooked through, about 30 minutes.

PER SERVING Calories: 372 | Fat: 5.1g | Protein: 57g | Sodium: 569mg | Fiber: 4.6g | Carbohydrates: 29g | Sugar: 10g

Scalloped Chicken

You will love how the tender, velvety texture of the chicken contrasts with the crispy and browned crumb topping. Serve with oven-roasted Brussels sprouts or another favorite vegetable.

INGREDIENTS | SERVES 6

1 tablespoon butter
1 onion, diced
4 garlic cloves, minced
4 cups low-sodium chicken broth
3 eggs, beaten
4 cups cooked cubed chicken
2 cups frozen baby peas
3 cups soft whole-wheat bread crumbs
½ cup grated Parmesan cheese

1. Preheat the oven to 350°F. Spray a 3-quart shallow casserole dish lightly with nonstick spray.

2. Melt the butter in a large saucepan over medium heat. Add the onion and garlic. Cook, stirring frequently, until tender, about 5 minutes. Remove from heat and add the chicken broth, then whisk the beaten eggs into the chicken broth mixture.

3. In a bowl, combine chicken and peas; mix to combine. In another bowl, combine crumbs with cheese and mix well. Alternate layering the crumb mixture with the chicken mixture in the prepared casserole, beginning and ending with crumb mixture.

4. Pour the chicken broth mixture slowly into casserole. Bake until casserole is brown and bubbly, about 1 hour.

PER SERVING Calories: 429 | Fat: 11g | Protein: 31g | Sodium: 1,027mg | Fiber: 4.8g | Carbohydrates: 47g | Sugar: 5.9g

Chicken Oven Stew with Olives and Warm Spices

This is a hearty winter dish that will warm you to your core. Best of all, it only improves the next day! Wash the leeks thoroughly to get rid of any clinging sand. Serve over a hearty grain like quinoa or brown rice.

INGREDIENTS | SERVES 6

4 pounds split bone-in chicken breasts

2 tablespoons olive oil

2 large leeks, white and green parts only, sliced into rounds

3 garlic cloves, minced

2 tablespoons tomato paste

1 cup dry red wine

1 (28-ounce) can diced tomatoes, drained

1 cinnamon stick

2 bay leaves

⅔ cup pitted roughly chopped green olives

½ teaspoon salt

¼ teaspoon pepper

Cinnamon

Cinnamon is harvested primarily from the inner bark of two species of tropical evergreen trees, Cinnamomum zeylanicum and Cinnamomum cassia. Cinnamon cassia, with its deep ruddy coloring and bold, spicy flavor, is the type that is most often used for cooking and baking.

1. Preheat the oven to 350°F. Remove the chicken skin and halve the chicken breasts crosswise so that each split breast yields 2 pieces; keep breasts refrigerated while you make the sauce.

2. Heat the oil over medium-low heat in a 3-quart Dutch oven. When hot, add the leeks and garlic. Cook, covered, until the leeks soften and begin to "melt," 10–15 minutes.

3. Add the tomato paste and stir to coat the vegetables. Stir in the wine, tomatoes, cinnamon stick, bay leaves, olives, salt, and pepper. Bring the sauce to a gentle simmer and continue to cook until the sauce thickens, about 25 minutes. Add the chicken breasts, stirring to cover with sauce.

4. Cover the pot with a lid and bake on the center rack in the oven until the chicken is cooked through, about 30 minutes.

PER SERVING Calories: 344 | Fat: 7.9g | Protein: 56g | Sodium: 566mg | Fiber: 2.8g | Carbohydrates: 14g | Sugar: 6.7g

Chicken Oven Stew with Root Vegetables

A rutabaga is a yellow turnip with a lovely sweet flavor. If you can't find them in your supermarket, substitute an equal quantity of turnips. If you choose to omit the wine, add an equal amount of chicken broth.

INGREDIENTS | SERVES 8

2 tablespoons olive oil

1 large sweet onion, diced

3 garlic cloves, minced

¼ cup all-purpose flour

1 teaspoon dried thyme

½ teaspoon salt

½ cup dry white wine

3 cups low-sodium chicken broth

3 pounds boneless, skinless chicken breasts, cut into 1" chunks

4 carrots, peeled and cut into 1" chunks

4 parsnips, peeled and cut into 1" chunks

2 medium rutabagas, peeled and cut into 1" chunks

Stewing Technique

Stewing is a moist-heat cooking method that produces exceptionally tender food because the food cooks at a constant, gentle temperature that never goes above 212°F. To ensure even cooking, cut all food pieces in roughly equivalent sizes so that they cook at about the same time.

1. Preheat the oven to 350°F.

2. Heat the oil over medium-high heat in a 3-quart Dutch oven. When hot, add the onion and cook, stirring often, until it begins to soften and turn translucent, about 5 minutes. Add the garlic and cook for 1 minute more. Stir in the flour, thyme, and salt.

3. Whisk in the wine and chicken broth; bring the liquid to a simmer. Add the chicken breasts, carrots, parsnips, and rutabagas; give the pot a final stir.

4. Cover the pot with a lid and bake on the center rack in the oven until the chicken is cooked through, about 30 minutes.

PER SERVING Calories: 331 | Fat: 5.5g | Protein: 36g | Sodium: 445mg | Fiber: 9.7g | Carbohydrates: 38g | Sugar: 19g

Every Chicken in a Potpie

The streusel topping becomes crunchy and toasty as the pie bakes. If you prefer a more classic biscuit topping, use the Whole-Wheat Biscuits in the Vegetable Potpie recipe (see Chapter 4).

INGREDIENTS | SERVES 6

2 tablespoons butter

½ medium onion, diced

2 carrots, peeled and diced

2 celery stalks, diced

½ cup sliced leeks

¼ cup flour

3 cups low-sodium chicken broth

1 bay leaf

1 cup frozen peas

½ cup Mock Cream (see Chapter 14)

½ teaspoon salt

¼ teaspoon pepper

4 boneless, skinless chicken breasts, cut into 1" chunks

¼ cup chopped chives

1 recipe Savory Streusel (see sidebar in this recipe)

Savory Streusel

Combine ⅓ cup finely chopped walnuts, ½ cup whole-wheat flour, ½ cup quick-cooking oats, ⅓ cup melted butter, and ½ teaspoon poultry seasoning in a bowl until thoroughly combined. Keep refrigerated until ready to use.

1. Heat the butter in a 3-quart Dutch oven over medium heat; add the onion, carrots, celery, and leeks. Cook, stirring occasionally, until the vegetables are just tender. Dust with flour, stir, and cook for 2–3 minutes. Add the chicken broth and bay leaf, then bring to a gentle simmer. Cook until the liquid thickens and the vegetables are tender, about 15–20 minutes.

2. Stir in the peas, Mock Cream, and chicken; remove from the heat. Remove the bay leaf, season with salt and pepper, and stir in chopped chives.

3. Preheat the oven to 400°F and spray a 9" × 13" casserole dish lightly with nonstick spray. Pour the filling into the prepared casserole dish and place on a rimmed baking sheet lined with foil.

4. Sprinkle the streusel topping over the filling and bake until the topping is crunchy and golden and the chicken is cooked through, 25–30 minutes.

PER SERVING Calories: 382 | Fat: 20g | Protein: 30g | Sodium: 503mg | Fiber: 4.9g | Carbohydrates: 24g | Sugar: 4g

Chicken-Stuffed Apples

This recipe is like an inside-out stuffed chicken. Each person gets 2 apple halves to enjoy.

INGREDIENTS | SERVES 6

6 large baking apples

3 tablespoons lemon juice

1 cup crushed croutons

2 cups diced cooked chicken

½ cup dried currants

¼ cup finely chopped walnuts

½ teaspoon salt

1 teaspoon dried thyme leaves

⅛ teaspoon pepper

¼ cup butter, melted

1 cup low-sodium chicken broth, divided

½ cup apple juice

1. Preheat the oven to 400°F and spray a 2-quart casserole dish (with lid) lightly with nonstick spray. Cut the apples in half and remove cores. Carefully remove the apple flesh, leaving a ½" shell. Chop the removed flesh and place in a medium bowl, then stir in 2 tablespoons lemon juice. Brush the apple shells with remaining 1 tablespoon lemon juice.

2. Add the croutons, chicken, currants, walnuts, salt, thyme, pepper, butter, and 3 tablespoons chicken broth to the chopped apples and mix gently, but thoroughly.

3. Cut a thin slice off bottoms of the apple shells so that they will sit without tipping. Divide the chicken mixture evenly among the shells and arrange in prepared casserole dish.

4. Pour the remaining chicken broth and apple juice into the dish and cover. Bake for 35–45 minutes, basting apples occasionally with the liquid in dish, until apples are tender.

PER SERVING Calories: 267 | Fat: 12g | Protein: 9.2g | Sodium: 418mg | Fiber: 3.9g | Carbohydrates: 33g | Sugar: 23g

Tuscan Chicken

A crispy seasoned bread and cheese topping helps keep the chicken moist as it bakes. Serve with a fennel salad dressed with lemon juice, olive oil, and Parmesan cheese.

INGREDIENTS | SERVES 6

6 boneless, skinless chicken breasts

1 teaspoon salt

⅛ teaspoon pepper

2 tomatoes

6 slices provolone cheese, cut in half

1 cup dry bread crumbs

¼ cup grated Parmesan cheese

3 tablespoons olive oil

3 cloves garlic, minced

1 teaspoon dried basil leaves

½ teaspoon dried oregano leaves

1 teaspoon dried thyme leaves

1 cup low-sodium chicken broth

The Cooking of Tuscany

Tuscan cuisine is characterized by the use of pristine, field-fresh ingredients, fruity extra-virgin olive oil, roast meats, hearth-baked breads, and truly seasonal cooking.

1. Preheat the oven to 400°F and lightly spray a 9" × 13" glass baking dish with nonstick spray. Arrange the chicken breasts in the prepared dish so that they do not overlap and sprinkle each breast with salt and pepper.

2. Slice the tomatoes. Cover each chicken breast with half a slice of cheese and 2 tomato slices, then top with an additional half slice of cheese.

3. In a small bowl, combine bread crumbs, Parmesan cheese, oil, garlic, basil, oregano, and thyme. Mix crumbs and sprinkle over chicken. Pour chicken broth into dish around chicken.

4. Bake chicken, covered, for 25 minutes. Then uncover chicken and bake for 15–20 minutes longer until chicken is thoroughly cooked.

PER SERVING Calories: 362 | Fat: 14g | Protein: 43g | Sodium: 803mg | Fiber: 1.6g | Carbohydrates: 16g | Sugar: 2.8g

Tex-Mex Chicken Casserole

To keep this truly a one-pot dish, everything could be stirred into and baked in the Dutch oven, but it is much prettier if this casserole is baked in a casserole dish.

INGREDIENTS | SERVES 8–10

2 pounds boneless, skinless chicken breasts, cubed

2½ cups low-sodium chicken broth

½ cup dry white wine

¼ cup coarsely chopped fresh cilantro leaves

1½ tablespoons fresh lime juice

2 garlic cloves, smashed

1 teaspoon black peppercorns

¼ teaspoon dried Mexican oregano

2 bay leaves

3 tablespoons butter

1 pound white button mushrooms, cleaned and sliced

¼ teaspoon salt

¼ teaspoon pepper

4 tablespoons all-purpose flour

1½ cups fat-free milk

12 cups baked tortilla chips

2 large yellow onions, diced

2 green bell peppers, seeded and diced

2 jalapeño peppers, seeded and minced

8 ounces pepper jack cheese, grated

2 teaspoons chili powder

1 teaspoon ground cumin

½ teaspoon paprika

¼ teaspoon freshly ground black pepper

½ teaspoon ground coriander

Pinch cayenne pepper

1 teaspoon garlic powder

Pinch dried red pepper flakes, crushed

1 cup chopped canned tomatoes, drained

1 (4-ounce) can diced green chilies, drained

1. Combine the chicken, broth, wine, cilantro, lime juice, garlic, peppercorns, oregano, and bay leaves in a 3-quart Dutch oven over medium-high heat; bring to a boil. Reduce heat to a simmer and cook, uncovered, for 10 minutes. Pour all contents into a bowl and allow to cool.

2. Preheat the oven to 350°F and spray a 9" × 13" casserole dish lightly with nonstick spray.

3. Wipe out the Dutch oven, place over medium heat, and melt butter. Add the mushrooms, salt, and pepper; cook, stirring occasionally, for 6 minutes or until the mushrooms are browned and all the liquid has evaporated. Sprinkle with the flour, stir to blend, and cook for 1 minute. Slowly whisk in the milk, scraping up any bits from the bottom. Cook until the mixture begins to thicken. Stir in about 1½ cups of the chicken cooking liquid; simmer for 10 minutes, stirring occasionally. Remove from the heat.

4. Crush the tortilla chips and add them in a layer to the bottom of the dish. Pour the remaining broth over the chips. Once the broth is absorbed by the crushed chips, scatter the chicken over the top of the tortilla layer. Spread the onions, bell peppers, and jalapeños in layers evenly over the chicken. Top with half of the grated cheese.

5. Mix together the chili powder, cumin, paprika, black pepper, coriander, cayenne pepper, garlic powder, and red pepper flakes; sprinkle over the cheese. Spoon the mushroom mixture evenly over the top of the spices, then top with the tomatoes and green chilies. Cover with all the remaining cheese. Bake, uncovered, for 45 minutes or until the cheese is bubbly and the casserole is heated through. Let sit for 5 minutes before serving.

PER SERVING Calories: 387 | Fat: 19g | Protein: 29g | Sodium: 452mg | Fiber: 3g | Carbohydrates: 31g | Sugar: 1.6g

Chicken Tetrazzini

This classic recipe looks complicated, but it goes together quickly.
It's a money saver too—it feeds a crowd with only 3 chicken breasts!

INGREDIENTS | SERVES 8

2 tablespoons olive oil

2 tablespoons butter

1 onion, chopped

4 cloves garlic, minced

3 cooked chicken breasts

2 (4-ounce) cans mushroom pieces

¼ cup all-purpose flour

½ teaspoon salt

⅛ teaspoon pepper

½ teaspoon thyme leaves

1 (16-ounce) package spaghetti pasta

1 cup low-sodium chicken broth

1 cup light cream or whole milk

1 tablespoon mustard

½ cup sour cream

1 cup shredded Muenster cheese

⅓ cup grated Parmesan cheese

Tetrazzini Trivia

Turkey Tetrazzini comes to us not from far-away Italian shores, but from one of the big culinary cities of California: San Francisco. It is rumored to be named for the famous opera soprano, Luisa Tetrazzini, who resided in the city for several years.

1. Preheat the oven to 350°F and spray a 2-quart casserole dish lightly with nonstick spray. Bring a large pot of salted water to a boil. In a large saucepan, combine olive oil and butter over medium heat. When the butter melts, add the onion and garlic; cook and stir until crisp-tender, about 4 minutes.

2. Cube the chicken into ½" cubes. Drain the mushrooms, reserving the juice. Add the mushrooms to the saucepan and cook for 1 minute. Sprinkle with flour, salt, pepper, and thyme leaves; cook and stir until bubbly, about 3 minutes.

3. Cook the pasta until almost al dente according to the package directions. Add the broth, light cream, and reserved mushroom liquid to the flour mixture in the saucepan and bring to a simmer. Cook until thickened, about 5 minutes.

4. Drain pasta and add to the sauce along with chicken. Stir in the mustard, sour cream, and Muenster cheese and pour into the prepared casserole. Sprinkle with Parmesan cheese and bake for 30–40 minutes or until casserole bubbles and begins to brown on top. Serve immediately.

PER SERVING Calories: 353 | Fat: 18g | Protein: 24g | Sodium: 554mg | Fiber: 2g | Carbohydrates: 25g | Sugar: 1.2g

Chicken in a Nutty Green Sauce

Have fun with this dish by experimenting with different types and amounts of chili peppers.

INGREDIENTS | SERVES 4

1 (2½- to 3½-pound) chicken

2 cups low-sodium chicken broth

6 habanero chilies, stems and seeds removed

1 medium yellow onion, peeled and quartered

4 garlic cloves, peeled and halved

6 green tomatoes, stems removed, cut into quarters

1 green bell pepper, stem and seeds removed, cut into quarters

1 bunch fresh cilantro, stems removed

½ cup blanched almond slivers

½ cup chopped walnuts

1 teaspoon salt

1 teaspoon ground black pepper

1 tablespoon olive oil

½ cup dry sherry

1. Preheat the oven to 300°F.

2. Wash the chicken, remove the skin, and cut into 8 serving pieces.

3. Place the chicken and broth in a 3-quart Dutch oven dish. Cover and bake on the middle oven rack for 30 minutes.

4. Combine the chilies, onion, garlic, tomatoes, bell pepper, cilantro, almonds, walnuts, salt, pepper, olive oil, and sherry in a mixing bowl. Scoop out about 1 cup at a time and place in a blender or food processor. Blend until all the ingredients are melded but not puréed. Repeat until all the ingredients are blended.

5. Drain off and discard the chicken broth from the chicken. Pour the sauce over the chicken, cover, and replace in the oven. Cook for 1½ hours.

PER SERVING Calories: 563 | Fat: 25g | Protein: 63g | Sodium: 1,022mg | Fiber: 5.4g | Carbohydrates: 24g | Sugar: 13g

Green Chicken with Almond Sauce

Serve with brown rice and a tomato and cucumber salad dressed with lime and cilantro.

INGREDIENTS | SERVES 4

1 fryer chicken

1 cup blanched almonds

4 fresh tomatillos, peeled and quartered

4 fresh serrano chilies, stems and seeds removed

1 large white onion, peeled and quartered

1 handful fresh cilantro, thick stems removed

1 handful fresh parsley, thick stems removed

1 cup dry sherry

1 cup low-sodium chicken broth

½ teaspoon garlic salt

¼ teaspoon ground white pepper

1. Preheat the oven to 350°F and spray a deep 3-quart casserole dish lightly with nonstick spray.

2. Cut the chicken into 8 serving pieces and remove the skin. Chop the almonds into small pieces.

3. Put the tomatillos, chilies, onion, cilantro, parsley, sherry, broth, garlic salt, and pepper in a blender. Blend on medium speed until puréed. Stir in the almonds.

4. Place the chicken in the prepared casserole dish and pour the tomatillo mixture over the chicken. Cover and bake until the chicken is tender and cooked through, about 1 hour.

PER SERVING Calories: 346 | Fat: 16g | Protein: 37g | Sodium: 324mg | Fiber: 3.7g | Carbohydrates: 11g | Sugar: 5.1g

Alcohol-Free Cooking

Alcohol doesn't completely disappear after cooking, so if you prefer to cook without it, substitute an equal amount of broth with a squeeze of lemon or a splash of vinegar.

Creamy Red Chicken with Mushrooms

For a milder flavor, omit the jalapeño peppers and use 1 poblano pepper instead.

INGREDIENTS | SERVES 4

4 boneless, skinless chicken breasts

1 pound fresh white button mushrooms, thinly sliced

1 large red onion, peeled and sliced into ¼" rounds

2 cups low-sodium chicken broth

1 garlic clove, peeled and quartered

2 medium red tomatoes, peeled, stems removed

1 red bell pepper, stem and seeds removed, cut into quarters

2 fresh jalapeño peppers, stem and seeds removed, cut into ¼" rounds

½ cup Mock Cream (see Chapter 14)

Taming the Heat

The heat from chili peppers comes from a compound called capsaicin, which is stored throughout the entire pepper but is found in the highest concentration in the seeds and in the ribs. If you still want the flavor of the chili pepper, but want to tame some of its heat, cut out the seeds and ribs and use the remainder of the pepper in your recipe. Always wear gloves and never touch your eyes when working with chili peppers.

1. Preheat the oven to 350°F and spray a deep 3-quart casserole dish lightly with nonstick spray.

2. Place the chicken breasts into the prepared casserole dish. Add the mushrooms and onion slices on top. Pour 1 cup of the chicken broth over the top. Cover and bake for 1 hour.

3. In the meantime, combine the remaining 1 cup chicken broth, garlic, tomatoes, red pepper, and jalapeños in a blender; blend on medium speed until puréed.

4. Pour the mixture into a medium skillet over medium heat. Gently stir in the Mock Cream until it is well mixed, making sure the mixture does not boil.

5. Pour the creamy mixture over the chicken. Replace the cover and bake for an additional 15 minutes.

PER SERVING Calories: 267 | Fat: 7.7g | Protein: 41g | Sodium: 317g | Fiber: 3g | Carbohydrates: 14g | Sugar: 6.1g

Apricot and Pistachio Couscous Chicken Roulades

Dried apricots and pistachios add flavor and fiber to the pasta stuffing for these chicken breasts. Couscous is so versatile that you can mix it with anything you'd ordinarily make with rice.

INGREDIENTS | SERVES 4

2 cups cooked couscous

¼ cup chopped dried apricots

¼ cup chopped pistachios

4 boneless, skinless chicken breast fillets, pounded thin

Salt and pepper, to taste

½ cup apricot preserves

2 tablespoons butter

Couscous

Couscous is a small granular type of pasta made from semolina flour. Traditionally it is steamed over cooking stews and takes a good amount of time to prepare; however, there are many "instant" brands available that can take as few as 5 minutes to cook. Couscous can be used in salads, soups, stews, appetizers, and even desserts!

1. Preheat the oven to 350°F and spray a 9" × 13" casserole dish lightly with nonstick spray. Combine the couscous with the dried apricots and pistachios. Lay chicken breasts out on plastic wrap and sprinkle them with a pinch of salt and pepper.

2. Divide the couscous mixture evenly among the chicken breasts, placing a pile of the mixture in the middle of each breast. Roll the chicken around the mixture and place the rolls seam side down in the prepared casserole dish.

3. Melt the apricot preserves with the butter and pour it over the chicken rolls; bake, uncovered, until the chicken cooks through and the glaze thickens, about 45 minutes.

PER SERVING Calories: 449 | Fat: 11g | Protein: 40g | Sodium: 80mg | Fiber: 2.6g | Carbohydrates: 51g | Sugar: 31g

Turkey, Orzo, and Feta Cheese Bake

Briny feta and zippy lemon unite in this casserole that makes good use of leftover turkey. Serve with sautéed or grilled zucchini and a crunchy cucumber salad.

INGREDIENTS | SERVES 4

1 tablespoon olive oil

1 medium onion, diced

1 rib celery, diced

1 red bell pepper, finely diced

1 garlic clove

½ teaspoon salt

2 teaspoons dried oregano

2½ cups low-sodium chicken broth

1 cup orzo

Zest and 2 tablespoons juice from 1 lemon

½ cup Mock Cream (see Chapter 14)

2 cups diced cooked turkey

⅔ cup crumbled feta cheese

Feta Cheese

This cheese hails from Greece and is traditionally made from goat's or sheep's milk, though many producers now make it from cow's milk. Feta is cured in a salt brine and has a sharp, tangy flavor. Use it in small quantities to pep up salads.

1. Preheat the oven to 350°F and spray a 2½-quart casserole dish lightly with nonstick spray.

2. Heat the oil in a medium saucepan over medium-high heat. When hot, add the onion and celery and cook, stirring occasionally, until the vegetables just begin to soften, about 5 minutes. Add the bell pepper and garlic and cook for 1 minute.

3. Add the salt, oregano, and chicken broth; bring to a boil over high heat. Add the orzo and cook, uncovered, until the orzo is just cooked, about 10 minutes.

4. Stir in the lemon zest and juice, Mock Cream, turkey, and half the feta cheese. Pour mixture into prepared casserole and sprinkle remaining feta over the top.

5. Bake, uncovered, until the flavors blend and the casserole bubbles, about 20 minutes.

PER SERVING Calories: 240 | Fat: 10g | Protein: 20g | Sodium: 1,247mg | Fiber: 1.6g | Carbohydrates: 18g | Sugar: 4g

Low-Fat Turkey and Cranberry Tetrazzini

You can easily make this dish ahead of time and refrigerate it until you're ready to eat. Just add 15 minutes or so to the baking time.

INGREDIENTS | SERVES 8

2 tablespoons butter

1 tablespoon olive oil

1 onion, chopped

4 garlic cloves, minced

2 stalks celery, chopped

¼ cup flour

½ teaspoon salt

⅛ teaspoon pepper

½ teaspoon dried mint leaves

1 teaspoon dried thyme leaves

1 cup dried cranberries

2 cups low-sodium chicken broth

1 cup 1% milk

3 cups cooked cubed turkey

1 (12-ounce) package spaghetti

1 cup shredded low-fat Swiss cheese

3 tablespoons grated Parmesan cheese

1. Preheat the oven to 350°F. Bring a large pot of salted water to a boil. Spray a 2½-quart casserole with nonstick spray; set aside. In a large saucepan, melt butter and olive oil over medium heat. Add onion and garlic; cook and stir until tender, about 6 minutes. Add celery; cook and stir for 2 minutes longer.

2. Add flour, salt, pepper, mint, and thyme to saucepan; cook and stir until bubbly. Add cranberries, chicken broth, and milk; cook and stir until mixture bubbles and starts to thicken. Add turkey and stir.

3. Cook pasta according to package directions until al dente. Drain and add to saucepan with turkey. Add Swiss cheese and cook until melted. Pour into prepared casserole dish.

4. Sprinkle with Parmesan cheese. Bake for 45–50 minutes or until casserole bubbles and its top starts to brown.

PER SERVING Calories: 355 | Fat: 10g | Protein: 20g | Sodium: 382mg | Fiber: 4g | Carbohydrates: 41g | Sugar: 12g

Turkey "Lasagna" Pie

Cook the lasagna noodles in the same Dutch oven in which you'll eventually assemble the lasagna. Baking in a deep Dutch oven means you don't have to worry about the lasagna boiling over, and it cooks more evenly than it would in a rectangular pan.

INGREDIENTS | SERVES 8

12 dried whole-wheat lasagna noodles

½ cup Basil Pesto (see Chapter 14)

1 teaspoon grated lemon zest

1 large egg, beaten

1 (15-ounce) carton part-skim ricotta cheese

2 cups reduced-fat mozzarella cheese, grated

¼ teaspoon salt

¼ teaspoon ground black pepper

2 cups fresh spinach, chopped

½ cup chopped walnuts, toasted if desired

2 cups cooked turkey, chopped

1 (24-ounce) bottle marinara or pasta sauce

1 (8-ounce) package fresh button or cremini mushrooms, cleaned and thinly sliced

½ cup dry red wine

Optional: fresh Italian flat-leaf parsley leaves

1. Preheat the oven to 375°F.

2. Cook the noodles according to the package directions until almost tender. Drain in a colander and rinse in cold water to stop the cooking. Drain well and set aside.

3. In a small bowl, mix together the pesto and lemon zest; set aside. Add the egg, ricotta cheese, 1 cup of the mozzarella cheese, salt, and pepper to a medium bowl and mix well.

4. Lightly coat the Dutch oven with nonstick spray. Arrange 4 cooked noodles in the bottom of the pan, trimming and overlapping them to cover. Top with the spinach. Sprinkle with half of the walnuts. Spread half of the ricotta cheese mixture evenly over walnuts. Spread half of the pesto mixture evenly over the ricotta, then sprinkle half of the turkey over the pesto. Pour half of the pasta sauce evenly over the turkey. Top with another layer of noodles. Top with the mushrooms. Spread the remaining ricotta cheese mixture over mushrooms. Spread the remaining pesto mixture over the ricotta. Sprinkle the remaining turkey over the pesto and then pour the rest of the pasta sauce over the turkey. Top with another layer of noodles.

5. Pour the wine into the empty marinara sauce jar, screw on the lid and shake to mix with any sauce remaining in the jar. Pour over the top layer of noodles. Cover the pan and bake for 45 minutes.

6. Remove the cover. Sprinkle the remaining mozzarella cheese over the top. Bake for an additional 15–30 minutes or until the cheese is melted and bubbly and the lasagna is hot in the center. Let set for 10 minutes and then garnish with parsley if desired. To serve, cut the lasagna into pizza slice–style wedges.

PER SERVING Calories: 521 | Fat: 22g | Protein: 32g | Sodium: 1,145mg | Fiber: 3.1g | Carbohydrates: 51g | Sugar: 11g

Turkey and Noodles Casserole

This is comfort food at its best. Serve this with a chopped salad dressed with a zippy balsamic vinaigrette.

INGREDIENTS | SERVES 8

1 pound dried extra-wide egg noodles

1 tablespoon extra-virgin olive oil

4 slices turkey bacon, chopped

2½ pounds lean ground turkey

1 pound white mushrooms, cleaned and sliced

1 large yellow onion, diced

½ teaspoon salt

¼ teaspoon freshly ground black pepper

1 tablespoon dried thyme

1 cup dry white wine

2 cups low-sodium chicken broth

1 cup Mock Cream (see Chapter 14)

¼ teaspoon freshly grated nutmeg

8 ounces Gruyère cheese, grated

1 cup plain bread crumbs

2 tablespoons butter, melted

1. Cook the noodles in a 3-quart Dutch oven according to package directions. Drain, set aside, and keep warm.

2. Preheat the oven to 350°F.

3. Wipe out the Dutch oven and heat the oil over medium-high heat. Add the bacon and cook for 3 minutes to render the bacon fat and until the bacon begins to brown at the edges. Add the ground turkey and brown, breaking up clumps with a wooden spoon. Add the mushrooms and onions and cook for 3–5 minutes or until the onions are translucent and the meat loses its pink color. Sprinkle with salt, pepper, and thyme.

4. Stir in the wine and scrape up any browned bits clinging to the bottom of the pan. Stir in the broth and bring to a simmer. Whisk in the Mock Cream. Stir in the nutmeg and Gruyère cheese. Stir in the noodles. Top with the bread crumbs; drizzle the butter over the crumbs. Bake until the casserole is bubbly and the crumbs are browned, about 30 minutes.

PER SERVING Calories: 476 | Fat: 24g | Protein: 37g | Sodium: 563mg | Fiber: 1.9g | Carbohydrates: 27g | Sugar: 2.2g

CHAPTER 10

Pork, Beef, and Lamb

Mini Spinach Casserole with Brown Rice and Ham

*This is a hearty, delicious meal for a cold fall or winter day.
It also makes great leftovers!*

INGREDIENTS | SERVES 2

2 cups fresh baby spinach

½ cup low-fat ricotta cheese

Salt and pepper to taste

1 cup brown rice, cooked

¼ cup Italian dressing

1 ounce Virginia ham, chopped

1. Preheat the oven to 350°F and spray an 8" × 8" casserole dish lightly with nonstick spray. Purée the spinach and ricotta in the blender.

2. Mix all the ingredients together in the prepared casserole dish and bake until hot and bubbly, about 20–30 minutes.

PER SERVING Calories: 342 | Fat: 19g | Protein: 16g | Sodium: 593mg | Fiber: 1g | Carbohydrates: 32g | Sugar: 2.4g

Main Dish Pork and Beans

The pork in this casserole is really just for flavor; it's the beans that give this recipe a bounty of lean protein. Substitute apple juice if you don't have cider on hand.

INGREDIENTS | SERVES 4

1⅓ cups cooked pinto beans

2 tablespoons ketchup

¼ teaspoon Dijon mustard

¼ teaspoon dry mustard

1 teaspoon cider vinegar

4 tablespoons diced red onion

1 tablespoon pure maple syrup

1 teaspoon brown sugar

¼ pound (4 ounces) slow-cooked, shredded pork

2 tablespoons apple cider

1. Preheat the oven to 350°F and spray a 9" × 13" casserole dish with nonstick spray. Add the beans, ketchup, mustards, vinegar, onion, maple syrup, and brown sugar; stir gently to combine. Layer the meat over the top of the bean mixture, then pour the cider over the pork.

2. Cover the beans with foil and bake until the mixture is well heated and bubbling, 20–30 minutes. Stir well before serving.

PER SERVING Calories: 153 | Fat: 2g | Protein: 11g | Sodium: 146mg | Fiber: 5g | Carbohydrates: 24g | Sugar: 5.9g

Baked Pork Tenderloin au Lait

Cooking meat in a bath of milk is not a new technique at all. French and Italian chefs have used this method for centuries to keep tender cuts moist and flavorful. Skim or reduced-fat milk will not work in this recipe.

INGREDIENTS | SERVES 4

4 (4-ounce) pork tenderloin cutlets, tenderized

2 teaspoons brown sugar

1 teaspoon ground ginger

1 teaspoon ground mustard

½ teaspoon salt

¼ teaspoon pepper

2 cups whole milk

1. Preheat the oven to 350°F and spray an 8" × 8" casserole dish lightly with nonstick spray.

2. Lay the pork in the baking dish and sprinkle with the brown sugar, ginger, ground mustard, salt, and pepper. Pour the milk over the meat.

3. Bake until the milk has reduced to a thick gravy and the pork is tender, 1–1½ hours.

PER SERVING Calories: 292 | Fat: 17g | Protein: 26g | Sodium: 385mg | Fiber: 1g | Carbohydrates: 5.5g | Sugar: 0g

Pork Loin Casserole

This hearty casserole is resplendent with autumnal flavors: earthy potatoes, sweet apples, and woodsy rosemary.

INGREDIENTS | SERVES 4

4 small Yukon Gold potatoes, peeled and sliced into thin rounds

2 (2-ounce) pieces trimmed boneless pork loin, pounded flat

1 tablespoon fresh rosemary

½ teaspoon salt

¼ teaspoon pepper

1 apple, peeled, cored, and sliced into thin rounds

4 dried apricot halves, finely chopped

1 tablespoon chopped red onion

⅛ cup apple cider

1 tablespoon olive oil

1. Preheat the oven to 350°F and spray a 9" × 13" casserole dish lightly with nonstick spray.

2. Layer half of the potato slices evenly over the bottom of the dish. Top with the flattened pork loins and sprinkle with the rosemary, salt, and pepper. Arrange the apple slices over the top of the loin and sprinkle the apricots and red onion over the apples. Layer the remaining potatoes on top. Drizzle the apple cider and olive oil over the top of the casserole.

3. Cover and bake for 45 minutes to 1 hour or until the potatoes are tender. Uncover the dish during the last 15 minutes of baking so that the potatoes brown slightly. Allow casserole to set for 10 minutes after you remove it from the oven to slice it easily.

PER SERVING Calories: 224 | Fat: 5.2g | Protein: 8g | Sodium: 382mg | Fiber: 4.2g | Carbohydrates: 38g | Sugar: 6.8g

Pork Chops and Fruited Veggies Bake

The bone in the pork chops helps to keep them tender and juicy.
Do not substitute canned peaches for the frozen or they will become mushy during cooking.

INGREDIENTS | SERVES 4

4 large Yukon gold potatoes, washed and sliced into thin rounds

1 (10-ounce) package frozen whole green beans, thawed

4 (6-ounce) bone-in pork loin chops

8 cloves garlic, crushed

¼ teaspoon freshly ground black pepper

¼ teaspoon dried thyme

¼ teaspoon dried rosemary

⅛ teaspoon dried oregano

1 cup peeled baby carrots

1 (10-ounce) package frozen organic sliced peaches, thawed

2 teaspoons brown sugar

¼ teaspoon ground cinnamon

Pinch ground cloves

1. Preheat the oven to 425°F and lightly spray a 9" × 13" casserole dish with nonstick spray.

2. Evenly spread the sliced potatoes and green beans across the bottom of the prepared casserole dish.

3. Rub the pork chops with the garlic. Place the garlic cloves and pork chops on top of the vegetables. Sprinkle with the pepper, thyme, rosemary, and oregano.

4. Place the carrots, peaches, brown sugar, cinnamon, and cloves in a medium bowl; stir gently to mix. Spread the carrot and peach mixture on top of the pork chops and vegetables.

5. Bake, uncovered, until the meat, potatoes, and carrots are tender, about 30 minutes.

PER SERVING Calories: 553 | Fat: 19g | Protein: 42g | Fiber: 11g | Carbohydrates: 78g | Sugar: 12g

Fruit Swap

You can substitute 4 peeled and sliced apples or pears for the peaches in the Pork Chops and Fruited Veggies Bake recipe. Toss the slices with 1 tablespoon of lemon juice before mixing them with the brown sugar, cinnamon, and cloves to help preserve their color.

Ground Pork and Eggplant Casserole

If you prefer, this dish will fit in a 2-quart baking dish, but using a 4-quart Dutch oven will give you plenty of room to mix the meat and vegetables together and let you do the stovetop cooking and baking in one pot.

INGREDIENTS | SERVES 10

2 tablespoons extra-virgin olive oil

2 pounds lean ground pork

2 large yellow onions, chopped

3 celery stalks, chopped

1 green bell pepper, seeded and chopped

6 cloves garlic, minced

4 medium eggplants, cut into ½" pieces

⅛ teaspoon dried thyme, crushed

2 tablespoons fresh parsley

3 tablespoons tomato paste

1 teaspoon hot sauce

2 teaspoons Worcestershire sauce

½ teaspoon salt

¼ teaspoon pepper

1 large egg, beaten

½ cup whole-wheat bread crumbs

1 tablespoon melted butter

1. Preheat the oven to 350°F.

2. Heat the oil in a 3-quart Dutch oven over medium-high heat and add the ground pork, breaking it apart with a wooden spoon as it cooks. When no longer pink, remove to a bowl and drain all but 1 tablespoon fat from the pot.

3. Add the onion, celery, and green pepper; cook over medium heat until the onion is transparent, about 7 minutes. Add the garlic, eggplant, thyme, parsley, and tomato paste. Stir to combine. Cover and simmer, stirring often, for 20 minutes or until the vegetables are tender. Return the ground pork to the pot. Off the heat, add the hot sauce, Worcestershire sauce, salt, pepper, and egg; stir to combine. Sprinkle the bread crumbs over the top and drizzle with the melted butter. Bake for 40 minutes or until the crumb topping is lightly browned and the casserole is hot in the center.

PER SERVING Calories: 304 | Fat: 17g | Protein: 20g | Sodium: 246mg | Fiber: 7.1g | Carbohydrates: 17g | Sugar: 5.3g

Why Choose Freshly Ground Black Pepper?

Bottled ground black pepper has less kick than fresh and contains anticaking agents that can make some people feel stomach discomfort.

Easy Oven Beef Burgundy

Serve this dish with a green salad and some crusty whole-wheat bread to sop up the luscious sauce.

INGREDIENTS | SERVES 4

1 pound beef round, cubed
2 tablespoons all-purpose flour
2 tablespoons canola oil
1 cup carrots, sliced
1 cup onions, chopped
1 cup celery, sliced
1 clove garlic, finely chopped
¼ teaspoon pepper
¼ teaspoon marjoram
¼ teaspoon thyme
½ teaspoon salt
2 tablespoons balsamic vinegar
½ cup dry red wine
½ cup low-sodium beef broth
1 cup fresh mushrooms, sliced

1. Preheat the oven to 325°F.

2. Dredge the meat cubes in flour and heat 1 tablespoon of the oil in a 3-quart Dutch oven over medium-high heat. Brown half the meat, making sure not to scorch the bottom of the pot, and remove to a plate. Repeat with remaining oil and beef.

3. Pour off any fat remaining in the pot, then add the beef, carrots, onions, celery, garlic, pepper, marjoram, thyme, salt, and vinegar. Pour the wine and beef broth over the mixture; stir to combine. Cover and bake for 1 hour.

4. Remove the pot from oven and mix in mushrooms.

5. Continue to cook until the beef cubes are tender, about 1 hour more.

PER SERVING Calories: 341 | Fat: 20g | Protein: 29g | Sodium: 304mg | Fiber: 2g | Carbohydrates: 9.6g | Sugar: 4.4g

Mushroom Meatballs in Tomato Sauce

To make quick work of dinner, make the meatballs in advance when you have a spare moment and refrigerate or freeze them until you are ready to bake the casserole. Substitute fresh homemade Basic Tomato Sauce (see Chapter 14) instead of jarred if you wish.

INGREDIENTS | YIELDS 16 MEATBALLS; SERVING SIZE: 2 MEATBALLS

¾ pound 93% lean ground beef

1 (8-ounce) package brown mushrooms, finely chopped

1 teaspoon salt

¼ teaspoon black pepper

1 whole egg

1 teaspoon dried oregano

¼ cup whole-wheat bread crumbs

3 cups jarred tomato sauce

3 tablespoons chopped fresh basil

Grass-Fed Beef

Although it is slightly more expensive, grass-fed beef is leaner and more flavorful, and has a more beneficial ratio of omega-3 to omega-6 fatty acids than grain-fed beef. Use as you would in standard beef recipes.

1. Preheat the oven to 425°F and spray a 9" × 13" casserole dish lightly with nonstick spray.

2. Mix the beef, mushrooms, salt, pepper, egg, oregano, and bread crumbs in a bowl. Form into 16 balls and place in the prepared casserole dish. Bake, uncovered, on the top oven rack until the meatballs begin to brown, about 15 minutes.

3. Discard any fat in the casserole dish and cover with the tomato sauce. Reduce the oven temperature to 350°F. Cover the dish tightly with foil and cook for 45 minutes on the middle oven rack until bubbly and cooked through. Sprinkle basil on top before serving.

PER SERVING Calories: 135 | Fat: 3.9g | Protein: 14g | Sodium: 362mg | Fiber: 1.8g | Carbohydrates: 10g | Sugar: 4.5g

Marzetti Casserole

This casserole can be made the night before, covered, and refrigerated until ready to bake.

INGREDIENTS | SERVES 8

8 ounces dried medium egg noodles

1 tablespoon olive oil

1 pound 93% lean ground beef

1 medium yellow onion, chopped

2 stalks celery, diced

1 (16-ounce) jar spaghetti sauce with mushrooms

1 green pepper, seeded and cut into thin strips

1 cup frozen peas

1 cup tomato juice

1 tablespoon Worcestershire sauce

½ teaspoon dried oregano, crushed

½ teaspoon salt

¼ teaspoon ground pepper, or to taste

8 ounces Cheddar cheese, grated

Day Two

If you're baking the Marzetti Casserole the next day, you can add another flavor dimension by mixing 1 cup of dried bread crumbs with 1 tablespoon of melted butter or extra-virgin olive oil. Sprinkle the crumb mixture and some Parmigiano-Reggiano cheese over the top of the casserole. Bake until the casserole is heated through and the bread crumbs are golden brown.

1. Preheat the oven to 375°F and spray a 9" × 13" casserole dish lightly with nonstick spray. In a 4-quart Dutch oven, prepare the egg noodles according to the package directions. Drain in a colander and keep warm.

2. Heat the oil in the Dutch oven over medium heat and brown the beef, breaking up clumps with a wooden spoon. Once the beef has lost its pink color, add the onion and celery; cook until the vegetables are tender and translucent.

3. Drain off any excess fat and add the sauce, green pepper, peas, tomato juice, Worcestershire sauce, oregano, salt, and pepper. Lower the heat and simmer, covered, for 10 minutes. Stir in the noodles and pour the mixture into the prepared casserole pan.

4. Sprinkle the top of the casserole with the Cheddar cheese. Bake until bubbly, about 15–20 minutes.

PER SERVING Calories: 426 | Fat: 18g | Protein: 28g | Sodium: 663mg | Fiber: 4.1g | Carbohydrates: 35g | Sugar: 7.8g

Shepherd's Pie

This version of shepherd's pie uses lean ground beef instead of the traditional (and fattier) ground lamb. The cheese and sour cream in the mashed potatoes help the potato crust to crisp and turn golden in the oven.

INGREDIENTS | SERVES 10

1½ pounds 93% lean ground beef

2 onions, chopped

3 cloves garlic, minced

3 tablespoons flour

1 teaspoon dried marjoram leaves

⅛ teaspoon pepper

3 tablespoons Worcestershire sauce

1 cup beef broth

½ cup chili sauce

¼ cup ketchup

1 (10-ounce) package frozen peas and carrots

1 (10-ounce) package frozen green beans

3 cups mashed potatoes

⅓ cup low-fat sour cream

⅓ cup shredded reduced fat Cheddar cheese

1. Preheat the oven to 375°F and spray a 9" × 13" casserole dish with nonstick spray. In a large nonstick skillet, cook the ground beef with the onion and garlic until the beef is browned and the onion and garlic are soft, about 15 minutes. Drain the fat, then return the pan to the heat. Add the flour, marjoram, and pepper. Cook, stirring frequently, for 4 minutes, then add Worcestershire sauce, beef broth, chili sauce, and ketchup.

2. Simmer the beef mixture for 10 minutes, then add the frozen vegetables and stir gently to combine. Pour the mixture into the prepared casserole dish.

3. In a large bowl, combine the potatoes with the sour cream and Cheddar cheese. Spread the potato mixture evenly over the meat mixture with a rubber spatula.

4. Bake until casserole bubbles and potatoes brown and crisp, about 35–40 minutes.

PER SERVING Calories: 246 | Fat: 6.6g | Protein: 23g | Sodium: 510mg | Fiber: 3.1g | Carbohydrates: 22g | Sugar: 3.5g

Mashed Potatoes

Make your own mashed potatoes instead of using the refrigerated variety. Just peel and cube 5 potatoes. Boil until tender, then drain and mash with 2 tablespoons butter, salt, pepper, and ½ cup skim milk.

Moussaka

Use vegetable protein crumbles to make a meatless version of this dish. For a more traditional flavor, substitute lean ground lamb for the beef. Pair with a side of grilled vegetables for a tasty meal.

INGREDIENTS | SERVES 10

2 eggplants, peeled
2 teaspoons salt
2 tablespoons olive oil
2 onions, chopped
4 cloves garlic, minced
¾ pound 93% lean ground beef
1 (6-ounce) can tomato paste
1 (8-ounce) can tomato sauce
1 teaspoon dried oregano leaves
½ teaspoon cinnamon
1 tablespoon chopped fresh basil leaves
2 tablespoons butter
2 tablespoons flour
⅛ teaspoon white pepper
1½ cups milk
2 eggs
¾ cup grated Romano cheese
¼ cup grated Parmesan cheese
¼ cup dried whole-wheat bread crumbs

1. Slice the eggplant into ½"-thick rounds. Sprinkle with 1 teaspoon of the salt and allow to drain in a colander set over a large bowl while preparing the rest of the recipe.

2. Heat 1 tablespoon of oil over medium heat in a large saucepan. Add the onions, stirring frequently, until they become translucent, about 5 minutes. Add the garlic and cook until fragrant, about 1 minute. Add the beef and cook until no longer pink. Drain any fat before proceeding with the recipe. Stir in the tomato paste and let the mixture brown slightly, scraping the bottom so that the mixture does not burn. Stir in the tomato sauce, oregano, cinnamon, basil, and ½ teaspoon salt; simmer over low heat for 15 minutes.

3. Heat the butter over medium heat in a medium saucepan. Add the flour, ½ teaspoon salt, and pepper. Cook, stirring frequently, until pale golden, about 1 minute. Quickly whisk in the milk and simmer until thickened, then remove from heat. Whisk the eggs and Romano together in a bowl. Dribble in the hot milk mixture, whisking constantly, until all the milk mixture has been combined with the eggs.

4. Rinse the eggplant, pat dry, and brush with the remaining olive oil. Broil on high for 7–8 minutes, turning once, until the eggplant is well-browned (not burned).

5. Preheat the oven to 350°F and lightly spray a 9" × 13" casserole dish with nonstick spray. Place a layer of eggplant in the bottom, top with tomato sauce, then layer the remaining eggplant on top. Pour the white sauce over the eggplant and sprinkle with the Parmesan and bread crumbs.

6. Bake for 40–50 minutes until top is golden brown. Cool for 10 minutes, then cut into squares to serve.

PER SERVING Calories: 239 | Fat: 12g | Protein: 17g | Sodium: 723mg | Fiber: 4.3g | Carbohydrates: 15g | Sugar: 5.1g

Tamale Spoon Bread Casserole

This recipe requires one pot for the cooking and a separate casserole dish for the baking.

INGREDIENTS | SERVES 10

1 tablespoon extra-virgin olive oil

1½ pounds 93% lean ground beef

1 large yellow onion, chopped

1 clove garlic, minced

1 green bell pepper, seeded and chopped

1 cup cornmeal

1 cup water

2 (14.5-ounce) cans chopped tomatoes, slightly drained

1 (12-ounce) can whole-kernel corn

1 tablespoon plus 1 teaspoon chili powder

½ teaspoon salt

¼ teaspoon freshly ground black pepper

½ cup sliced, pitted ripe olives

1½ cups milk

2 tablespoons butter

1 cup grated extra-sharp reduced-fat Cheddar cheese

2 eggs, slightly beaten

Quickest and Easiest

You can assemble this casserole the night before or earlier in the day. Cover the casserole dish with plastic wrap and refrigerate until needed. Remove the plastic wrap and bake for 75–90 minutes. The extra cooking time lets you bake the casserole without letting it come to room temperature before you put it in the oven.

1. Preheat the oven to 350°F and spray a 9" × 13" casserole dish lightly with nonstick spray.

2. Heat the olive oil in a deep nonstick skillet over medium-high heat. Add the ground beef and brown the meat, breaking up clumps with a wooden spoon. Add the onion, garlic, and green pepper to the skillet; cook, stirring, until the onion is slightly browned. Drain the fat from the skillet.

3. Mix together ½ cup of the cornmeal and 1 cup water and stir it into the skillet; cover and simmer for 10 minutes. Stir in the tomatoes, corn, chili powder, salt, and pepper; simmer for 5 minutes longer. Mix in the olives, then spoon the meat mixture into the prepared casserole dish.

4. Heat the milk and butter in a large saucepan over medium heat. When the milk begins to simmer, slowly whisk in the remaining ½ cup cornmeal. Lower the heat and continue to simmer while stirring or whisking until it thickens. Remove from the heat and whisk in the cheese and eggs. Pour the cornmeal mixture over the meat mixture. Bake, uncovered, for 1 hour or until the entire casserole is hot and bubbly.

PER SERVING Calories: 415 | Fat: 16g | Protein: 27g | Sodium: 308mg | Fiber: 4.6g | Carbohydrates: 40g | Sugar: 0.38g

Tamale Pie

This hearty casserole feeds a crowd. The spicier the sausage, the spicier the casserole.
If you like it really hot, add more jalapeño peppers.

INGREDIENTS | SERVES 8

2 cups low-sodium chicken broth

1 cup water

1 cup yellow cornmeal

½ pound spicy lean pork sausage

½ pound 93% lean ground beef

2 medium onions, chopped

4 garlic cloves, minced

2 jalapeño peppers, minced

1 green bell pepper, chopped

1 red bell pepper, chopped

2 (14.5-ounce) cans diced tomatoes

2 (14.5-ounce) cans black beans, drained

1 tablespoon chili powder

1 teaspoon cumin

½ teaspoon salt

⅛ teaspoon pepper

½ cup shredded Muenster cheese

¼ cup grated Cotija cheese

1. Preheat the oven to 400°F and spray a 3-quart casserole dish with nonstick spray.

2. In a medium saucepan, bring the broth and water to a boil. Add the cornmeal, bring to a simmer, then lower heat and cover. Simmer for 15–20 minutes, stirring frequently until thickened. Set aside.

3. In a large saucepan, cook the sausage and beef with the onion, garlic, and jalapeños until the meat is brown and the vegetables are tender, 10–15 minutes. Add the bell peppers and cook for 5 minutes longer. Drain the mixture of fat before proceeding to the next step.

4. Add the tomatoes, beans, chili powder, cumin, salt, and pepper. Simmer until the mixture is heated through and the flavors blend, about 15 minutes.

5. Stir the Muenster cheese into the cornmeal mixture. Place half of the cornmeal mixture in bottom of the prepared casserole dish. Top with sausage mixture, then spread the remaining cornmeal mixture on top. Sprinkle with the Cotija cheese.

6. Bake until the casserole is bubbling and cornmeal topping is golden brown, about 30–40 minutes. Let the casserole stand for 5 minutes before serving.

PER SERVING Calories: 515 | Fat: 9.1g | Protein: 35g | Sodium: 817mg | Fiber: 15g | Carbohydrates: 73g | Sugar: 4g

Taco Skillet Casserole

Serve with a side of beans and warmed whole-wheat tortillas.

INGREDIENTS | SERVES 6

1½ pounds 93% lean ground beef

1 small yellow onion, chopped into ¼" pieces

1 garlic clove, minced

1 teaspoon salt

½ teaspoon ground black pepper

1 teaspoon chili powder

2 cups canned tomato sauce

1 ounce unsalted, baked tortilla chips, crumbled

½ cup grated Cheddar cheese

¼ head lettuce, shredded

Corn Husks as Spice

The Mexican culture is unique for using corn husks to spice food. Most often used in corn tamales, the husks are also used as a wrapper for other foods such as candy. Even when leaving the husk on for cooking the corn, you notice a distinctly earthy taste that is transferred to the food.

1. Crumble the ground beef into a large nonstick skillet and brown over medium heat, breaking up clumps with a wooden spoon. Drain off any fat and return the skillet to the heat.

2. Add the onion and garlic and cook until the onion is soft, about 5 minutes.

3. Stir in the salt, pepper, chili powder, and tomato sauce; continue cooking over low heat for about 15 minutes longer, stirring frequently.

4. Stir the tortilla chips into the meat mixture and cook for about 5 minutes, stirring frequently.

5. Sprinkle with cheese. As soon as the cheese melts, remove from heat. Top with shredded lettuce and serve immediately.

PER SERVING Calories: 295 | Fat: 12g | Protein: 34g | Sodium: 539mg | Fiber: 1.5g | Carbohydrates: 10g | Sugar: 3.5g

Unstuffed Cabbage Rolls

Use Italian-seasoned tomatoes and cooked orzo pasta instead of rice to give this dish a Tuscan flair. If you prefer German flavors, add 1 teaspoon of caraway seeds and 2 teaspoons of brown sugar.

INGREDIENTS | SERVES 8

2 tablespoons extra-virgin olive oil

6 stalks celery, diced

6 large carrots, peeled and diced

1 large yellow onion, diced

1 pound 93% lean ground beef

2 cloves garlic, minced

4 cups coleslaw mix

2 (15-ounce) cans diced tomatoes

2 cups cooked rice

1½ cups chicken broth

½ cup dry white wine

½ teaspoon salt

¼ teaspoon freshly ground black pepper

1. Preheat the oven to 350°F.

2. Heat the oil in an ovenproof 3-quart Dutch oven over medium heat. Add the celery, carrots, and onion. Cook for 5 minutes, then add the ground beef and garlic. Cook until the beef is no longer pink and the onion is translucent. Drain off and discard any excess fat.

3. Add the coleslaw mix, canned tomatoes, rice, broth, wine, salt, and pepper. Stir into the beef mixture and use the back of a spoon to press the mixture down evenly in the Dutch oven. Cover and bake for 45 minutes. Uncover and bake for an additional 15 minutes or until most of the liquid has evaporated.

PER SERVING Calories: 268 | Fat: 7.6g | Protein: 19g | Sodium: 596mg | Fiber: 5.4g | Carbohydrates: 31g | Sugar: 11g

Cabbage Rolls

Cabbage is the perfect vessel for nutty brown rice, crunchy hazelnuts, and lean beef and pork.
If your store doesn't carry lean ground pork, grind your own from pork loin.

INGREDIENTS | SERVES 4; SERVING SIZE: 3 ROLLS

12 large cabbage leaves
1 cup cooked brown rice
¼ cup currants
¼ cup toasted hazelnuts
¼ cup minced onion
¾ teaspoon salt
Pepper, to taste
½ pound lean ground pork
½ pound 93% lean ground beef
1 tablespoon olive oil
2 garlic cloves, finely minced
2 cups tomato sauce
1 tablespoon brown sugar

Vegetarian Cabbage Rolls

For a meatless version, substitute chopped mushrooms for the ground beef and pork. You will also have to double the quantity of rice, add extra currants, and perhaps toss in some chopped celery and nuts. You can also increase the amount of onions in this recipe for a vegetarian version. Increase the protein by adding an egg or two to the filling.

1. Preheat the oven to 350°F and lightly spray a 9" × 13" casserole dish with nonstick spray.

2. Blanch the cabbage leaves in boiling water for 4 minutes. Remove and lay flat on a tray. Chill in the refrigerator while you make the filling.

3. Combine the cooked brown rice, currants, hazelnuts, onion, salt, and pepper in a bowl. Add ground pork and beef and mix well. Remove cabbage leaves from the refrigerator and blot with paper towels. Place about ¼ cup meat mixture on each cabbage leaf. Fold in sides and then roll up leaf to completely enclose filling. Place the cabbage rolls in the prepared dish, seam side down.

4. Heat the olive oil in a large saucepan. Add the garlic and cook until just fragrant, about 1 minute. Add the tomato sauce and brown sugar; stir to combine.

5. Spoon the sauce over the rolls, cover with foil, and bake until the filling is cooked through and the cabbage leaves are very tender, about 1 hour. Serve hot.

PER SERVING Calories: 447 | Fat: 20g | Protein: 30g | Sodium: 550mg | Fiber: 6.5g | Carbohydrates: 23g | Sugar: 8.1g

Unstuffed Green Peppers Casserole

You can use a can of whole tomatoes instead of diced, if you prefer.
Just crush or cut up the tomatoes when you add them (and their juices) to the casserole.

INGREDIENTS | SERVES 6

1 tablespoon olive oil

¾ pound 93% lean ground beef

1 medium yellow onion, chopped

1 (14.5-ounce) can chopped tomatoes

1 (8-ounce) can whole-kernel corn, drained

2½ cups whole-wheat bread crumbs

3 large green bell peppers, seeded and cut into large dice

1 tablespoon melted butter

1. Preheat the oven to 400°F.

2. Heat the olive oil over medium heat in a 4-quart oven-proof Dutch oven. Add the beef and brown, breaking up clumps with a wooden spoon. Add the onion and cook until translucent, about 5 minutes more. Pour off any excess fat. Add the tomatoes, corn, 2 cups bread crumbs, and green pepper. Mix well.

3. Cover and bake for 25 minutes or until the green peppers are tender. In a small bowl, mix the remaining bread crumbs with the melted butter. Remove the cover from the casserole and sprinkle the bread crumbs over the top. Bake for an additional 5 minutes or until the bread crumbs are golden brown.

PER SERVING Calories: 490 | Fat: 12g | Protein: 25g | Sodium: 547mg | Fiber: 7g | Carbohydrates: 69g | Sugar: 5.5g

Stuffed Bell Peppers

These stuffed peppers are chock-full of lean meat, vegetables, and whole-grain fiber.

INGREDIENTS | SERVES 6

3 large green bell peppers
2 large red bell peppers
2 large yellow bell peppers
¾ pound 93% lean ground beef
¼ cup Grape-Nuts cereal
1 cup cooked brown rice
½ cup diced onion
¼ cup diced carrots
¼ cup diced celery
2 cups tomato sauce
Salt and pepper, to taste

Bell Peppers: Native to the New World

Although bell peppers are used widely in food preparations across world cultures, they are actually a new world food. Bell peppers come in a variety of colors and are a great source of vitamins A and C.

1. Preheat the oven to 350°F and spray a 9" × 13" casserole dish lightly with nonstick spray.

2. Cut the peppers in half through the stem and discard seeds, stem, and membrane. Lay the pepper cups in the prepared casserole dish.

3. Mix together the meat, cereal, rice, onion, carrots, celery, and ½ cup tomato sauce. Season the mixture with salt and pepper.

4. Divide the meat mixture evenly among the pepper cups. Pour remaining tomato sauce over tops of stuffed peppers, cover with foil, and bake until bubbling and cooked through, 45–50 minutes.

PER SERVING Calories: 328 | Fat: 18g | Protein: 21g | Sodium: 81mg | Fiber: 4.5g | Sugar: 5g

Baked Stuffed Kibbe

If you have trouble finding bulgur wheat in your supermarket, look for packaged taboule wheat salad mix. It is essentially the same thing—just discard the seasoning packet.

INGREDIENTS | SERVES 8

¾ cup bulgur wheat, fine grind

2 cups boiling water

1 pound lean ground lamb

1 cup onion, grated

1 teaspoon salt

¼ teaspoon pepper

Small bowl ice water

3 tablespoons butter

¼ cup pine nuts

¼ teaspoon cinnamon

¼ teaspoon allspice

Making Lean Ground Lamb

Unless you have a butcher, very lean ground lamb is difficult to find. Make it yourself using chunks of meat trimmed from a leg of lamb. Be sure to remove all visible fat from the lamb and grind twice using a medium or fine grinder blade. Removing all visible fat prevents lamb from having a strong "mutton" taste.

1. Preheat the oven to 350°F and spray a 9" × 9" baking dish with nonstick spray.

2. Put the bulgur wheat in a small heatproof bowl. Cover with the boiling water and allow the wheat to absorb the liquid, 15–20 minutes.

3. Line a colander with a small piece of cheesecloth. Drop the bulgur wheat into cloth; drain and squeeze as much liquid out of the wheat as possible.

4. On large cutting board, combine lamb, half the grated onions, wheat, salt, and pepper. Knead all the ingredients together with your hands.

5. Divide meat mixture in half. Place the first half in the bottom of baking dish by dipping your hands into ice water to spread meat mixture evenly and smoothly over the bottom of the dish.

6. In a small pan, melt half of the butter over medium heat. Sauté the remaining onions, pine nuts, cinnamon, and allspice until the onions are soft.

7. Spread the onion and pine nut mixture evenly over first layer of meat in the baking dish. Take remaining meat mixture and spread it smoothly on top, using the procedure in Step 5.

8. Score top in diamond shapes with a knife dipped in cold water. Melt the remaining butter and drizzle over the meat. Bake on the middle oven rack for approximately 40–45 minutes or until golden brown.

PER SERVING Calories: 226 | Fat: 12g | Protein: 18g | Sodium: 343mg | Fiber: 3g | Carbohydrates: 13g | Sugar: 0g

Greek Lamb and Pasta Casserole

Mint adds a delightfully fresh flavor to an otherwise hearty dish.
Serve with a fresh green salad dressed with a lemony vinaigrette.

INGREDIENTS | SERVES 6

1 tablespoon olive oil

1 pound lean ground lamb

1 large sweet onion, chopped

4 garlic cloves, minced

½ cup currants

½ teaspoon cinnamon

½ teaspoon salt

¼ teaspoon pepper

1 tablespoon fresh chopped mint

3 cups parboiled orzo

½ cup low-sodium chicken broth

½ cup toasted pine nuts

1. Preheat the oven to 350°F. Spray a 9" × 13" casserole dish lightly with nonstick spray.

2. Heat the olive oil in a large nonstick skillet over medium heat. Sauté the lamb, onion, and garlic, stirring constantly, until the lamb is no longer pink and the onion is softened, about 15 minutes. Drain off any fat, then add the currants, cinnamon, salt, pepper, and mint.

3. Add the orzo and broth; pour the mixture into the casserole dish. Sprinkle with pine nuts. Bake until hot and bubbly, about 30 minutes.

PER SERVING Calories: 360 | Fat: 19g | Protein: 20g | Sodium: 282mg | Fiber: 2g | Carbohydrates: 28g | Sugar: 3.3g

Greek Cooking Trivia

The ancient Greeks didn't have processed sugar. They used honey for desserts and cooked with fruit such as figs or grapes to bring sweetness to other dishes. This recipe adds a balanced, mild, sweet flavor with onions and currants.

CHAPTER 11

Potatoes, Tubers, and Roots

Roasted Carrot and Cumin Bake

Cumin and carrots are a natural pairing. Add mint, and you've got a very special dish.

INGREDIENTS | SERVES 6

2 pounds carrots, peeled and sliced into 1" pieces
¼ cup olive oil
1 teaspoon cumin
¼ teaspoon salt
¼ cup chopped fresh mint
2 teaspoons lemon juice

1. Preheat the oven to 400°F and spray a 9" × 13" casserole dish lightly with nonstick spray.

2. Toss the carrots together with the olive oil, cumin, and salt and pour in an even layer into the prepared casserole dish.

3. Roast the carrots until they are tender and slightly browned, about 40–45 minutes. Toss with the mint and lemon juice just before serving.

PER SERVING Calories: 143 | Fat: 9.4g | Protein: 1.6g | Sodium: 105mg | Fiber: 4.6g | Carbohydrates: 15g | Sugar: 7.6g

Sweet Potato Puff

This is a Southern specialty that usually involves a lot of sugar, but this recipe adds natural sweetness with orange juice. You can use virtually any nut to top it, but pecans work well with the sweet flavors.

INGREDIENTS | SERVES 8

3 cups cooked cubed sweet potatoes
4 egg whites
¼ cup brown sugar
1 teaspoon vanilla
½ cup orange juice
2 tablespoons flour
1 teaspoon salt
½ cup chopped pecans

1. Preheat the oven to 350°F and spray a 3-quart casserole dish lightly with nonstick spray.

2. Place the sweet potatoes, egg whites, brown sugar, vanilla, orange juice, flour, and salt in the bowl of a food processor. Purée the mixture until smooth and transfer to the prepared casserole dish.

3. Sprinkle the chopped pecans on top of the casserole dish and bake until puffed and brown, about 30 minutes.

PER SERVING Calories: 145 | Fat: 6g | Protein: 4g | Sodium: 328mg | Fiber: 3g | Carbohydrates: 21g | Sugar: 10g

Scalloped Potatoes with Aromatic Vegetables

*Layered casseroles are a great choice to serve at potlucks or with
simple meats like baked chicken or pork chops.*

INGREDIENTS | SERVES 8

2 carrots, peeled and sliced

2 parsnips, peeled and sliced

3 russet potatoes, sliced

¼ cup olive oil

⅛ teaspoon salt

⅛ teaspoon white pepper

1 onion, finely chopped

4 cloves garlic, minced

⅓ cup grated Parmesan cheese

¾ cup dry bread crumbs

1 cup milk

1. Preheat the oven to 375°F and spray a 9" × 13" baking dish lightly with nonstick spray.

2. In a large bowl, combine the carrots, parsnips, and potatoes. Drizzle the vegetables with the olive oil, sprinkle with salt and pepper, and toss to coat. Layer the vegetables in prepared baking dish, sprinkling each layer with onion, garlic, Parmesan cheese, and bread crumbs, finishing with bread crumbs.

3. Pour milk into casserole. Cover tightly with foil. Bake for 45 minutes, then uncover. Bake for 15–25 minutes longer or until vegetables are tender and top is browned.

PER SERVING Calories: 272 | Fat: 9g | Protein: 5.9g | Sodium: 212mg | Fiber: 5.5g | Carbohydrates: 30g | Sugar: 4.3g

Chili-Spiced Hash Browns

*These lightened hash browns are the perfect accompaniment to egg dishes served at brunch.
The chili powder adds smooth, mellow heat. Feel free to add more if you want to dial up the spice.*

INGREDIENTS | SERVES 6

1 (15-ounce) bag hash browns

1 teaspoon chili powder

½ teaspoon garlic powder

¼ teaspoon salt

¼ teaspoon pepper

3 tablespoons olive oil

1 large egg, beaten

1. Preheat the oven to 425°F and spray a rimmed baking sheet lightly with nonstick spray.

2. Blot the hash browns between layers of paper towels and toss them together with the chili powder, garlic powder, salt, pepper, olive oil, and egg.

3. Place the baking sheet on the middle oven rack to preheat for 3 minutes. When hot, carefully remove it from the oven and spread the hash brown mixture evenly into the pan.

4. Bake the hash browns until the top is browned and the edges are crispy, about 45 minutes.

PER SERVING Calories: 227 | Fat: 16g | Protein: 3.2g | Sodium: 132mg | Fiber: 1.4g | Carbohydrates: 20g | Sugar: 1.1g

Traditional Potatoes Au Gratin Casserole

You'll never miss the boxed version after trying these easy potatoes!

INGREDIENTS | SERVES 4

1 onion, chopped

2 tablespoons flour

2 cups 2% milk

½ teaspoon salt

½ teaspoon paprika

½ teaspoon mustard powder

¼ teaspoon pepper

1½ pounds russet potatoes

3 ounces grated Monterey jack cheese

Slicing Potatoes

Although you can certainly cut potatoes by hand, it's far more expedient (and easier) to use a mandolin when trying to slice them evenly and thinly. Inexpensive mandolins are readily found in most kitchen stores. Look for models that are easy to clean with a dial setting that can adjust to make slices of varying sizes.

1. Preheat the oven to 375°F and spray an 8" × 8" baking dish lightly with nonstick spray.

2. Heat the butter over medium heat in a large saucepan. When hot, add the onion and cook, stirring occasionally, until the onion softens, 5 minutes.

3. Whisk in the flour and slowly stream in the milk, whisking constantly to avoid lumps. Whisk in the salt, paprika, mustard powder, and pepper. Cook the sauce over medium heat until it thickens, about 5 minutes. Remove the sauce from the heat.

4. Peel and slice the potatoes ⅛" thick, gently stirring the slices into the sauce mixture. Transfer the contents of the pot to the prepared casserole dish, spreading the potatoes so that they form an even layer and are submerged in the sauce. Sprinkle the casserole with the cheese.

5. Bake the casserole, covered tightly with foil, until the potatoes are tender and cooked through, about 45 minutes. Remove the foil and cook for another 15–20 minutes until the top browns. Allow the casserole to cool for at least 10 minutes before serving, as sauce will thicken as it cools.

PER SERVING Calories: 338 | Fat: 12g | Protein: 14g | Sodium: 529mg | Fiber: 2.4g | Carbohydrates: 41g | Sugar: 7.6g

Vegan Potatoes Au Gratin Casserole

You won't miss the dairy in these vegan potatoes.
Serve them with sautéed vegetables and Vegan TVP-Stuffed Peppers (see Chapter 7).

INGREDIENTS | SERVES 4

1 tablespoon vegan margarine
1 onion, chopped
2 tablespoons flour
2 cups unsweetened soymilk
2 teaspoons onion powder
1 teaspoon garlic powder
2 tablespoons nutritional yeast
1 teaspoon lemon juice
½ teaspoon salt
4 russet potatoes, peeled
¾ teaspoon paprika
½ teaspoon black pepper
¾ cup vegan bread crumbs

1. Preheat the oven to 375°F and spray a 9" × 9" casserole dish lightly with nonstick spray.

2. Melt the margarine over medium heat in a medium saucepan. When hot, add the onion and cook until softened, about 5 minutes. Add the flour, stirring to make a paste. Whisk in the soymilk, onion powder, garlic powder, nutritional yeast, lemon juice, and salt. Whisk the sauce over low heat until it has thickened, about 2–3 minutes.

3. Slice the potatoes thinly into a large bowl, pour the sauce over them, and toss lightly to combine.

4. Transfer the mixture to the prepared casserole dish; sprinkle with paprika and black pepper and top with the bread crumbs.

5. Cover the casserole tightly with foil and bake for 45 minutes. Uncover and bake an additional 10 minutes until the crumbs are browned.

PER SERVING Calories: 264 | Fat: 5g | Protein: 9g | Sodium: 406mg | Fiber: 7g | Carbohydrates: 55g | Sugar: 2.9g

Ham and Artichoke Hearts Scalloped Potatoes

Ham lends a slightly smoky flavor and savory edge to this lightened cheesy casserole.

INGREDIENTS | SERVES 4

2 cups frozen artichoke hearts

1 cup chopped onion

4 small potatoes, thinly sliced

¼ teaspoon salt

⅛ teaspoon black pepper

1 tablespoon lemon juice

1 tablespoon dry white wine

1 cup Mock Cream (see Chapter 14)

½ cup nonfat cottage cheese

1 teaspoon dried parsley

1 teaspoon garlic powder

⅛ cup freshly grated Parmesan cheese

¼ pound (4 ounces) lean ham, cubed

2 ounces Cheddar cheese, grated (to yield ½ cup)

Simple Substitutions

For a less expensive alternative, substitute cabbage, broccoli, or cauliflower (or a mixture of all three) for the artichokes.

1. Preheat the oven to 300°F and spray a deep 3-quart casserole dish lightly with nonstick spray.

2. Thaw the artichoke hearts and pat them dry with a paper towel. Layer the artichokes, onion, and potatoes in the prepared casserole dish and lightly sprinkle the salt and pepper over the top of each layer.

3. In a food processor or blender, combine the lemon juice, wine, Mock Cream, cottage cheese, parsley, garlic powder, and Parmesan cheese and process until smooth. Pour the mixture over the layered vegetables. Top with the ham. Cover the casserole dish tightly with foil and bake until the potatoes are cooked through, 35–40 minutes.

4. Remove the cover, top the casserole with the Cheddar cheese, and bake until the cheese melts, about 10 minutes. Allow the casserole to rest for 10 minutes before cutting.

PER SERVING Calories: 269 | Fat: 7.58g | Protein: 21.5g | Sodium: 762mg | Fiber: 6g | Carbohydrates: 31g | Sugar: 1g

Potato, Cauliflower, and Onion Bake

*The potatoes and onions harmonize with the cauliflower in this recipe,
making for a slightly different twist on a classic bistro side.*

INGREDIENTS | SERVES 8

1 tablespoon olive oil

2 medium sweet onions, diced

2 cloves garlic, minced

3 tablespoons butter

3 tablespoons flour

3 cups 2% milk

½ teaspoon salt

¼ teaspoon pepper

½ teaspoon mustard powder

¼ cup shredded Gruyère cheese

2 pounds russet potatoes

4 cups cauliflower, cut into miniflorets

Cruciferous Vegetables

This family of vegetables takes their name from the shape of their flowers, whose petals form the shape of the cross. Cauliflower, broccoli, and cabbage belong to this family and are noted for their high concentration of vitamin C and soluble fiber. Cruciferous vegetables also contain phytonutrients that may have potential anticancer properties.

1. Preheat the oven to 350°F and spray a 9" × 13" casserole dish lightly with nonstick spray.

2. Heat the olive oil in a medium nonstick skillet over medium-low heat. When hot, add the onions and garlic and cook, stirring occasionally, until tender, 10–15 minutes. Do not let the onions brown.

3. While the vegetables are cooking, heat the butter in a medium saucepan over medium heat. When melted, add the flour and stir to combine. Slowly stream in the milk, whisking constantly to avoid lumps. Whisk in the salt, pepper, and mustard powder. Simmer the sauce, whisking often, until thickened, about 3 minutes. Remove the sauce from the heat and whisk in the Gruyère cheese.

4. Peel and slice the potatoes into thin ⅛" thick rounds and spread them evenly along the bottom of the casserole dish. Layer the onion mixture over the potatoes, then spread the cauliflower over the onions. Pour the sauce mixture over the vegetables, cover tightly with foil, and bake until the potatoes are just tender, 45 minutes.

5. Remove the foil from the casserole and bake an additional 15–20 minutes until the top of the casserole is browned and bubbly and the vegetables are completely tender. Allow the casserole to rest for 10 minutes before slicing.

PER SERVING Calories: 261 | Fat: 9.4g | Protein: 9.3g | Sodium: 285mg | Fiber: 3.8g | Carbohydrates: 37g | Sugar: 11g

Fennel and Potato Bake

The sweet anise flavor of fennel is bright and fresh.
Enjoy this dish alongside a crisp green salad and grilled chicken or fish.

INGREDIENTS | SERVES 6

3 tablespoons butter

1 onion chopped

2 cloves garlic

2 tablespoons flour

2 cups 2% milk

½ teaspoon salt

½ teaspoon mustard powder

½ teaspoon fennel seeds

¼ teaspoon pepper

1½ pounds russet potatoes

2 small fennel bulbs

1. Preheat the oven to 375°F and spray a 9" × 13" baking dish lightly with nonstick spray.

2. Heat the butter over medium heat in a large saucepan. When hot, add the onion and garlic and cook, stirring occasionally, until the vegetables soften, 5 minutes.

3. Whisk in the flour and slowly stream in the milk, whisking constantly to avoid lumps. Whisk in the salt, mustard powder, fennel seeds, and pepper. Cook the sauce over medium heat until it thickens, about 5 minutes. Remove the sauce from the heat.

4. Peel and slice the potatoes ⅛" thick and slice the fennel into ⅛"-thick rounds. Gently stir the vegetables into the sauce mixture to coat. Transfer the contents of the saucepan to the prepared casserole dish, spreading the vegetables so that they form an even layer and are submerged in the sauce.

5. Bake the casserole, covered tightly with foil, until the vegetables are tender and cooked through, about 45 minutes. Remove the foil and cook for another 15–20 minutes until the top browns. Allow the casserole to cool for at least 10 minutes before serving, as sauce will thicken as it cools.

PER SERVING Calories: 228 | Fat: 7.7g | Protein: 7g | Sodium: 347mg | Fiber: 4.1g | Carbohydrates: 33g | Sugar: 5g

Potato, Pepper, and Sweet Basil Casserole

The flavors of Italy and the colors of the Italian flag are both mirrored in this casserole. You may substitute jarred red peppers packed in olive oil for the fresh peppers, but do not use peppers packed in vinegar.

INGREDIENTS | SERVES 4 TO 6

3 tablespoons butter

2 tablespoons flour

1 cup 2% milk

1 cup low-sodium chicken broth

2 tablespoons dry sherry

½ teaspoon salt

⅛ teaspoon pepper

½ cup grated fontina cheese

4 russet potatoes

3 roasted red peppers, peeled and seeded

¼ cup chopped basil

Roasting Peppers

Place the peppers directly over a gas burner set at high heat or under an electric broiler. Using tongs, rotate the peppers so that the skin blisters evenly. When the peppers are charred and blistered, remove them to a bowl and cover tightly with plastic wrap. Allow the peppers to steam for 15 minutes. The skin and seeds should then be removed easily.

1. Preheat the oven to 350°F and spray an 8" × 8" casserole dish lightly with nonstick spray.

2. Heat the butter over medium heat in a large saucepan. When hot, whisk in the flour, then slowly stream in the milk, chicken broth, and sherry, whisking constantly to avoid lumps. Whisk in the salt and pepper and simmer the sauce until it thickens, about 3 minutes. Remove the sauce from the heat and whisk in the fontina cheese.

3. Peel and slice the potatoes into ⅛"-thick rounds and cut the peppers into wide strips. Alternate layers of potato, red pepper, and basil in the prepared casserole dish, allowing a few peppers and pieces of basil to peep out from the top layer.

4. Pour the sauce over the potatoes, cover tightly with foil, and bake until the potatoes are tender, about 45–50 minutes.

5. Remove the foil from the casserole and bake for an additional 15–20 minutes until the top of the casserole is browned and bubbly. Allow the casserole to rest for 10 minutes before slicing.

PER SERVING Calories: 224 | Fat: 10g | Protein: 7.7g | Sodium: 505mg | Fiber: 1.6g | Carbohydrates: 26g | Sugar: 3.5g

Potato Soufflé

This soufflé isn't as light as others; it's more like a potato puff.
Serve it with a fruit salad for a nice lunch.

INGREDIENTS | SERVES 4

2 Yukon Gold potatoes

1 tablespoon olive oil

⅛ teaspoon nutmeg

¼ teaspoon onion salt

⅛ teaspoon cayenne pepper

⅓ cup fat-free half-and-half

¼ cup grated Parmesan cheese

4 egg whites

¼ teaspoon cream of tartar

1 cup chopped grape tomatoes

¼ cup chopped fresh basil

Cooking Potatoes

When you are cooking potatoes, be sure to place them in cold water to cover as they are being peeled or chopped. Potatoes turn brown very quickly when exposed to the air, and this slows the process. Do not overcook potatoes; cook them just until they are tender when pierced with a knife. Drain well and shake in a hot pot to remove excess moisture.

1. Preheat the oven to 450°F and spray a 2-quart casserole or soufflé dish lightly with nonstick spray.

2. Peel and thinly slice the potatoes, adding them to a pot of cold water as you work. Bring the potatoes to a boil over high heat, then reduce the heat and simmer until tender, about 12–15 minutes.

3. Drain the potatoes and return them to the hot pot; shake for 1 minute. Add the olive oil, nutmeg, onion salt, and cayenne pepper; mash until smooth. Beat in the half-and-half and Parmesan cheese.

4. In a large bowl, combine the egg whites with the cream of tartar and beat until stiff peaks form. Stir a dollop of the egg whites into the potato mixture and mix. Fold in the remaining egg whites.

5. Spoon the potato mixture into the casserole. Bake for 20 minutes, then reduce the heat to 375°F and bake for another 12–17 minutes or until soufflé is golden brown and puffed.

6. While the soufflé is baking, combine the tomatoes and basil in a small bowl and mix gently. Serve immediately with tomato mixture on top of the soufflé.

PER SERVING Calories: 208 | Fat: 5.6g | Protein: 11g | Sodium: 344mg | Fiber: 3g | Carbohydrates: 30g | Sugar: 2.3g

Mashed Potato and Spinach Casserole

This elegant casserole puffs into a gorgeous potato soufflé.
Enjoy alongside roasted or grilled meats and your favorite vegetables.

INGREDIENTS | SERVES 4

2 Yukon Gold potatoes

3 tablespoons olive oil

1 small onion, minced

1 (16-ounce) bag baby spinach

⅛ teaspoon nutmeg

¼ teaspoon onion salt

⅛ teaspoon cayenne pepper

⅓ cup fat-free half-and-half

¼ cup grated Parmesan cheese

4 egg whites

¼ teaspoon cream of tartar

1. Preheat the oven to 450°F and spray a 2-quart casserole or soufflé dish lightly with nonstick spray.

2. Peel and thinly slice the potatoes, adding them to a pot of cold water as you work. Bring the potatoes to a boil over high heat, then reduce the heat and simmer until tender, about 12–15 minutes.

3. While the potatoes are cooking, heat 1 tablespoon of the olive oil in a large skillet over medium heat. When hot, add the onion and cook, stirring occasionally, until the onion is very tender, 10 minutes. Turn up the heat to high and add the spinach. Cook the spinach, tossing with tongs, until wilted. Remove the vegetables from the heat and allow to cool slightly, then roughly chop, squeezing out extra moisture from the spinach.

4. Drain the potatoes and return them to the hot pot; shake for 1 minute. Add the remaining 2 tablespoons olive oil, nutmeg, onion salt, and cayenne pepper; mash until smooth. Beat in the half-and-half and Parmesan cheese, then fold in the spinach mixture.

5. In a large bowl, combine the egg whites with the cream of tartar and beat until stiff peaks form. Stir a dollop of the egg whites into the potato mixture and mix. Fold in the remaining egg whites.

6. Spoon the potato mixture into the casserole. Bake for 20 minutes, then reduce the heat to 375°F and bake for another 12–17 minutes or until soufflé is golden brown and puffed.

PER SERVING Calories: 311 | Fat: 12g | Protein: 15g | Sodium: 349mg | Fiber: 6.9g | Carbohydrates: 38g | Sugar: 5.2g

Potato and Mushroom Bake

Dried porcini mushrooms can be found in the specialty foods aisle in your supermarket or in many natural foods stores. If you cannot find them, simply increase the mushrooms called for in the recipe by 8 ounces.

INGREDIENTS | SERVES 4

1 ounce dried porcini mushrooms

1 cup boiling water

2 tablespoons olive oil

1 pound sliced cremini mushrooms

3 tablespoons butter

1 onion, chopped

2 tablespoons flour

1 cup 2% milk

3 tablespoons dry sherry or vermouth

½ teaspoon salt

¼ teaspoon pepper

1½ pounds russet potatoes

1 tablespoon chopped fresh thyme

Porcini Mushrooms

Fresh porcini mushrooms have a natural meaty and woodsy flavor and are a favorite ingredient used widely in Italian cuisine. Fresh porcini mushrooms are costly and difficult to find, but dried porcinis still offer the same flavor at a fraction of the cost. To use, place the dried porcinis in a bowl, cover with boiling water, and allow them to rehydrate for 20 minutes. Simply drain the porcinis (reserving the flavorful mushroom liquid for another use), chop, and use as you would fresh mushrooms in cooked preparations.

1. Preheat the oven to 375°F and spray an 8" × 8" baking dish lightly with nonstick spray. Place the porcini in a heat-safe bowl and pour the boiling water over the top. After 20 minutes, remove the mushrooms with a slotted spoon and roughly chop them. Reserve the liquid and strain through a fine-meshed strainer or piece of cheesecloth.

2. Heat the olive oil in a large skillet over medium-high heat. When hot, add the cremini mushrooms and cook without stirring until they begin to lose some of their moisture and start to brown, about 5 minutes. Stir the cremini mushrooms and cook until tender and browned, 3–5 minutes more.

3. While the mushrooms are cooking, heat the butter over medium heat in a large saucepan. When hot, add the onion and cook, stirring occasionally, until the onion softens, 5 minutes.

4. Whisk in the flour and slowly stream in the milk, whisking constantly to avoid lumps. Whisk in the reserved porcini liquid, sherry, salt, and pepper. Cook the sauce over medium heat, whisking often, until it thickens, about 5 minutes. Remove the sauce from the heat.

5. Peel and slice the potatoes ⅛" thick, gently stirring the slices into the sauce mixture with the thyme; add the creminis and porcinis. Transfer the contents of the pot to the prepared casserole dish, spreading the vegetables so that they form an even layer and are submerged in the sauce.

6. Bake the casserole, covered tightly with foil, until the potatoes are tender and cooked through, about 45 minutes. Remove the foil and cook for another 15–20 minutes until the top browns. Allow the casserole to cool for at least 10 minutes before serving.

PER SERVING Calories: 356 | Fat: 17g | Protein: 9.6g | Sodium: 431mg | Fiber: 3.1g | Carbohydrates: 42g | Sugar: 6.4g

Two-Potato Gratin

Serve this creamy and crunchy dish alongside some grilled hamburgers or with the roasted Thanksgiving turkey.

INGREDIENTS | SERVES 6

2 slices whole-wheat bread

4 tablespoons butter, divided

2 tablespoons grated Parmesan cheese

1 onion, chopped

2 tablespoons all-purpose flour

1 teaspoon salt

⅛ teaspoon white pepper

1¼ cups milk

2 tablespoons mustard

½ teaspoon dried dill weed

1 sweet potato

2 russet potatoes

1. Preheat the oven to 350°F and spray a 2-quart baking dish lightly with nonstick spray. Pulse the bread in a food processor until the crumbs are the size of small peas and remove to a small bowl. In a small microwave-safe dish, melt 2 tablespoons butter. Drizzle over bread crumbs and add Parmesan cheese; toss and set aside.

2. In a medium saucepan, combine 2 tablespoons butter and the onion. Cook, stirring often, until the onion is tender, about 5 minutes. Sprinkle with the flour, salt, and pepper; cook until bubbly, about 3 minutes. Stream in the milk, whisking constantly, and cook until thickened, about 5 minutes. Whisk in mustard and dill weed.

3. Peel the potatoes and grate them directly into the baking dish. Top with sauce, stirring gently to coat. Sprinkle the top of the casserole with the bread crumb mixture.

4. Bake the casserole for 40–50 minutes or until potatoes are tender and the top is golden brown and crusty.

PER SERVING Calories: 195 | Fat: 9.3g | Protein: 5.3g | Sodium: 589mg | Fiber: 2g | Carbohydrates: 24g | Sugar: 1.2g

Curried Sweet Potato Gratin

The inspiration for this dish is Thai massaman curry, which features sweet potatoes, coconut, and peanuts. Serve with baked fish and your favorite green vegetable.

INGREDIENTS | SERVES 8

1 tablespoon canola oil

2 teaspoons sweet curry powder

1 medium onion, minced

3 cloves garlic, minced

1 tablespoon minced fresh ginger

½ teaspoon salt

1 (14-ounce) can light coconut milk

2 pounds sweet potatoes

⅓ cup chopped peanuts

1. Preheat the oven to 375°F and spray a 9" × 13" casserole dish lightly with nonstick spray.

2. Heat the canola oil over medium-high heat in a medium saucepan. When hot, add the curry powder and onion. Cook until the onion becomes tender, about 5 minutes. Add the garlic, ginger, and salt; cook until fragrant, 1 minute. Stir in the coconut milk, bring to a bare simmer, and remove from the heat.

3. Peel the sweet potatoes and cut thinly into ⅛" circles. Layer the potatoes in the prepared casserole dish, then pour the coconut curry sauce over the top. Sprinkle on the peanuts.

4. Bake the casserole, uncovered, until the liquid is absorbed and the potatoes are tender, about 45 minutes.

PER SERVING Calories: 261 | Fat: 16g | Protein: 4.7g | Sodium: 70mg | Fiber: 4g | Carbohydrates: 27g | Sugar: 4.8g

Tropical Sweet Potatoes

*The tropical flavors of ginger, lime, and coconut enhance
the flavor of the sweet potatoes without masking them in syrupy sweetness.*

INGREDIENTS | SERVES 8

3 cups cooked cubed sweet potatoes

4 egg whites

¼ cup brown sugar

1 tablespoon grated lime zest

1 tablespoon grated fresh ginger

½ cup light coconut milk

2 tablespoons flour

1 teaspoon salt

Ginger

Select young, unblemished, and wrinkle-free specimens of ginger that feel heavy for their size. Older ginger is drier and stringy. Store fresh ginger in the vegetable crisper in your refrigerator for up to a week.

1. Preheat the oven to 350°F and spray a 3-quart casserole dish lightly with nonstick spray.

2. Place the sweet potatoes, egg whites, brown sugar, lime zest, ginger, coconut milk, flour, and salt in the bowl of a food processor. Purée the mixture until smooth and transfer to the prepared casserole dish.

3. Bake the casserole until it puffs and browns, about 30 minutes.

PER SERVING Calories: 109 | Fat: 3.1g | Protein: 3.7g | Sodium: 355mg | Fiber: 1.5g | Carbohydrates: 17g | Sugar: 8.5g

Vegan Gingered and Pralined Sweet Potatoes

Keep this recipe handy during the holiday season.
Who needs marshmallows anyway?

INGREDIENTS | SERVES 4

4 baked sweet potatoes

⅓ cup flour

¼ cup soymilk

¼ cup orange juice

½ teaspoon salt

½ cup chopped pecans

2 tablespoons vegan margarine

⅓ cup maple syrup

⅓ cup crystallized (candied) ginger

Why Aren't Marshmallows Vegan?

They aren't even technically vegetarian! Marshmallows contain gelatin, which is extracted from boiled animal bones or hides. Online specialty stores and some natural foods stores may stock vegan marshmallows, but candied ginger adds an elegant twist to this holiday favorite!

1. Preheat the oven to 350°F and spray a 2½-quart casserole dish lightly with nonstick spray.

2. Mash together the sweet potatoes, flour, soymilk, orange juice, and salt until smooth and creamy. Transfer to the prepared casserole dish.

3. In a small bowl, combine the pecans, margarine, maple syrup, and ginger and spread over the top of the sweet potatoes.

4. Bake the casserole until heated through and bubbly around the edges, about 30 minutes.

PER SERVING Calories: 436 | Fat: 17g | Protein: 5g | Sodium: 443mg | Fiber: 6g | Carbohydrates: 57g | Sugar: 23g

Sweet Potatoes Roasted with Maple and Walnuts

*The maple syrup helps the sweet potato chunks to caramelize,
and the walnuts lend this recipe a pleasing crunch.*

INGREDIENTS | SERVES 4

3 large sweet potatoes, peeled and cubed into ½" chunks

½ cup pure maple syrup

2 tablespoons butter, melted

2 teaspoons lemon juice

½ teaspoon salt

½ cup walnut pieces, toasted

Maple Syrup

When choosing maple syrup for cooking, select grade B syrup. Although it is slightly thinner than grade A syrup, grade B has deeper maple flavor and is considerably less expensive.

1. Preheat the oven to 400°F and spray a 9" × 13" casserole dish lightly with nonstick spray.

2. Place the sweet potatoes in the prepared casserole dish and drizzle with maple syrup, butter, lemon juice, and salt; toss to coat the potatoes with the other ingredients.

3. Cover the casserole dish tightly with foil and roast the sweet potatoes for 15 minutes.

4. Uncover the sweet potatoes and continue to roast, stirring a few times during cooking, until the potatoes are tender, about 45 minutes more. Sprinkle the walnuts over the top just before serving.

PER SERVING Calories: 308 | Fat: 15g | Protein: 3.6g | Sodium: 389mg | Fiber: 2.9g | Carbohydrates: 42g | Sugar: 27g

Celery Root and Celery Gratin

This potato alternative is fresh and bright.
Celery and celery root are layered in a creamlike sauce and baked until bubbly and brown.

INGREDIENTS | SERVES 6

1 tablespoon olive oil

1 large onion, chopped

3 tablespoons butter

2 tablespoons flour

2 cups 2% milk

2 tablespoons prepared horseradish

½ teaspoon salt

1 head celery, cleaned and sliced into ⅛"-thick slices

1 pound celery root, peeled, halved, and sliced into ⅛"-thick slices

Celery Root

This nubby brown root is also known as celeriac and is a member of the celery family. It tastes like a cross between celery and parsley, and may be eaten raw or cooked. Choose relatively small roots with a minimum of knobs and craters as it will be easier to peel. Prepare the celery root by slicing off the brown peel and, if the root is especially large, slicing it in half.

1. Preheat the oven to 350°F and spray a 9" × 13" casserole dish lightly with nonstick spray.

2. Heat the oil over medium-high heat in a skillet. When hot, add the onion and cook, stirring occasionally, until it becomes translucent and tender, about 7 minutes.

3. While the onion is cooking, heat the butter in a medium saucepan. When melted, whisk in the flour, then slowly stream in the milk, whisking constantly to avoid lumps. Whisk in the horseradish and salt and bring the sauce to a simmer. Cook until the sauce thickens slightly, about 5 minutes.

4. Layer the celery root and celery together in the prepared casserole dish and sprinkle with the onion. Pour the sauce over the top and cover tightly with foil.

5. Bake the casserole for 20 minutes, then remove the foil and continue to bake until the casserole browns and the vegetables become tender, about 25–30 minutes more.

PER SERVING Calories: 152 | Fat: 9.9g | Protein: 4.8g | Sodium: 411mg | Fiber: 2.6g | Carbohydrates: 11g | Sugar: 7.1g

Roasted Root Vegetables with Thyme and Parmesan

These vegetables are a favorite served with roasts and braised dishes.
They add a little life to even the dullest of winter days.

INGREDIENTS | SERVES 6

1 pound carrots, peeled and chopped into 1" pieces

½ pound parsnips, peeled and chopped into 1" pieces

½ pound turnips, peeled and chopped into 1" pieces

½ pound celery root, peeled and chopped into 1" pieces

½ pound Yukon Gold potatoes, washed and cut into 1" pieces

¼ cup olive oil

½ teaspoon salt

¼ teaspoon pepper

2 tablespoons chopped fresh thyme

⅛ cup grated Parmesan cheese

1. Preheat the oven to 400°F and spray two 9" × 13" casserole dishes lightly with nonstick spray.

2. Toss the carrots, parsnips, turnips, celery root, and potatoes together with the olive oil, salt, and pepper in a large bowl. Divide the mixture between the two casserole dishes.

3. Roast the vegetables on the middle and upper middle racks for 30 minutes, stirring occasionally. Reverse the position of the casserole dishes.

4. Continue to roast, stirring occasionally, until the vegetables are tender and lightly browned in spots, 40–45 minutes longer. Sprinkle the thyme and Parmesan over the vegetables and serve.

PER SERVING Calories: 205 | Fat: 10g | Protein: 3.6g | Sodium: 342mg | Fiber: 6.6g | Carbohydrates: 27g | Sugar: 8g

Layered Carrot and Parsnip Casserole

Make quick work of shredding the vegetables by using your food processor.
Otherwise, grate them through the large holes of a box grater.

INGREDIENTS | SERVES 8

1 tablespoon olive oil

1 large onion, diced

2 pounds carrots, peeled and shredded

2 pounds parsnips, peeled and shredded

2 tablespoons butter

2 tablespoons flour

1½ cups 2% milk

1 teaspoon dried dill

¼ teaspoon salt

½ cup shredded light Cheddar cheese

½ cup coarse bread crumbs

1. Preheat the oven to 350°F and spray a 9" × 9" casserole dish lightly with nonstick spray.

2. Heat the olive oil over medium-high heat in a skillet. When hot, add the onion and cook, stirring frequently, until it becomes tender, about 7 minutes.

3. Layer the carrots, parsnips, and onions together in the prepared casserole dish.

4. Heat the butter in a medium saucepan over medium heat. When melted, whisk in the flour and slowly stream in the milk, whisking constantly to avoid lumps. Whisk in the dill and salt and bring the sauce to a simmer. Cook, whisking often, until the sauce thickens, about 5 minutes. Off the heat, whisk in the Cheddar cheese.

5. Pour the cheese sauce over the vegetables, then layer the crumbs on top. Spray the crumb topping lightly with non-stick spray and bake the casserole until the vegetables are tender and the topping is brown, 30–35 minutes.

PER SERVING Calories: 263 | Fat: 9.2g | Protein: 7g | Sodium: 319mg | Fiber: 9.4g | Carbohydrates: 39g | Sugar: 14g

Baked Pastas

Country Lasagna

Using macaroni instead of lasagna noodles helps reduce the cost and also makes this hearty dish easier to prepare.

INGREDIENTS | SERVES 10

¼ pound lean ground pork sausage

¼ pound 93% lean ground beef

1 onion, chopped

3 cloves garlic, minced

1 green bell pepper, chopped

2 (4-ounce) cans mushroom pieces, undrained

1 (14-ounce) can diced tomatoes, undrained

1 (6-ounce) can tomato paste

1 tablespoon Worcestershire sauce

1 teaspoon dried Italian seasoning

½ teaspoon salt

½ cup water

⅛ teaspoon cayenne pepper

1 pound macaroni

2 tablespoons butter

½ cup shredded reduced-fat Cheddar cheese

1 cup shredded mozzarella cheese

⅓ cup grated Parmesan cheese

1. Bring a large pot of salted water to a boil. Meanwhile, in a large saucepan, combine the sausage, beef, onion, and garlic over medium heat. Cook, breaking up the meat with the back of a spoon, until the meat is cooked, 10–12 minutes.

2. Drain the fat from the meat and add the bell pepper to the saucepan; cook until just softened, stirring occasionally, 3 minutes. Stir in the mushrooms, tomatoes, tomato paste, Worcestershire sauce, Italian seasoning, salt, water, and cayenne pepper; bring the sauce to a simmer and cook for 10 minutes.

3. Cook the macaroni until al dente according to package directions. Drain and return to the pot; add the butter and let melt.

4. Preheat the oven to 350°F and spray a 9" × 13" glass baking dish with nonstick cooking spray. Put ½ cup of the meat sauce in the bottom, then top with ⅓ of the macaroni. Dot with ⅓ of the Cheddar cheese. Repeat the layers, ending with the meat sauce. Sprinkle with mozzarella and Parmesan cheese.

5. Bake until casserole is bubbling and cheese is melted and beginning to brown, 35–45 minutes.

PER SERVING Calories: 365 | Fat: 13g | Protein: 19g | Sodium: 500mg | Fiber: 3.7g | Carbohydrates: 43g | Sugar: 3.4g

Black Bean Lasagna

No one will miss the meat in this rich and indulgent casserole.
It feeds a crowd easily.

INGREDIENTS | SERVES 12

2 tablespoons olive oil

1 onion, chopped

4 cloves garlic, minced

2 jalapeño peppers, minced

1 (14.5-ounce) can refried beans

2 (14.5-ounce) cans black beans, drained, divided

1 tablespoon chili powder

½ teaspoon cumin

¼ teaspoon cayenne pepper

1 cup sour cream

1 cup part-skim ricotta cheese

1 (4-ounce) can diced green chilies, drained

2 cups vegetable broth

3 cups salsa

12 dry lasagna noodles

2 cups shredded part-skim mozzarella cheese

½ cup grated Cotija cheese

Refried Beans

Refried beans are cooked beans that have been mashed and cooked with lard or vegetable oil and seasoned. Many grocery stores sell lower-fat and lower-sodium versions. Look for them in the international foods aisle of your grocery store.

1. Spray a 9" × 13" casserole dish lightly with nonstick cooking spray. In a large skillet, heat the olive oil over medium heat. Add the onion, garlic, and jalapeños; cook until tender, about 6 minutes. Add the refried beans, 1 can of black beans, chili powder, cumin, and cayenne pepper; simmer for 3 minutes.

2. Meanwhile, in a medium bowl, combine the sour cream, ricotta cheese, green chilies, and the remaining can of black beans; mix gently.

3. Combine the broth and salsa in another bowl and mix. Place ½ cup broth mixture in the bottom of the prepared baking dish. Top with 4 lasagna noodles, one-third of the refried bean mixture, one-third of the sour cream mixture, and one-third of the mozzarella cheese. Repeat the layers. Pour the remaining salsa mixture over the top of the lasagna.

4. Cover the casserole and refrigerate for 12–24 hours. When ready to eat, preheat the oven to 350°F. Bake for 1½ hours, then uncover and sprinkle with the Cotija cheese. Bake for 10–15 minutes longer until the casserole is bubbly and pasta is tender. Let stand for 15 minutes, then serve.

PER SERVING Calories: 482 | Fat: 10g | Protein: 24g | Sodium: 507mg | Fiber: 14g | Carbohydrates: 76g | Sugar: 5.4g

Vegan Basic Tofu Lasagna

Seasoned tofu takes the place of ricotta cheese and really does look and taste like the real thing. Fresh parsley adds flavor, and with store-bought sauce, it's quick to get in the oven.

INGREDIENTS | SERVES 6

1 block firm tofu

1 (12-ounce) block silken tofu

¼ cup nutritional yeast

1 tablespoon lemon juice

1 tablespoon soy sauce

1 teaspoon garlic powder

2 teaspoons basil

3 tablespoons chopped fresh parsley

1 teaspoon salt

4 cups spaghetti sauce

1 (16-ounce) package lasagna noodles, cooked

1. Preheat the oven to 350°F.

2. In a large bowl, mash together the firm tofu, silken tofu, nutritional yeast, lemon juice, soy sauce, garlic powder, basil, parsley, and salt until combined and crumbly like ricotta cheese.

3. To assemble the lasagna, spread about ⅔ cup spaghetti sauce on the bottom of a lasagna pan, then add a layer of noodles.

4. Spread about half the tofu mixture on top of the noodles, followed by another layer of sauce. Place a second layer of noodles on top, followed by the remaining tofu and more sauce. Finish it off with a third layer of noodles and the rest of the sauce.

5. Cover and bake until the lasagna is bubbly and the pasta tender, 25–30 minutes.

PER SERVING Calories: 510 | Fat: 10g | Protein: 21g | Sodium: 1,016mg | Fiber: 9g | Carbohydrates: 88g | Sugar: 21g

Vegan White Lasagna with Spinach

This lasagna will make you dream of Italian opera houses or old Tuscany.
To bring a bit of Italy into your kitchen, enjoy this chic cashew-butter lasagna while listening to Pavarotti.

INGREDIENTS | SERVES 8

2 tablespoons olive oil

½ onion, diced

4 cloves garlic, minced

1 (10-ounce) box frozen spinach, thawed and pressed to remove moisture

½ teaspoon salt

1 block firm tofu, crumbled

¾ cup jarred cashew nut butter

2 cups soymilk

1 tablespoon miso

2 tablespoons soy sauce

2 tablespoons lemon juice

3 tablespoons nutritional yeast

2 teaspoons onion powder

1 (12-ounce) package lasagna noodles

Like the Mona Lisa

Although you might not be the next Michelangelo, lasagna is a bit of an art form. Many variants affect the outcome: moisture, temperature, assembly, the thickness of the noodles. If you're worried about presenting a crumbly lasagna, prepare it in advance and allow to cool completely. Then reheat just before slicing and serving.

1. Heat the olive oil over medium-high heat in a large skillet. When hot, add the onion and garlic and cook, stirring often, until just tender, about 7 minutes. Add the spinach and salt, stirring to combine well and cooking just until spinach is heated through. Add the crumbled tofu and mix well; then cool completely.

2. In a small saucepan over low heat, combine the cashew butter, soymilk, miso, soy sauce, lemon juice, nutritional yeast, and onion powder until smooth and creamy.

3. Prepare lasagna noodles according to the package instructions. Preheat the oven to 350°F and spray a 9" × 13" casserole dish lightly with nonstick spray.

4. Place a thin layer of cashew sauce and then a layer of noodles in the prepared casserole dish. Next add spinach and more sauce, then a layer of noodles, continuing until all ingredients are used up. The top layer should be spinach and then sauce.

5. Bake until bubbly and lightly browned, about 40 minutes. Allow to cool for at least 10 minutes before serving.

PER SERVING Calories: 490 | Fat: 25g | Protein: 24g | Sodium: 675mg | Fiber: 5.1g | Carbohydrates: 50g | Sugar: 2.3g

Updated Seafood Lasagna

Make this elegant dish ahead of time and refrigerate it.
Then when you're ready to entertain, just pop it in the oven.

INGREDIENTS | SERVES 12

2 tablespoons olive oil

1 tablespoon butter

1 onion, chopped

3 cloves garlic, minced

⅓ cup flour

2 cups 1% milk

1 (8-ounce) package low-fat cream cheese, cubed

¾ cup shredded Havarti cheese

¾ cup shredded part-skim mozzarella cheese

¼ teaspoon nutmeg

½ teaspoon salt

¼ teaspoon white pepper

1 (10-ounce) package frozen cut-leaf spinach, thawed and drained

1 pound medium cooked shrimp, thawed

1 (8-ounce) package imitation crabmeat, thawed

2 cups frozen baby peas, thawed

2 tablespoons lemon juice

9 whole-wheat lasagna noodles

⅓ cup grated Parmesan cheese

1. Preheat the oven to 350°F and spray a 9" × 13" casserole dish lightly with nonstick spray. Bring a large pot of water to a boil over high heat.

2. In a large skillet, heat the olive oil and butter over medium heat. Add the onion and garlic; cook until tender, about 6–7 minutes. Add the flour; cook and stir until bubbly.

3. Stream in the milk, whisking constantly to avoid lumps. Whisk in the cream cheese, Havarti cheese, and mozzarella cheese; cook until melted and smooth. Remove the sauce from the heat and add the nutmeg, salt, and pepper.

4. In a large bowl, combine spinach, shrimp, crabmeat, peas, and lemon juice; mix gently. Cook the noodles in boiling water until almost al dente; drain well.

5. Spoon a thin layer of the cheese sauce in bottom of the prepared casserole dish. Top with three noodles, some of the seafood mixture, and more cheese sauce. Repeat the layers, ending with cheese sauce. Sprinkle with Parmesan cheese.

6. Bake for 50–60 minutes or until the casserole is bubbling and the cheese on top begins to brown. If you refrigerated the casserole, bake an additional 15–20 minutes until bubbly. Let stand for 10 minutes, then cut into squares to serve.

PER SERVING Calories: 305 | Fat: 13g | Protein: 21g | Sodium: 530mg | Fiber: 2.5g | Carbohydrates: 26g | Sugar: 2.1g

Vegan Baked Macaroni and "Cheese"

Vegan chefs all take pride in seeing who can create the best dairy-free macaroni and cheese ever. Join in the friendly rivalry with this recipe. Don't tell anyone that the silken tofu is the secret ingredient for super creaminess.

INGREDIENTS | SERVES 6

1 (12-ounce) package macaroni

1 block silken tofu

1 cup soymilk

2 tablespoons tahini

2 tablespoons lemon juice

1 tablespoon miso

1 teaspoon garlic powder

1 teaspoon onion powder

¼ cup nutritional yeast

2 tablespoons vegan margarine

1 cup bread crumbs

⅓ teaspoon nutmeg (optional)

½ teaspoon salt

½ teaspoon pepper

Miso

This Japanese seasoning is made by fermenting barley, rice, and soybeans with salt and kojikin (a type of fungus). The resulting paste is used to add umami (a savory meat-like quality) flavor to soups and sauces. Purchase miso in the refrigerated section of your supermarket.

1. Preheat the oven to 350°F and spray a 9" × 13" casserole dish lightly with nonstick spray. Cook the macaroni according to the package instructions. Drain well and place in the prepared casserole dish.

2. In a blender or food processor, purée together the tofu, soymilk, tahini, lemon juice, miso, garlic and onion powders, and nutritional yeast until smooth and creamy, scraping the sides to blend well.

3. Combine the tofu mixture with the macaroni in the casserole dish.

4. In a small skillet, melt the vegan margarine and add bread crumbs, stirring to coat. Spread bread crumbs on top of macaroni and sprinkle with the nutmeg, salt, and pepper.

5. Bake until the topping is browned and crisp, about 20–25 minutes.

PER SERVING Calories: 409 | Fat: 16g | Protein: 16g | Sodium: 486mg | Fiber: 4g | Carbohydrates: 53g | Sugar: 2.5g

Squash Baked Macaroni and Cheese

Butternut squash adds a nice, sweet flavor that harmonizes with the creamy cheese and savory thyme in the casserole.

INGREDIENTS | SERVES 8

1 (12-ounce) package macaroni

1 small butternut squash, peeled and seeds removed

3 tablespoons butter

1 small shallot, minced

2 teaspoons chopped thyme

¼ cup flour

2½ cups 1% milk

¼ cup Parmesan cheese

½ cup fontina cheese

1 cup reduced-fat Cheddar cheese

Butternut Squash

Butternut squash not only tastes good but is also a nutrition powerhouse. It's a good source of folate, calcium, and magnesium, and a very good source of vitamins A and C, potassium, and manganese.

1. Preheat the oven to 350°F and spray a 9" × 13" casserole dish lightly with nonstick spray. Cook the macaroni according to the package instructions until just al dente. Drain well and place in the prepared casserole dish.

2. While the macaroni is cooking, chop the squash into ¼" pieces. Heat the butter in a large lidded saucepan over medium-low heat. When melted, add the squash, shallot, and thyme and cook until the squash is tender but not falling apart, 12–15 minutes. Add the flour and stir to coat the vegetables. Slowly stream in the milk, stirring constantly to avoid lumps. Bring to a gentle simmer and cook until the sauce thickens, 2 minutes. Stir in the Parmesan, fontina, and Cheddar cheeses; heat just until the cheese begins to melt.

3. Pour the sauce over the macaroni, stir to combine and cover the casserole tightly with foil.

4. Bake until the casserole bubbles and the macaroni and squash are tender, about 30 minutes. Uncover and bake until the top is just golden, 5 minutes. Allow to stand for 5 minutes before serving.

PER SERVING Calories: 354 | Fat: 11g | Protein: 17g | Sodium: 308mg | Fiber: 2.9g | Carbohydrates: 48g | Sugar: 2.4g

Vegan Cheesy Macaroni and "Hamburger" Casserole

Reminiscent of the boxed version, this is guilt-free vegan comfort food at its finest.

INGREDIENTS | SERVES 6

1 (12-ounce) bag macaroni noodles

1 tablespoon olive oil

4 veggie burgers, thawed and crumbled, or 1 (12-ounce) package vegan beef crumbles

1 tomato, diced

1 teaspoon chili powder

2 tablespoons vegan margarine

2 tablespoons flour

1 cup soymilk

1 teaspoon garlic powder

1 teaspoon onion powder

¼ cup nutritional yeast

¼ teaspoon salt

¼ teaspoon pepper

1. Preheat the oven to 350°F and spray a 9" × 13" casserole dish lightly with nonstick spray. Cook the macaroni according to the package instructions until just al dente. Drain well and place in the prepared casserole dish.

2. Heat the oil in a large skillet and cook the veggie burgers until they are lightly browned. Add the tomatoes and chili powder; stir into the macaroni.

3. In a separate small skillet, melt the margarine, then stir in the flour. Whisk in the soymilk, stirring constantly to avoid lumps; cook until thickened, about 3 minutes. Stir in the garlic and onion powders, nutritional yeast, salt, and pepper.

4. Pour the sauce over the macaroni and stir to combine. Cover tightly with foil and bake until bubbly and heated through, about 20 minutes.

PER SERVING Calories: 395 | Fat: 12g | Protein: 21g | Sodium: 259mg | Fiber: 5g | Carbohydrates: 46g | Sugar: 2.2g

Vegan Italian Veggie and Pasta Casserole

Veggies and pasta are baked into an Italian-spiced casserole with a crumbly topping.
Add in a handful of TVP crumbles or some kidney beans if you want a protein boost.

INGREDIENTS | SERVES 8

1 (16-ounce) package pasta (use a medium pasta like bow ties, corkscrews, or small shells)

2 tablespoons olive oil

1 onion, chopped

3 zucchini, sliced

1 red bell pepper, chopped

4 cloves garlic, minced

1 (28-ounce) can diced tomatoes

¾ cup corn kernels

1 teaspoon parsley

1 teaspoon basil

½ teaspoon oregano

½ teaspoon crushed red pepper flakes

¼ teaspoon black pepper

1 cup bread crumbs

½ cup grated vegan cheese

1. Preheat the oven to 425°F and spray a 9" × 13" casserole dish lightly with nonstick spray. Cook the macaroni according to the package instructions until just al dente. Drain well and place in the prepared casserole dish.

2. Heat the oil in a large skillet over medium-high heat. When hot, add the onion, zucchini, bell pepper, and garlic. Cook the vegetables just until soft, about 3–4 minutes. Add the tomatoes, corn, parsley, basil, oregano, and crushed red pepper. Simmer the sauce for 8–10 minutes and season with black pepper.

3. Toss the pasta with zucchini and tomato mixture. Sprinkle with the bread crumbs and vegan cheese.

4. Bake the casserole, uncovered, until heated through and browned on top, 10–12 minutes.

PER SERVING Calories: 362 | Fat: 8.2g | Protein: 12g | Sodium: 285mg | Fiber: 5.7g | Carbohydrates: 62g | Sugar: 2.2g

What Is Vegan Cheese?

These days there are many brands to choose from, and the primary ingredient in each differs from brand to brand. The overwhelming majority of vegan cheeses have soy as their base, though they can also be made from rice and nuts. When choosing vegan cheese to cook with, look for varieties that can be melted.

Seafood-Stuffed Shells

Now this is one elegant dish! You will be proud to serve it to guests, even your boss.

INGREDIENTS | SERVES 6

1 tablespoon butter

1 onion, finely chopped

1 green bell pepper, chopped

1 (8-ounce) package Neufchâtel cream cheese

½ cup skim milk

½ teaspoon salt

⅛ teaspoon pepper

½ teaspoon dried thyme leaves

1 (6-ounce) can crabmeat

4 ounces frozen, cooked small shrimp, thawed

⅓ cup grated Parmesan cheese

1 cup prepared salsa

1 (12-ounce) package jumbo macaroni shells

1 cup shredded Swiss cheese

About Seafood

You can substitute most seafood for other types in most recipes. Crab is a good substitute for shrimp, which is a good substitute for clams or mussels. Seafood should always smell sweet or slightly briny, never fishy. If you buy it fresh, use it within 1–2 days or freeze it immediately in freezer-proof bags or wraps.

1. Preheat the oven to 400°F and spray a 9" × 13" casserole dish with nonstick spray. Bring a large pot of salted water to a boil.

2. In a medium saucepan, melt the butter over medium heat. Add the onion and bell pepper. Cook, stirring occasionally, until crisp-tender, about 4 minutes. Cut the cream cheese into cubes and add to the saucepan with the milk, salt, pepper, and thyme. Bring to a simmer and cook, stirring, until sauce blends. Reserve ½ cup sauce.

3. Drain the crab and pick over the meat. Discard any shell or cartilage. Add the crab to the mixture in the saucepan along with the shrimp and Parmesan cheese. Stir in half of the salsa and set aside.

4. Cook the shells in water until almost al dente according to the package directions. Drain, rinse shells in cold water, and drain again. Stuff shells with the seafood mixture.

5. Combine the remaining salsa with the reserved sauce and place in the prepared casserole dish. Add the shells, seam side up, and sprinkle with Swiss cheese. Bake until the casserole is hot and the cheese melts, 20–25 minutes.

PER SERVING Calories: 482 | Fat: 18g | Protein: 28g | Sodium: 948mg | Fiber: 2.3g | Carbohydrates: 51g | Sugar: 2g

Lentil-Stuffed Shells

The lentils are a nice variation from either cheese- or meat-stuffed shells.
Serve them with an arugula salad dressed with lemon vinaigrette.

INGREDIENTS | SERVES 6

1 pound jumbo shells

2 tablespoons extra-virgin olive oil

2 garlic cloves, minced

2 shallots, minced

1 celery stalk, minced

1 carrot, minced

1 cup lentils

3 cups vegetable broth

¼ teaspoon salt

½ cup Parmesan cheese

3 tablespoons chopped fresh basil

1 recipe Basic Tomato Sauce (see Chapter 14)

Preparing Pasta

If cooking pasta that will later be stuffed, rinse, drain it well, and spread it out on a rimmed baking sheet. This will keep the pasta from sticking together. If holding the pasta for more than a few minutes before stuffing, place a damp towel over the pasta so that it does not dry out.

1. Cook the shells according to the package directions, then spread them out on a clean rimmed baking sheet to cool.

2. Heat the olive oil in a medium saucepan over medium heat. When hot, add the garlic, shallots, celery, and carrot. Cook the vegetables until they are just tender, about 7 minutes. Add the lentils, vegetable broth, and salt; simmer until the lentils are tender, 20–30 minutes. (If the lentils begin to dry out before they are cooked, add more water.) Drain the lentils and remove to a bowl.

3. Stir ¼ cup Parmesan cheese and the basil into the lentils and mash them gently with the back of a spoon until about half are mashed. Stir to combine with the whole lentils.

4. Preheat the oven to 350°F and spray a 9" × 13" casserole dish lightly with nonstick spray.

5. Spread 1½ cups of the sauce on the bottom of the prepared casserole dish. Divide the filling among the cooked shells and place seam side up in the baking dish. When all the shells are filled, pour the remaining sauce over the shells, sprinkle with the remaining Parmesan cheese, and wrap tightly with foil.

6. Bake until the casserole bubbles and the pasta and filling are cooked through, about 45 minutes.

PER SERVING Calories: 524 | Fat: 9.1g | Protein: 23g | Sodium: 259mg | Fiber: 16g | Carbohydrates: 90g | Sugar: 10g

Vegan Tofu "Ricotta" Manicotti

Check the label on your manicotti package, as some need to be precooked and some can be placed straight into the oven.

INGREDIENTS | SERVES 4

12 large manicotti

2 blocks firm tofu, crumbled

2 tablespoons lemon juice

2 tablespoons olive oil

2 tablespoons soymilk

¼ cup nutritional yeast

½ teaspoon garlic powder

½ teaspoon onion powder

¼ teaspoon salt

1 teaspoon basil

2 tablespoons fresh chopped parsley

3 cups prepared marinara sauce

⅓ cup grated vegan cheese (optional)

Mani—Canne—What?

If you can't find manicotti noodles (sometimes called cannelloni), use a large shell pasta. Or cook some lasagna noodles al dente, then place the filling on top of a noodle and roll it up. Place seam side down in your casserole dish and stuff them in tight to get them to stick together.

1. Precook the manicotti shells according to package instructions (if needed). Preheat the oven to 350°F and spray a 9" × 13" casserole dish lightly with nonstick spray.

2. In a large bowl, mash together the tofu, lemon juice, olive oil, soymilk, nutritional yeast, garlic and onion powders, salt, basil, and parsley until well mixed, crumbly, and almost smooth.

3. Stuff each manicotti noodle with the tofu mixture.

4. Spread half of the marinara sauce in the bottom of the prepared casserole dish, then place the manicotti on top. Sprinkle with grated vegan cheese if desired and cover with the remaining sauce.

5. Cover and bake until bubbly and heated through, about 30 minutes.

PER SERVING Calories: 570 | Fat: 20g | Protein: 26g | Sodium: 964mg | Fiber: 9g | Carbohydrates: 62g | Sugar: 17g

Baked Penne, Prosciutto, and Garlicky Greens with Tomato Sauce

The mild sweetness of the tomatoes and prosciutto mellow the flavor of the slightly bitter garlicky greens in this recipe. Serve with crusty bread and a leafy salad.

INGREDIENTS | SERVES 8

1 (16-ounce) package penne pasta
3 tablespoons olive oil
3 cloves garlic, minced
½ teaspoon red pepper flakes
¼ cup diced prosciutto
1 bunch kale, rinsed and finely chopped (about 4 packed cups)
1 (28-ounce) can crushed tomatoes
1 teaspoon sugar
¼ teaspoon salt
¾ cup grated Parmesan cheese

1. Preheat the oven to 350°F and spray a 9" × 13" casserole dish lightly with nonstick spray. Cook the penne according to the package directions, until just al dente; rinse, drain well, and place in the prepared casserole dish.

2. Heat the olive oil in a large lidded saucepan over medium heat. When hot, add the garlic, red pepper flakes, and prosciutto. Cook until the garlic is fragrant and the prosciutto just heated through, about 2 minutes. Add the kale and cook, covered, until the kale wilts and becomes tender, about 20 minutes. Add the tomatoes, sugar, and salt. Cook until the flavors of the sauce come together, about 10 minutes.

3. Stir ½ cup Parmesan cheese into the sauce and pour over the pasta. Sprinkle the top with the remaining Parmesan cheese; cover tightly with foil.

4. Bake the pasta until it is cooked through and bubbling, 20 minutes. Remove the foil carefully and allow the topping to brown for 5 minutes.

PER SERVING Calories: 343 | Fat: 9.8g | Protein: 15g | Sodium: 463mg | Fiber: 4.6g | Carbohydrates: 53g | Sugar: 1.1g

Penne Baked with Chicken, Butternut Squash, and Sage

Butternut squash and sage are a classic pairing in Italian cuisine, most often seen in butternut squash ravioli. This is a simplified, but no less tasty, version of this dish.

INGREDIENTS | SERVES 8

1 (16-ounce) package penne pasta

3 tablespoons olive oil

1 large onion, minced

3 cloves garlic, minced

1 small butternut squash, peeled and seeds removed

2 teaspoons chopped fresh sage

¼ cup flour

2½ cups 1% milk

¼ cup Parmesan cheese

½ cup shredded fontina cheese

2 cups cubed, cooked chicken

1 cup coarse bread crumbs

1 tablespoon melted butter

Storing Dried Herbs

Dried herbs begin to lose their flavor after a year or so—especially if they've been stored exposed to light. Keep them in a cool, dark cabinet and replace herbs after 1 year.

1. Preheat the oven to 350°F and spray a 9" × 13" casserole dish lightly with nonstick spray. Cook the penne according to the package directions, until just al dente; rinse, drain well, and place in the prepared casserole dish.

2. Heat the olive oil in a large lidded saucepan over medium heat. When hot, add the onion and cook until just tender, about 5 minutes. Add the garlic and cook for 1 minute. Add the squash and sage and cover, stirring occasionally, until the squash is just tender, about 10 minutes.

3. Add the flour, stirring to coat the vegetables. Slowly stream in the milk, stirring continuously to avoid lumps. Cook until the sauce thickens slightly, about 3 minutes. Off the heat, stir in the Parmesan cheese, fontina cheese, and chicken. Pour the sauce over the pasta and stir gently to combine. Toss the bread crumbs with the butter in a small bowl and sprinkle over the pasta.

4. Bake until the pasta becomes tender and bubbles and the topping browns, about 35–40 minutes.

PER SERVING Calories: 412 | Fat: 13g | Protein: 20g | Sodium: 176mg | Fiber: 3.1g | Carbohydrates: 55g | Sugar: 1.9g

Penne with Emerald Sauce and Greens

This dish looks dazzling out of the oven and shines with the flavors of fresh basil, garlic, and Parmesan cheese. Enjoy with grilled vegetables and garlic bread.

INGREDIENTS | SERVES 8

1 (16-ounce) package whole-wheat penne pasta

3 tablespoons olive oil

3 cloves garlic, minced

½ teaspoon red pepper flakes

1 pound baby spinach

1 pound Swiss chard, finely chopped

⅔ cup fresh Three-Herb Pesto (see Chapter 14)

¼ cup Parmesan cheese

Adding More Whole Grains to Your Eating Plan

The nutrition scientists behind the Dietary Guidelines for Americans recommend making half of the grains you eat every day whole grains. Try using whole-wheat pasta instead of pasta made from white flour or substituting brown rice for white or whole-grain breads for white breads.

1. Preheat the oven to 350°F and spray a 9" × 13" casserole dish lightly with nonstick spray. Cook the penne according to the package directions, until just al dente; rinse, drain well, and place in the prepared casserole dish.

2. In a large pot or 3-quart Dutch oven, heat the olive oil over medium heat. When hot, add the garlic and cook until fragrant, 1 minute. Add the red pepper flakes, baby spinach, and chard. Cover, stirring occasionally, until wilted and tender, 7–10 minutes.

3. Stir the wilted greens and their juices into the penne with the Three-Herb Pesto. Sprinkle with the Parmesan cheese and bake until the pasta is cooked through and the Parmesan cheese melted, about 25 minutes.

PER SERVING Calories: 257 | Fat: 3.6g | Protein: 13g | Sodium: 219mg | Fiber: 7.9g | Carbohydrates: 48g | Sugar: 1g

Penne with Broccoli Rabe, Sausage, and Mozzarella

Chicken sausage and velouté sauce lighten this dish from the traditional version made with pork sausage and heavy cream.

INGREDIENTS | SERVES 8

1 (16-ounce) package whole-wheat penne pasta

1 tablespoon olive oil

2 links sweet chicken Italian sausage, crumbled

3 garlic cloves, minced

1 pound broccoli rabe, chopped

¼ cup water

2 tablespoons butter

¼ cup flour

2 cups chicken broth

½ teaspoon salt

¼ teaspoon nutmeg

¼ cup shredded part-skim mozzarella

Broccoli Rabe

Also known as rapini, broccoli rabe has a distinctive peppery bite—much like its close relative, the turnip. It is a very good source of vitamins C and A and dietary fiber.

1. Preheat the oven to 350°F and spray a 9" × 13" casserole dish lightly with nonstick spray. Cook the penne according to the package directions, until just al dente; rinse, drain well, and place in the prepared casserole dish.

2. In a large pot or 3-quart Dutch oven, heat the olive oil over medium heat. When hot, add the sausage and brown, breaking up clumps with the back of a spoon. Add the garlic and cook until fragrant, 1 minute. Add the broccoli rabe and water, then turn the heat to low; cook, covered, until just tender, 7–10 minutes. Toss the vegetable and sausage mixture with the penne and return the Dutch oven to the heat.

3. Melt the butter and whisk in the flour. Pour the chicken broth into the pot, whisking constantly, in a slow, steady stream. Add the salt and nutmeg and cook until the sauce thickens slightly, 5 minutes. Pour the sauce over the pasta, toss, and cover with the mozzarella cheese.

4. Bake until the cheese is melted and the casserole bubbles, 25–30 minutes.

PER SERVING Calories: 310 | Fat: 8.2g | Protein: 16g | Sodium: 478mg | Fiber: 6.4g | Carbohydrates: 45g | Sugar: 0g

Creamy Whole-Wheat Pasta with Chickpeas, Spinach, and Chipotle

The surprise kick of the chipotle is mellowed by the creamy sauce and nutty chickpeas. Adjust the level of spice by adding more or less adobo sauce. Serve with a shaved fennel salad to create the taste of Italy in your own home.

INGREDIENTS | SERVES 8

1 (16-ounce) package whole-wheat penne pasta

3 tablespoons olive oil

1 medium onion, minced

2 cloves garlic, minced

¼ cup flour

2½ cups 2% milk

½ teaspoon salt

1 tablespoon adobo sauce from a can of chipotles

¼ cup shredded fontina cheese

1 pound frozen chopped spinach, thawed and well drained

1 (14.5-ounce) can chickpeas

1. Preheat the oven to 350°F and spray a 9" × 13" casserole dish lightly with nonstick spray. Cook the penne according to the package directions, until just al dente; rinse, drain well, and place in the prepared casserole dish.

2. In a large pot or 3-quart Dutch oven, heat the olive oil over medium heat. When hot, add the onion and cook until translucent, 5 minutes. Add the garlic and cook until fragrant, 1 minute.

3. Stir in the flour and pour in the milk in a steady stream, stirring constantly to avoid lumps. Add the salt and adobo sauce and cook until the sauce thickens slightly, 5 minutes. Stir in the fontina cheese and pour the sauce over the pasta, then add the spinach and chickpeas, tossing to coat.

4. Bake the casserole until the cheese bubbles and the sauce just begins to brown, 25–30 minutes.

PER SERVING Calories: 395 | Fat: 9.7g | Protein: 18g | Sodium: 424mg | Fiber: 8.9g | Carbohydrates: 64g | Sugar: 4.6g

Ziti Baked with Sun-Dried Tomatoes, Mozzarella, and Chicken

Sun-dried tomatoes give this pasta extra tomato flavor, and the basil adds a nice sparkle of herb flavor. Serve with your favorite grilled vegetables.

INGREDIENTS | SERVES 8

1 (16-ounce) package ziti pasta

¼ cup sun-dried tomatoes, minced

1 cup boiling water

3 tablespoons olive oil

3 cloves garlic, minced

1 (28-ounce) can crushed tomatoes

1 teaspoon sugar

¼ teaspoon salt

¾ cup grated part-skim mozzarella cheese

1½ cups diced cooked chicken

¼ cup chopped fresh basil

1. Preheat the oven to 350°F and spray a 9" × 13" casserole dish lightly with nonstick spray. Cook the ziti according to the package directions, until just al dente; rinse, drain well, and place in the prepared casserole dish. Plump the sun-dried tomatoes in boiling water for 10 minutes, then drain.

2. Heat the olive oil in a large saucepan over medium heat. When hot, add the garlic and cook until fragrant, about 1 minute. Add the tomatoes, sugar, salt, and sun-dried tomatoes. Cook until the flavors of the sauce come together, about 10 minutes.

3. Pour the sauce over the pasta, stir in ½ cup of the mozzarella cheese, the chicken, and the basil. Sprinkle the top with the remaining mozzarella cheese.

4. Bake the pasta until it bubbles and the cheese melts, 20 minutes.

PER SERVING Calories: 356 | Fat: 9.7g | Protein: 19g | Sodium: 320mg | Fiber: 4.1g | Carbohydrates: 51g | Sugar: 2.2g

Baked Ziti with Mushrooms and Mozzarella

Use a selection of mushrooms such as shiitake, button, cremini, or portobello for the deepest mushroom flavor.

INGREDIENTS | SERVES 8

1 (16-ounce) package ziti pasta

3 tablespoons olive oil

2 pounds mixed, sliced mushrooms

3 garlic cloves, minced

1 (28-ounce) can crushed tomatoes

1 teaspoon sugar

¼ teaspoon salt

¾ cup grated part-skim mozzarella cheese

¼ cup chopped fresh basil

Mushroom Storage

Store mushrooms once you get them home from the store in the package they come in. If you plan to store them for a day or two longer before using, remove them from the packaging, place them on a rimmed baking sheet, and cover lightly with a slightly damp paper towel.

1. Preheat the oven to 350°F and spray a 9" × 13" casserole dish lightly with nonstick spray. Cook the ziti according to the package directions, until just al dente; rinse, drain well, and place in the prepared casserole dish.

2. Heat the olive oil in a large skillet over medium-high heat. When hot, add the mushrooms and cook without moving until they begin to brown on one side, about 7 minutes. Stir and continue to cook until they lose most of their liquid, another 3–4 minutes. Add the garlic and cook until fragrant, about 1 minute. Add the tomatoes, sugar, and salt. Cook until the flavors of the sauce come together, about 10 minutes.

3. Pour the sauce over the pasta and stir in ½ cup mozzarella cheese and the basil. Sprinkle the top with the remaining mozzarella cheese.

4. Bake the pasta until it bubbles and the cheese melts, 20 minutes.

PER SERVING Calories: 341 | Fat: 9.3g | Protein: 15g | Sodium: 275mg | Fiber: 5g | Carbohydrates: 54g | Sugar: 3.4g

Summer Squash and Pesto Baked Pasta

Delicate summer squash and flavorful pesto blend together harmoniously in this lightened cream sauce. Enjoy with a salad made from bitter greens served with balsamic vinaigrette.

INGREDIENTS | SERVES 8

1 (16-ounce) package whole-wheat pasta

3 tablespoons olive oil

1 large onion, minced

3 garlic cloves, minced

¼ cup flour

2½ cups 1% milk

1 small zucchini, julienned

1 small yellow squash, julienned

3 tablespoons pesto

¼ cup shredded fontina cheese

1 cup bread coarse bread crumbs

1 tablespoon melted butter

1. Preheat the oven to 350°F and spray a 9" × 13" casserole dish lightly with nonstick spray. Cook the pasta according to the package directions, until just al dente; rinse, drain well, and place in the prepared casserole dish.

2. Heat the olive oil in a medium saucepan over medium-high heat. When hot, add the onion and cook until just tender, about 5 minutes. Add garlic and cook until fragrant, about 30 seconds.

3. Add the flour, stirring to coat the onions and garlic. Slowly stream in the milk, stirring continuously to avoid lumps. Stir in the zucchini and yellow squash and cook the mixture until the sauce thickens slightly and the vegetables soften, about 5 minutes. Off the heat, stir in the pesto and fontina cheese. Pour the sauce over the pasta and stir gently to combine. Toss the bread crumbs with the butter in a small bowl and sprinkle over the pasta.

4. Bake until the pasta becomes tender and bubbles and the topping browns, about 35–40 minutes.

PER SERVING Calories: 358 | Fat: 7g | Protein: 16g | Sodium: 197mg | Fiber: 6.1g | Carbohydrates: 62g | Sugar: 1.8g

Artichoke and Spinach Pasta Bake

*More sophisticated than macaroni and cheese, but just as tasty,
this recipe will get even the pickiest eaters to eat their vegetables.*

INGREDIENTS | SERVES 8

1 (16-ounce) package whole-wheat pasta

3 tablespoons olive oil

1 large onion, minced

3 garlic cloves, minced

¼ cup flour

2½ cups 1% milk

1 (14.5-ounce) can artichokes, drained and rinsed

1 (16-ounce) package of frozen spinach, thawed and drained

¼ cup basil

¼ cup shredded Parmesan cheese

1 cup coarse bread crumbs

1 tablespoon melted butter

Canned Artichokes

When using canned artichokes, rinse them under cool running water before adding them to dishes. Rinsing removes some of the citric acid flavor (which keeps them from turning brown) and makes them taste a little fresher. Alternately, use frozen artichokes in dishes.

1. Preheat the oven to 350°F and spray a 9" × 13" casserole dish lightly with nonstick spray. Cook the pasta according to the package directions, until just al dente; rinse, drain well, and place in the prepared casserole dish.

2. Heat the olive oil in a medium saucepan over medium-high heat. When hot, add the onion and cook until just tender, about 5 minutes. Add the garlic and cook until fragrant, about 30 seconds.

3. Add the flour, stirring to coat the onions and garlic. Slowly stream in the milk, stirring continuously to avoid lumps. Cook the sauce until it thickens slightly, about 5 minutes. Off the heat, stir in the artichokes, spinach, basil, and Parmesan cheese. Pour the sauce over the pasta and stir gently to combine. Toss the bread crumbs with the butter in a small bowl and sprinkle over the pasta.

4. Bake until the pasta becomes tender and bubbles and the topping browns, about 35–40 minutes.

PER SERVING Calories: 397 | Fat: 10g | Protein: 18g | Sodium: 277mg | Fiber: 9.2g | Carbohydrates: 63g | Sugar: 1.3g

Pasta Puttanesca Casserole

Make this casserole with your favorite type of whole-wheat pasta. Rotini and bow tie pasta both hold the sauce well. This version of puttanesca does not use anchovies. Add a few minced anchovies in with the garlic for a more authentic version.

INGREDIENTS | SERVES 8

1 (16-ounce) package whole-wheat pasta

3 tablespoons olive oil

3 garlic cloves, minced

1 (28-ounce) can crushed tomatoes

1 teaspoon sugar

¼ teaspoon salt

½ cup halved pitted olives

3 tablespoons capers, rinsed

¾ cup grated part-skim mozzarella cheese

¼ cup chopped fresh basil

Rinsing Capers

Capers are brined, which means that they are packed in salt. Rinse them in a couple changes of water or under cool running water to remove some of the salt before cooking. This same technique may be used for other brined foods, such as olives, if you are watching your sodium intake.

1. Preheat the oven to 350°F and spray a 9" × 13" casserole dish lightly with nonstick spray. Cook the pasta according to the package directions, until just al dente; rinse, drain well, and place in the prepared casserole dish.

2. Heat the olive oil in a large skillet over medium-high heat. When hot, add the garlic and cook until fragrant, about 1 minute. Add the tomatoes, sugar, salt, olives, and capers. Cook until the flavors of the sauce come together, about 10 minutes.

3. Pour the sauce over the pasta and stir in ½ cup mozzarella cheese and the basil. Sprinkle the top with the remaining mozzarella cheese.

4. Bake the pasta until it bubbles and the cheese melts, 20 minutes.

PER SERVING Calories: 317 | Fat: 9g | Protein: 13g | Sodium: 416mg | Fiber: 6.8g | Carbohydrates: 51g | Sugar: 1g

Kugel

Serve this recipe as part of a brunch or buffet. You can adjust the sweetness to your liking, or make a savory version by omitting the sugar entirely.

INGREDIENTS | SERVES 8

1 (12-ounce) package yolk-free egg noodles

2 tablespoons butter, melted

1 (16-ounce) container reduced-fat cottage cheese

1 (16-ounce) container reduced-fat sour cream

2 eggs, beaten

2 egg whites

½ cup sugar

2 tablespoons vanilla extract

1. Preheat the oven to 350°F and spray a 9" × 13" casserole dish lightly with nonstick spray. Cook the noodles according to the package directions, then drain and rinse with cold water; drain again.

2. Combine the noodles, butter, cottage cheese, sour cream, eggs, egg whites, sugar, and vanilla in a large bowl. Pour the mixture into the prepared casserole dish.

3. Bake the mixture for 1 hour until it bubbles and begins to brown.

PER SERVING Calories: 314 | Fat: 13g | Protein: 16g | Sodium: 335mg | Fiber: 1g | Carbohydrates: 32g | Sugar: 13g

Orecchiette Pasta Baked with Chicken and Lemon

Eat this pasta in the winter for a burst of bright lemon flavor that will shake up your taste buds and remind you of the summer months ahead.

INGREDIENTS | SERVES 8

1 (16-ounce) package orecchiette

3 tablespoons olive oil

1 large onion, minced

3 garlic cloves, minced

¼ cup flour

2½ cups low-sodium chicken broth

½ tablespoon glace de poulet (optional)

2 tablespoons lemon juice

1 tablespoon lemon zest

½ cup Parmesan cheese

2 tablespoons fresh thyme, chopped

2 cups cubed, cooked chicken

1 cup coarse bread crumbs

1 tablespoon melted butter

Glace de Poulet

Glace de poulet is concentrated and reduced chicken flavor, and is made by boiling down and concentrating chicken stock. It's used to add body and a ton of chicken flavor to sauces and soups. Find it in some supermarkets or specialty foods shops. A little goes a long way, so even though it's a little pricy, it lasts a long time. Once opened, store in the refrigerator. Do not substitute bouillon.

1. Preheat the oven to 350°F and spray a 9" × 13" casserole dish lightly with nonstick spray. Cook the orecchiette according to the package directions, until just al dente; rinse, drain well, and place in the prepared casserole dish.

2. Heat the olive oil in a large saucepan over medium heat. When hot, add the onion and cook until just tender, about 5 minutes. Add the garlic and cook for 1 minute.

3. Add the flour, stirring to coat the vegetables. Slowly stream in the chicken broth and stir in the glace de poulet (if using), stirring continuously to avoid lumps. Cook until the sauce thickens slightly, about 3 minutes. Off the heat, stir in the lemon juice, lemon zest, Parmesan cheese, thyme, and chicken. Pour the sauce over the pasta and stir gently to combine. Toss the bread crumbs with the butter in a small bowl and sprinkle over the pasta.

4. Bake until the pasta becomes tender and bubbles and the topping browns, about 35–40 minutes.

PER SERVING Calories: 401 | Fat: 11g | Protein: 21g | Sodium: 402mg | Fiber: 2.8g | Carbohydrates: 55g | Sugar: 1.9g

Bow Tie and Mushroom Casserole with Gorgonzola

Serve this with a sprinkling of toasted walnuts if you like for an extra-decadent flavor.

INGREDIENTS | SERVES 8

1 (16-ounce) package bow tie pasta

3 tablespoons olive oil

1 (16-ounce) package sliced mushrooms

1 large onion, minced

3 cloves garlic, minced

2 tablespoons fresh thyme, chopped

¼ cup flour

2½ cups fat-free milk

½ cup Gorgonzola cheese

1 cup coarse bread crumbs

1 tablespoon melted butter

1. Preheat the oven to 350°F and spray a 9" × 13" casserole dish lightly with nonstick spray. Cook the bow ties according to the package directions, until just al dente; rinse, drain well, and place in the prepared casserole dish.

2. Heat the olive oil in a large skillet over medium-high heat. When hot, add the mushrooms and cook without moving until the first side begins to brown, about 7 minutes. Stir the mushrooms and cook until they have released most of their juice, about 5 minutes more. Add the onion and cook until just tender, about 5 minutes. Add the garlic and thyme and cook for 1 minute.

3. Add the flour, stirring to coat the vegetables. Slowly stream in the milk, stirring continuously to avoid lumps. Cook until the sauce thickens slightly, about 3 minutes. Stir in the Gorgonzola cheese and heat until just melted through, about 1 minute. Pour the sauce over the pasta and stir gently to combine. Toss the bread crumbs with the butter in a small bowl and sprinkle over the pasta.

4. Bake until the pasta becomes tender and bubbles and the topping browns, about 35–40 minutes.

PER SERVING Calories: 470 | Fat: 17g | Protein: 19g | Sodium: 554mg | Fiber: 3.3g | Carbohydrates: 61g | Sugar: 3g

CHAPTER 13

International Favorites

Greek Shrimp Bake

Serve this dish with orzo, lemony rice, or with crusty whole-grain bread.

INGREDIENTS | SERVES 4

1½ pounds shrimp, peeled and deveined
3 tablespoons extra-virgin olive oil
2 garlic cloves, minced
1 tablespoon grated lemon zest
1 tablespoon chopped fresh oregano
¼ teaspoon black pepper
½ cup feta cheese
2 tablespoons lemon juice

1. Preheat the oven to 425°F and spray a 9" × 13" casserole dish lightly with nonstick spray.

2. Arrange the shrimp in the prepared casserole dish, drizzle with the olive oil, and sprinkle with the garlic, lemon zest, oregano, pepper, feta, and lemon juice.

3. Bake until the shrimp is cooked and pink and the cheese slightly melted, about 10–13 minutes.

PER SERVING Calories: 278 | Fat: 16g | Protein: 29g | Sodium: 404mg | Fiber: 0g | Carbohydrates: 3g | Sugar: 1g

Barley and Black Bean Enchiladas

These rich enchiladas are filled with parsley, vegetables, and black beans, making them colorful and delicious.

INGREDIENTS | SERVES 10

½ cup medium pearl barley

1 cup vegetable stock

1 tablespoon olive oil

1 onion, chopped

3 garlic cloves, minced

1 jalapeño pepper, minced

1 (15-ounce) can black beans, drained

1 cup frozen corn

2 tomatoes, chopped

1 tablespoon chili powder

12 (8") flour tortillas

1 cup shredded pepper jack cheese

1 cup shredded part-skim mozzarella cheese

1 (16-ounce) jar salsa

1 (8-ounce) can tomato sauce

¼ cup grated Cotija cheese

Cotija Cheese

Cotija cheese is a hard Mexican grating cheese that is similar to Parmesan and Romano cheese but with a more intense flavor. You can find it in chunks or pre-grated at Mexican markets and usually in larger grocery stores. You can substitute Parmesan or Romano cheese for it, but there's nothing truly like it.

1. Preheat the oven to 375°F and spray a 9" × 13" casserole dish lightly with nonstick spray. In a small saucepan, combine the barley and vegetable stock; bring to a simmer. Cover and simmer until barley is tender, about 35 minutes. Drain and set aside.

2. In a large skillet, heat the olive oil over medium heat. Add the onion, garlic, and jalapeño; cook and stir for 5 minutes. Stir in the black beans, corn, tomatoes, chili powder, and cooked barley; simmer for 10 minutes.

3. Divide the barley mixture among the tortillas; top with a mixture of pepper jack and mozzarella cheese. Roll up and place in the prepared casserole dish. Pour the salsa and tomato sauce over all; sprinkle with the Cotija cheese.

4. Bake the casserole until it bubbles and begins to brown, 45–55 minutes.

PER SERVING Calories: 408 | Fat: 12g | Protein: 22g | Sodium: 817mg | Fiber: 7.5g | Carbohydrates: 59g | Sugar: 3.7g

Sweet Potato Enchiladas

Sweet potatoes add great flavor, nutrition, and fiber to these wholesome and delicious enchiladas. Substitute homemade green or Red Chili Sauce or Green Chili Sauce (see Chapter 14) for the enchilada sauce.

INGREDIENTS | SERVES 8

2 tablespoons olive oil

1 onion, chopped

3 garlic cloves, minced

2 jalapeño peppers, minced

1 (14.5-ounce) can refried beans

1 tablespoon chili powder

1 teaspoon ground cumin

½ teaspoon salt

⅛ teaspoon pepper

3 tablespoons Dijon mustard

1 (20-ounce) can sweet potatoes, drained and chopped

1½ cups salsa, divided

12 (10") flour tortillas

2½ cups shredded Cheddar cheese, divided

1 (18-ounce) can enchilada sauce

Transport Tips

If taking this casserole to a party, bake it there so that it can be served piping hot. If you're the guest, make sure that the host knows that you need a 375°F oven to finish your contribution. Cover it well, using toothpicks or wire picks to hold the foil away from the dish, and bring the cheese along in a separate bag.

1. Spray a 9" × 13" casserole dish lightly with nonstick spray. In a large skillet, heat olive oil over medium heat. When hot, add the onions, garlic, and jalapeños. Cook, stirring occasionally, until the vegetables are tender, about 6 minutes.

2. Add the refried beans, chili powder, cumin, salt, pepper, and Dijon mustard; bring the mixture to a simmer. Add the sweet potatoes and ½ cup salsa; remove from the heat.

3. Place the tortillas on a clean work surface. Divide the sweet potato mixture among them; top each with 2 tablespoons Cheddar cheese. Roll up, enclosing the filling.

4. Combine the remaining 1 cup salsa with the enchilada sauce and mix well. Place ½ cup sauce in the prepared baking dish. Top with the enchiladas, then pour the remaining sauce over the top. Cover and chill the enchiladas for 12–24 hours in the refrigerator.

5. When ready to eat, preheat the oven to 375°F. Uncover and top with the remaining 1 cup cheese. Bake for 45–55 minutes until the casserole is hot and bubbling.

PER SERVING Calories: 502 | Fat: 22g | Protein: 20g | Sodium: 1,252mg | Fiber: 7.3g | Carbohydrates: 56g | Sugar: 6g

Vegetable Spanakopita

Be sure to thaw the phyllo according to package directions to make this classic Greek dish.

INGREDIENTS | SERVES 6

2 tablespoons olive oil, divided

1 onion, chopped

4 garlic cloves, minced

1 (8-ounce) package sliced mushrooms

1 (10-ounce) package frozen chopped spinach, thawed

1 cup chopped tomatoes

⅛ teaspoon pepper

2 tablespoons chopped fresh dill

½ cup part-skim ricotta cheese

3 egg whites

1 cup shredded part-skim mozzarella cheese

¼ cup crumbled feta cheese

1 tablespoon butter, melted

8 (9" × 14") sheets frozen phyllo dough, thawed

6 tablespoons wheat germ

Draining Frozen Spinach

Frozen spinach contains a large amount of water. Most recipes call for draining thawed frozen spinach. One way is to put the spinach in a kitchen towel, then squeeze over the sink until dry. You can also place the spinach between two plates; hold it vertically and squeeze it over the sink until dry.

1. Preheat the oven to 350°F and spray a 9" × 9" baking pan with nonstick spray and set aside. In a large skillet, heat 1 tablespoon of olive oil over medium heat. When hot, add the onion and garlic; cook, stirring occasionally, until the vegetables are crisp-tender. Add the mushrooms and cook for 4 minutes longer. Add the spinach and tomatoes and cook until the liquid evaporates, about 10–15 minutes longer. Remove the mixture from the heat and place the filling in a large bowl; allow the mixture to cool.

2. Add the pepper, dill, ricotta, egg whites, mozzarella, and feta to the filling and mix well. In a small bowl, combine the remaining tablespoon of olive oil with the butter.

3. Place a sheet of phyllo dough into the prepared pan, letting the edges hang over the pan. Brush with some of the olive oil mixture and sprinkle with 1 tablespoon wheat germ. Layer 4 more sheets of phyllo on top, alternately spraying with nonstick spray and brushing with olive oil mixture; top with the wheat germ. Pour the filling into the prepared pan.

4. Fold the edges of the dough over the filling. Top with the remaining phyllo, brushing with the olive oil mixture; tuck in the edges. Bake until it is golden brown, about 25–30 minutes.

PER SERVING Calories: 297 | Fat: 11g | Protein: 20g | Sodium: 522mg | Fiber: 4g | Carbohydrates: 28g | Sugar: 5g

Lobster Paella

If your budget is tight, substitute cooked shrimp for the lobster.

INGREDIENTS | SERVES 6

¼ cup extra-virgin olive oil

2 large yellow onions, diced

2 red bell peppers, seeded and sliced into ½" strips

4 garlic cloves, minced

2 cups uncooked white basmati rice

5 cups chicken broth

½ teaspoon saffron threads, crushed

¼ teaspoon crushed red pepper flakes

1 teaspoon sea or kosher salt

½ teaspoon freshly ground black pepper

⅓ cup licorice-flavored liqueur, such as Pernod

1½ pounds cooked lobster meat

1 pound kielbasa, cut into ¼" rounds

1 (10-ounce) package frozen peas

Fresh parsley, chopped, to taste

2 lemons, cut into wedges

1. Preheat the oven to 425°F.

2. Heat the oil in a 3-quart Dutch oven over medium-high heat. Add the onions and cook for 5 minutes, stirring occasionally. Add the bell peppers and cook for another 5 minutes. Lower the heat, add the garlic, and cook for 1 minute more. Stir in the rice, chicken broth, saffron, red pepper flakes, salt, and pepper; bring to a boil over medium-high heat. Cover, move the pot to the oven, and bake for 15 minutes. Take the pot out of the oven and remove the lid; gently stir the rice using a wooden spoon. Return the pot to the oven and bake, uncovered, for 10–15 minutes or until the rice is fully cooked.

3. Move the paella back to the stovetop; add the liqueur. Cook over medium heat for 1 minute or until the liqueur is absorbed by the rice. Turn off the heat and add the lobster, kielbasa, and peas, gently stirring to mix in the added ingredients. Cover and let it set for 10 minutes. Uncover, sprinkle with the parsley, garnish with lemon wedges, and serve hot.

PER SERVING Calories: 452 | Fat: 23g | Protein: 28g | Sodium: 1,526mg | Fiber: 2.9g | Carbohydrates: 29g | Sugar: 2.6g

Indian Chicken and Chickpea Casserole

Serve this dish with a drizzle of thinned yogurt and a sprinkle of chopped scallions.

INGREDIENTS | SERVES 4

1 tablespoon canola oil

2 medium onions, minced

3 garlic cloves, minced

1 tablespoon minced fresh ginger

½ teaspoon turmeric

2 teaspoons paprika

2 teaspoons curry powder

2 cups low-sodium chicken broth

¼ teaspoon salt

1 (14.5-ounce) can chickpeas, drained and rinsed

⅓ cup chopped fresh cilantro

4 boneless, skinless chicken breasts

Handling Poultry

Be careful when handling raw poultry because it may be contaminated with salmonella. Salmonella is a type of bacteria that can cause abdominal upset and fever if it is not killed first by cooking or proper sanitation. Wash all cutting boards, knives, work areas, and your hands with hot soapy water and leave all poultry in the refrigerator until it is ready to be cooked.

1. Preheat the oven to 450°F and spray a 9" × 13" casserole dish with nonstick spray.

2. Heat the oil over medium-high heat in a large skillet. When hot, add the onions and cook, stirring occasionally, until they begin to brown, about 10 minutes. Add the garlic, ginger, turmeric, paprika, and curry powder; cook until fragrant, about 1 minute. Add the chicken broth, salt, and chickpeas; bring the mixture to a boil.

3. Once the sauce has reached a boil, mash some of the chickpeas with the back of a wooden spoon or potato masher so that it thickens slightly. Add the cilantro and remove from the heat.

4. Place the chicken in the prepared casserole dish, pour the chickpea sauce over the top, and cover tightly with foil.

5. Bake until the chicken is cooked through and the sauce has thickened, 30–35 minutes.

PER SERVING Calories: 333 | Fat: 6.2g | Protein: 41g | Sodium: 730mg | Fiber: 4.5g | Carbohydrates: 24g | Sugar: 0g

Ginger-Flavored Chicken Curry

Use fresh, tender ginger for this recipe. Serve with naan bread or brown rice.

INGREDIENTS | SERVES 4

2 tablespoons grated ginger

1 teaspoon powdered coriander

1 teaspoon curry powder

½ teaspoon red chili powder

¾ cup plain nonfat yogurt

2 tablespoons vegetable oil

4 boneless, skinless chicken breasts, cut into 1" cubes

½ teaspoon cumin seeds

1 cardamom pod

1 bay leaf

1 cup tomato purée

Indian Cooking Oils

Indian cooking uses peanut, vegetable, mustard, sesame, and corn oils for cooking. There are two types of ghee that are used: vanaspathi (vegetable) and ghee (clarified butter). Indian cooking does not use any animal fat or lard as a cooking medium.

1. In a large bowl or resealable plastic bag, stir together the ginger, coriander, curry powder, chili powder, yogurt, and 1 tablespoon vegetable oil. Add the chicken and coat all pieces evenly with the marinade. Cover and refrigerate for 3–4 hours.

2. Preheat the oven to 350°F and heat the remaining table-spoon of oil in a 3-quart Dutch oven over medium-high heat. Add the cumin seeds, cardamom, and bay leaf. When the seeds begin to sizzle, add the tomato purée.

3. Cook the sauce over medium heat for about 3–4 minutes, then add the chicken and marinade to the pot with 1 cup of water. Bring the curry to a bare simmer, cover, and place in the oven.

4. Bake the curry until the chicken is cooked through and the sauce is somewhat thickened, 20–25 minutes. Remove the cardamom pod and bay leaf before serving.

PER SERVING Calories: 265 | Fat: 8.9g | Protein: 38g | Sodium: 54mg | Fiber: 1.3g | Carbohydrates: 9.5g | Sugar: 6.6g

Moroccan Chicken Bake

Serve this dish with whole-wheat couscous and mint tea for an authentic Moroccan meal.

INGREDIENTS | SERVES 4

1 tablespoon olive oil

1 large sweet onion, minced

2 teaspoons fresh minced ginger

3 garlic cloves, minced

1 teaspoon ground coriander

2 teaspoons sweet paprika

2 bay leaves

½ cup golden raisins

¼ teaspoon salt

2 cups low-sodium chicken broth

4 boneless, skinless chicken breasts

2 tablespoons lemon juice

½ cup pitted olives

2 tablespoons chopped fresh parsley

1. Preheat the oven to 350°F and spray a 9" × 13" casserole dish with nonstick cooking spray.

2. Heat the oil over medium-high heat in a medium saucepan. When hot, add the onion and cook until translucent, about 5 minutes. Stir in the ginger, garlic, coriander, and paprika. Cook the vegetables another minute, then add the bay leaves, raisins, salt, and chicken broth; bring the mixture to a boil.

3. Place the chicken in the prepared casserole dish and carefully pour the sauce over the chicken. Cover the casserole tightly with foil and bake until the chicken is cooked through and the sauce slightly reduced, 30–35 minutes.

4. Remove the casserole from the oven and stir in the lemon juice, olives, and parsley. Remove bay leaves. Serve hot.

PER SERVING Calories: 305 | Fat: 8.2g | Protein: 37g | Sodium: 557mg | Fiber: 1.9g | Carbohydrates: 25 g | Sugar: 16g

Arroz Con Pollo

Whole pimentos, green Spanish olives, and medium-grain rice can be found in the international foods section of your grocery store.

INGREDIENTS | SERVES 6

4 boneless, skinless chicken breasts, cut in half crosswise

3 tablespoons extra-virgin olive oil

6 garlic cloves, minced

1 tablespoon lemon zest

1 tablespoon dried oregano

¼ teaspoon salt

¼ teaspoon pepper

1 large onion, minced

1 green bell pepper, minced

2¼ cups low-sodium chicken broth

1 cup tomato sauce

3 cups medium-grain rice

⅓ cup chopped green Spanish olives

½ cup whole pimentos, diced

3 tablespoons lemon juice

¼ cup chopped cilantro

Arroz Con Pollo

The name of this dish literally translates to "rice with chicken" and is a representation of Latino comfort food at its finest. Serve with lemon or lime wedges for extra zip.

1. Prick the chicken breasts all over with the tines of a fork. Combine 2 tablespoons of the olive oil, garlic, lemon zest, oregano, salt, and pepper together in a medium bowl. Stir in the chicken, cover, and refrigerate for 30 minutes (or up to 8 hours) while you prepare the rest of the ingredients.

2. Preheat the oven to 350°F and heat the remaining olive oil in a 3-quart Dutch oven. When hot, add the onion and pepper and cook, stirring occasionally, until the vegetables are tender, about 10 minutes. Stir in the chicken broth and tomato sauce and bring to a simmer. Stir in the rice, olives, pimentos, chicken, and the marinade.

3. Cover the Dutch oven and transfer to the oven. Bake, stirring every 10 minutes, until the chicken is cooked through and the rice is tender, about 30 minutes. If the pot begins to look dry after about 20 minutes, stir in up to ¼ cup of water.

4. Stir in the lemon juice and cilantro just before serving.

PER SERVING Calories: 304 | Fat: 9.6g | Protein: 27g | Sodium: 368mg | Fiber: 1.6g | Carbohydrates: 28g | Sugar: 2.2g

Chicken Cacciatore

This is an easy weeknight version of a classic stew that's typically cooked for hours.
Enjoy the same flavors and have dinner on the table in just over half an hour.

INGREDIENTS | SERVES 4

2 tablespoons extra-virgin olive oil

1 small yellow onion, minced

1 green bell pepper, minced

3 garlic cloves, minced

1½ tablespoons minced fresh thyme

2 cups sliced button mushrooms

1 (28-ounce) can crushed tomatoes

¼ teaspoon salt

⅛ teaspoon pepper

½ cup dry white wine

4 boneless, skinless chicken breasts

¼ cup chopped parsley

Cacciatore

In Italian, cacciatore means "hunter." Food prepared in the cacciatore style therefore includes foods that might be gathered from the forests and fields: mushrooms, herbs, tomatoes, peppers, and sometimes wine.

1. Preheat the oven to 350°F and spray a 9" × 13" casserole dish with nonstick cooking spray.

2. Heat the olive oil in a skillet over medium heat. When hot, add the onion, bell pepper, and garlic; cook until the vegetables are just tender, stirring occasionally, 7 minutes. Add the thyme and mushrooms and cook until the mushrooms are almost cooked through, 5 minutes. Add the tomatoes, salt, pepper, and white wine; bring the sauce to a simmer.

3. Place the chicken breasts in the prepared casserole dish and pour the sauce over the top. Cover tightly with foil and bake until the chicken is cooked through and the sauce has reduced slightly, 30–35 minutes. Garnish with parsley just before serving.

PER SERVING Calories: 298 | Fat: 9g | Protein: 39g | Sodium: 412mg | Fiber: 4.2g | Carbohydrates: 16g | Sugar: 1g

Chicken Paprikash

Serve with yolk-free egg noodles and a tossed green salad.

INGREDIENTS | SERVES 4

1 tablespoon olive oil

1 large sweet onion, julienned

1 yellow bell pepper, stemmed, seeded, and julienned

1 red bell pepper, stemmed, seeded, and julienned

2 garlic cloves, minced

3 tablespoons paprika

2 tablespoons flour

1 cup low-sodium chicken broth

¼ teaspoon salt

⅛ teaspoon pepper

4 boneless, skinless chicken breasts cut into 1" pieces

½ cup reduced-fat sour cream

1. Preheat the oven to 350°F. Heat the oil in a 3-quart Dutch oven over medium-high heat. When hot, add the onion and cook until softened and just beginning to brown, 10 minutes.

2. Add the peppers and cook until just softened, 3 minutes. Add the garlic, paprika, and flour and stir to combine. Stir in the chicken broth, salt, and pepper; bring the mixture to a boil. Cook until the sauce thickens slightly, about 1 minute.

3. Stir in the chicken breasts, cover, and bake until the chicken is cooked through and the sauce slightly thickened, about 20 minutes. Remove the pot from the oven and stir in the sour cream before serving.

PER SERVING Calories: 298 | Fat: 9.5g | Protein: 39g | Sodium: 313mg | Fiber: 2g | Carbohydrates: 14g | Sugar: 4.2g

Cooking with Sour Cream

Sour cream will break and curdle if heated to a very high temperature. When adding sour cream to sauces, stir it in at the end of cooking time off the heat so that the sauce remains creamy.

Hahn Beef Casserole with Crispy Veggies

This casserole cooks into a beautifully satisfying main course with the flavors of Asia and the pleasantly chewy bite of udon noodles.

INGREDIENTS | SERVES 8

1 pound udon noodles

1 tablespoon canola oil

1 cup scallions, thinly sliced

1 tablespoon minced fresh ginger

3 garlic cloves, minced

½ pound 93% lean ground beef

8 ounces shiitake mushrooms, sliced

8 ounces (½ package) frozen stir-fry vegetables

1 teaspoon toasted sesame oil

3 tablespoons reduced-sodium soy sauce

½ cup low-sodium beef broth

2 eggs

2 egg whites

Udon Noodles

Udon noodles are a thick and chewy type of noodle from Japan. They are made from wheat flour and may be purchased in a fresh, dried, or frozen form. They are available in Asian markets and the international foods section of many grocery stores. Follow the cooking directions on the package of the udon as the cooking time varies from brand to brand.

1. Preheat the oven to 350°F and spray a 9" × 13" casserole dish with nonstick spray. Cook the udon noodles according to package directions until just al dente, then rinse under cool running water.

2. Heat the oil in a large skillet over medium-high heat. When hot, add the scallions, ginger, and garlic. Cook until fragrant, about 1 minute. Add the beef and cook, breaking up clumps with the back of a wooden spoon, until browned.

3. Push the beef to the side of the skillet and add the mushrooms. Cook, stirring occasionally, until the mushrooms are tender, about 7 minutes. Stir in the frozen stir-fry vegetables and remove the skillet from the heat.

4. Whisk the sesame oil, soy sauce, beef broth, eggs, and egg whites together in a large bowl. Stir in the udon and vegetable mixture, then pour into the prepared casserole dish.

5. Bake the casserole until it is set in the center, 25–30 minutes.

PER SERVING Calories: 322 | Fat: 6g | Protein: 20g | Sodium: 771mg | Fiber: 2g | Carbohydrates: 51g | Sugar: 1.3g

Pozole Casserole

Pozole is a traditional Mexican hominy stew. This version is a little less soupy and made with chicken instead of pork, but no less delicious. Serve with wedges of lime, chopped cilantro, oregano, and scallions.

INGREDIENTS | SERVES 8

6 cups low-sodium chicken broth

3 dried ancho chilies

2 tablespoons vegetable oil

2 medium onions, diced

4 garlic cloves, minced

¼ teaspoon salt

1 tablespoon minced oregano

1 tablespoon cumin

¼ cup flour

1 pound fresh green beans, cut into 1" lengths

3 (14-ounce) cans hominy

2 pounds boneless, skinless chicken breasts cut into 1" chunks

2 tablespoons lime juice

1. Microwave 1 cup of broth with the ancho chilies for 2 minutes. Let the chilies sit until they are rehydrated, about 10 minutes, then purée them with the chicken broth in a blender.

2. Preheat the oven to 350°F and heat the oil in a 3-quart Dutch oven over medium-high heat. When hot, add the onions and cook until they are just translucent, about 5 minutes. Add the garlic, salt, oregano, and cumin; cook until fragrant, about 1 minute. Stir in the flour and slowly stream in the remaining broth, stirring constantly to avoid lumps. Stir in the green beans, hominy, and chili purée.

3. Cover and bake for 1 hour, then add in the chicken. Cover and bake for another 30 minutes until the chicken is cooked through. Add the lime juice just before serving.

PER SERVING Calories: 293 | Fat: 5.9g | Protein: 25g | Sodium: 801mg | Fiber: 3.8g | Carbohydrates: 25g | Sugar: 1g

Cassoulet

Soak the beans the night before cooking the cassoulet, or quick soak the beans by bringing them up to a boil, allowing them to soak for 90 minutes, draining, and proceeding with the recipe.

INGREDIENTS | SERVES 10

BEANS
1 pound dried great northern beans that have been soaked overnight, drained
1 onion, peeled
1 carrot, peeled
1 stalk celery, trimmed

MEAT
2 tablespoons olive oil
3 pieces turkey bacon, diced
1 pound pork tenderloin, trimmed into 2" pieces
2 pounds boneless chicken thighs, skin and fat removed
1 large onion, diced
1 carrot, minced
1 stalk celery, minced
3 garlic cloves, minced
½ teaspoon kosher salt
2 tablespoons tomato paste
1 tablespoon fresh minced thyme
1 quart chicken broth
1 cup dry white wine
½ cup coarse bread crumbs

1. Place the beans in a large pot with enough water to cover by 2". Add the onion, carrot, and celery and cook at a gentle simmer until the beans are just tender but still slightly underdone, 1¼–1½ hours. Drain the beans and discard the vegetables.

2. Preheat the oven to 350°F. Heat the oil over medium heat in a 3-quart Dutch oven. When hot, add the bacon and cook until just crisp. Remove with a slotted spoon to drain on paper towels.

3. Turn the heat up to medium-high and brown the tenderloin on all sides; remove to a plate to drain. Brown the chicken in two batches and remove to a plate to drain. Add the onion, carrot, celery, garlic, and salt to the Dutch oven. Cook until the vegetables are just beginning to soften, about 5 minutes. Stir in the tomato paste, thyme, chicken broth, and wine.

4. Add the beans and meats back to the pot, cover, and cook until the beans and meats are both tender, about 1 hour.

5. Uncover the Dutch oven and scatter the bread crumbs over the top of the casserole. Bake until the crumbs are browned and crisp, about 15 minutes.

PER SERVING Calories: 428 | Fat: 10g | Protein: 47g | Sodium: 502mg | Fiber: 8g | Carbohydrates: 36g | Sugar: 3.8g

Cassoulet

Named for its cooking vessel, the cassole, cassoulet is a rich, slow-cooked white bean casserole that originated in the south of France. Pork sausages, braised pork, duck, goose, and mutton are traditional in this dish.

Brown Rice Vegetarian Paella

Substitute any flavor of vegetarian sausage (except breakfast sausage) for the vegetarian kielbasa if you can't find it in your supermarket.

INGREDIENTS | SERVES 6

¼ cup extra-virgin olive oil

1 (16-ounce) package vegetarian kielbasa, cut into ¼" rounds

2 large yellow onions, diced

2 red bell peppers, seeded and sliced into ½" strips

4 cloves garlic, minced

2 cups long-grain brown rice

3 cups vegetable broth

⅓ cup dry white wine

1 small zucchini, chopped

1 small yellow squash, chopped

½ pound haricot vert, cut into 1" lengths

½ teaspoon saffron threads, crushed

¼ teaspoon crushed red pepper flakes

1 teaspoon kosher salt

½ teaspoon freshly ground black pepper

1 (10-ounce) package frozen peas

1 tablespoon chopped fresh parsley

2 lemons, cut into wedges

1. Preheat the oven to 425°F.

2. Heat the oil in a 3-quart Dutch oven over medium-high heat. Add the vegetarian kielbasa and brown on all sides; remove to a plate. Add the onions and cook for 5 minutes, stirring occasionally. Add the bell peppers and cook for another 5 minutes. Lower the heat, add the garlic, and cook for 1 minute more.

3. Stir in the rice, vegetable broth, white wine, zucchini, yellow squash, haricot vert, saffron, red pepper flakes, salt, and pepper; bring to a boil over medium-high heat. Cover, move the pot to the oven, and bake for 15 minutes. Take the pot out of the oven and remove the lid; gently stir the rice using a wooden spoon. Add the kielbasa and return the pot to the oven. Bake, uncovered, for 10–15 minutes or until the rice is fully cooked.

4. Move the paella back to the stovetop and add the peas and parsley. Allow them to warm through for 5 minutes. Garnish with the lemon wedges and serve hot.

PER SERVING Calories: 601 | Fat: 24g | Protein: 20g | Sodium: 1,126mg | Fiber: 8.1g | Carbohydrates: 43g | Sugar: 9.6g

Baked Cioppino

Don't limit yourself to the seafood suggestions offered here. Simply substitute your favorite seafood combinations, or whatever happens to be freshest the day you are making the stew. For extra flavor, substitute Basic Fish Stock (see Chapter 14) for the chicken broth.

INGREDIENTS | SERVES 6

3 tablespoons extra-virgin olive oil

1 large onion, minced

1 red bell pepper, diced

3 garlic cloves, minced

2 teaspoons chopped oregano

½ teaspoon red pepper flakes

2 bay leaves

½ teaspoon salt

¼ teaspoon pepper

3 tablespoons tomato paste

1 (28-ounce) can diced tomatoes

2 cups low-sodium chicken broth

1 cup dry white wine

1 pound firm fleshed fish, such as halibut, cut into 1" chunks

1 pound (16:20) shrimp, peeled and deveined

1 pound sea scallops

¼ cup chopped basil

1. Preheat the oven to 350°F.

2. Heat the oil in a 3-quart Dutch oven over medium-high heat. When hot, add the onion, bell pepper, garlic, oregano, and pepper flakes. Cook until the vegetables just start to become tender, 7 minutes. Stir in the bay leaves, salt, pepper, tomato paste, diced tomatoes, chicken broth, and white wine. Cover and bake until the liquid reduces by about half, 30–35 minutes.

3. Remove the pot from the oven and gently stir in the fish, shrimp, and sea scallops. Re-cover and return the pot to the oven until the seafood is cooked through, 7–10 minutes. Remove bay leafs and garnish with the basil just before serving.

PER SERVING Calories: 340 | Fat: 10g | Protein: 43g | Sodium: 992mg | Fiber: 3.1g | Carbohydrates: 18g | Sugar: 8.5g

San Francisco Stew

Portuguese and Italian fishermen settled into the North Beach section of San Francisco, and first popularized this stew in the late 1800s. It was originally made out at sea from the catch of the day, then brought back closer to home as a food served in North Beach restaurants. Its name comes from the word ciuppin, which means "to chop" in the Ligurian dialect.

Chile Relleno Casserole

These are excellent served with any number of sauces and salsas such as the Zesty Black Bean Salsa or the Roasted Corn Salsa (see Chapter 14).

INGREDIENTS | SERVES 6

10 fresh large (5"–6") hot peppers

1 tablespoon oil

1 small white onion

2 large garlic cloves

2 large ripe tomatoes

5 large eggs

½ cup shredded pepper jack cheese

¼ teaspoon salt

⅛ teaspoon pepper

½ teaspoon cumin powder

1. Position the peppers 3" under the broiler or place them directly over a gas burner. Turn the peppers with tongs so that the skin chars evenly, then remove them to a bowl and cover them with plastic wrap. Allow the peppers to steam for 20 minutes. When cool enough to handle, peel the peppers and remove the seeds.

2. Preheat the oven to 350°F and spray a 1½-quart baking dish lightly with nonstick spray. Heat the oil in a skillet over medium-high heat. When hot, add the onion and cook until softened, about 7 minutes. Add the garlic and cook until fragrant, about 1 minute. Stir in the tomatoes and remove from heat.

3. Layer the peppers, then the onion mixture, in the prepared baking dish. Whisk the eggs, cheese, salt, pepper, and cumin powder together in a bowl. Pour over the vegetables.

4. Bake the casserole until the top browns and the center of the casserole is set, 35–40 minutes.

PER SERVING Calories: 131 | Fat: 7.6g | Protein: 8.7g | Sodium: 221mg | Fiber: 2g | Carbohydrates: 7.5g | Sugar: 3.5g

Bouillabaisse

Serve this sumptuous seafood stew with crusty bread and Rouille (see recipe in sidebar).

INGREDIENTS | SERVES 4

3 tablespoons extra-virgin olive oil

1 large onion, minced

1 stalk celery, minced

1 fennel bulb, minced

3 garlic cloves, minced

1 teaspoon fennel seed

1 pinch saffron

½ teaspoon chopped fresh thyme

2 bay leaves

½ teaspoon salt

¼ teaspoon pepper

3 tablespoons tomato paste

1 (14.5-ounce) can diced tomatoes

2 cups clam juice

1 cup dry white wine

1 pound firm fleshed fish, such as halibut, cut into 1" pieces

1 pound (16:20) shrimp, peeled and deveined

1 pound sea scallops

¼ cup chopped parsley

1. Preheat the oven to 350°F.

2. Heat the oil in a 3-quart Dutch oven over medium-high heat. When hot, add the onion, celery, fennel, garlic, fennel seed, saffron, and thyme. Cook until the vegetables just start to become tender, 7 minutes. Stir in the bay leaves, salt, pepper, tomato paste, diced tomatoes, clam juice, and white wine. Cover and bake until the vegetables are fully tender, 25–30 minutes.

3. Remove the pot from the oven and gently stir in the fish, shrimp, and sea scallops. Re-cover and return the pot to the oven until the seafood is cooked through, 7–10 minutes. Remove the bay leaves and garnish with the parsley just before serving.

PER SERVING Calories: 333 | Fat: 10g | Protein: 43g | Sodium: 821mg | Fiber: 3.4g | Carbohydrates: 17g | Sugar: 7g

Rouille

Combine 1 jarred roasted red pepper, 3 tablespoons reduced-fat mayo, 1 grated garlic clove, 1 pinch saffron, ½ teaspoon lemon juice, and 1 teaspoon extra-virgin olive oil together in a blender or food processor. Process until the sauce is very smooth. Serve with Bouillabaisse.

Tuscan White Bean Oven Stew

Serve this soup drizzled with a bit of Basil Pesto (see Chapter 14) or simply grate a bit of Parmesan cheese over the top before serving.

INGREDIENTS | SERVES 8

3 tablespoons olive oil

1 large onion, finely diced

2 carrots, peeled and finely diced

2 stalks celery, finely diced

3 garlic cloves, minced

1 teaspoon chopped fresh thyme

1 (14.5-ounce) can petite diced tomatoes

1 quart low-sodium chicken broth

½ teaspoon salt

2 (14.5-ounce) cans white beans, rinsed and drained

1. Preheat the oven to 350°F.

2. Heat the oil in a 3-quart Dutch oven over medium-high heat. When hot, add the onion, carrots, celery, garlic, and thyme. Cook, stirring occasionally, until the vegetables begin to soften, about 7 minutes.

3. Add the tomatoes, chicken broth, salt, and white beans; bring the stew to a simmer over high heat. Cover and bake the stew until the vegetables are tender and the broth is slightly thickened, 25–30 minutes.

4. Lightly mash the beans with the back of a spoon if you desire a slightly thicker soup.

PER SERVING Calories: 202 | Fat: 5.5g | Protein: 10g | Sodium: 571mg | Fiber: 7g | Carbohydrates: 30g | Sugar: 3.8g

Cuban Black Bean Oven Stew

Serve with lime wedges and chopped red onion for garnish.

INGREDIENTS | SERVES 8

3 tablespoons olive oil

1 large onion, finely diced

2 carrots, peeled and finely diced

2 stalks celery, finely diced

1 green pepper, finely diced

3 garlic cloves, minced

1 teaspoon chopped fresh oregano

2 teaspoons cumin

1 quart low-sodium chicken broth

½ teaspoon salt

2 (14.5-ounce) cans black beans, rinsed and drained

Cuban Cuisine

During colonial times, Cuba was an important port of trade, so its food is a reflection of the Spanish, African, and Caribbean influences that were introduced by traders, slaves, and settlers.

1. Preheat the oven to 350°F.

2. Heat the oil in a 3-quart Dutch oven over medium-high heat. When hot, add the onion, carrots, celery, green pepper, garlic, oregano, and cumin. Cook, stirring occasionally, until the vegetables begin to soften, about 7 minutes.

3. Add the chicken broth, salt, and black beans; bring the stew to a simmer over high heat. Cover and bake the stew until the vegetables are tender and the broth is slightly thickened, 25–30 minutes.

4. Lightly mash the beans with the back of a spoon if you desire a slightly thicker soup.

PER SERVING Calories: 420 | Fat: 6.6g | Protein: 24g | Sodium: 1,366mg | Fiber: 17g | Carbohydrates: 68g | Sugar: 4.2g

Spinach Lamb Curry

This dish graces menus at innumerable Indian restaurants. Serve with naan bread or brown rice.

INGREDIENTS | SERVES 4

½ pound frozen chopped spinach

2 tablespoons vegetable oil

2 bay leaves

1 cinnamon stick

4 cloves

2 black cardamom pods

2 medium red onions, minced

1 teaspoon grated fresh ginger

2 garlic cloves, minced

1¼ pounds boneless lean lamb, cut into 1" chunks

2 small tomatoes, finely chopped

1 teaspoon curry powder

½ teaspoon turmeric powder

¼ teaspoon salt

½ cup nonfat plain yogurt

½ cup water

1. Cook the spinach in boiling water until just wilted; drain. Purée in a food processor. Set aside.

2. Preheat the oven to 350°F.

3. In a 3-quart Dutch oven, heat the vegetable oil. When hot, add the bay leaves, cinnamon, cloves, and cardamom pods. When the spices begin to sizzle, add the onions. Stirring constantly, cook until the onions turn golden brown, 7–10 minutes. Add the ginger and garlic; cook for 1 minute.

4. Add the lamb and cook, stirring constantly, for 10 minutes.

5. Add the tomatoes, curry, turmeric, salt, yogurt, and water. Bring to a boil, stir well, cover, and bake.

6. Cook until the lamb is tender, about 45 minutes. Stir in the spinach and bake another 5 minutes until warmed through.

PER SERVING Calories: 409 | Fat: 27g | Protein: 29g | Sodium: 282mg | Fiber: 2.3g | Carbohydrates: 7.1g | Sugar: 4g

Thai Curry with Sweet Potatoes

This easy one-pot meal is fantastic on its own or served over brown rice. Look for Thai curry paste and fish sauce in the international foods aisle of your grocery store. Garnish with extra basil and lime wedges.

INGREDIENTS | SERVES 6

2 tablespoons vegetable oil

1 medium onion, diced

1 tablespoon Thai curry paste

1 red bell pepper, diced

1 yellow bell pepper, diced

1 (14-ounce) can light coconut milk

2 teaspoons fish sauce

¼ cup brown sugar

¼ cup chicken broth

1 (14.5-ounce) can diced tomatoes

2 medium sweet potatoes, cut into 1" chunks

1 pound boneless, skinless chicken breasts, cut into 1" chunks

¼ cup chopped basil

1 tablespoon lime juice

1. Preheat the oven to 350°F.

2. In a 3-quart Dutch oven, heat the vegetable oil. When hot, add the onion and curry paste. Cook until the onion is tender, about 10 minutes. Add the bell peppers, coconut milk, fish sauce, brown sugar, chicken broth, tomatoes, sweet potatoes, and chicken. Bring the curry to a simmer, cover, and bake.

3. Bake the curry, stirring once or twice, until the vegetables are tender, the chicken cooked through, and the sauce somewhat thickened, 30–35 minutes.

4. Stir in the basil and lime juice just before serving.

PER SERVING Calories: 351 | Fat: 19g | Protein: 17g | Sodium: 400mg | Fiber: 3.1g | Carbohydrates: 31g | Sugar: 16g

Fish Sauce

The unique flavor of Thai cuisine is owed in part to this unique condiment. It offers a depth of flavor that would otherwise be difficult to achieve without long cooking. Fish sauce is made from fermented fish and has a slightly sweet taste. It is a common ingredient in curries and other sauces.

CHAPTER 14

Sauces, Relishes, and Salsas

Basic Fish Stock

Do not use oily fish bones like those from tuna or salmon.
Light whitefish bones are a better option for this stock.

**INGREDIENTS | YIELDS 1 GALLON;
SERVING SIZE: 1 CUP**

4 pounds fish bones
3 large yellow onions
2 large carrots
3 stalks celery
½ bunch fresh parsley
8 sprigs fresh thyme
3 bay leaves
6 peppercorns
2 gallons cold water

1. Rinse the fish bones in ice-cold water. Peel and roughly chop the onions and carrots. Clean and roughly chop the celery. Rinse the parsley and thyme.

2. Place all the ingredients in a large stockpot and bring to a simmer. Cook over medium-low heat for 2 hours, uncovered.

3. Strain the broth through a fine-meshed sieve and discard the solids. Use in recipes as needed or let cool completely and store for later use.

PER SERVING Calories: 40 | Fat: 2g | Protein: 5g | Sodium: 364mg | Fiber: 0g | Carbohydrates: 0g | Sugar: 0g

Green Chili Sauce

Use as a green sauce for enchiladas or any other dish.

INGREDIENTS | YIELDS 2 CUPS

1 cup fresh green chilies (the type of your choice), roasted, stemmed, and seeded
1 cup canned tomatillos with juice
¼ cup parsley
¼ cup onion
1 garlic clove
½ cup canned jalapeño peppers, drained
¼ teaspoon salt
½ teaspoon pepper
¼ cup olive oil

1. Combine the chilies, tomatillos with their juice, parsley, onion, garlic, jalapeños, salt, and pepper in a food processor or blender. Purée until smooth.

2. Heat the oil in a medium skillet over medium heat. Add the sauce and cook for about 5 minutes, stirring constantly.

PER SERVING Calories: 130 | Fat: 14g | Protein: 0.36g | Sodium: 284mg | Fiber: 1g | Carbohydrates: 2.3g | Sugar: 0.34g

Fresh Peach-Mango Salsa

This makes a welcome addition to simple grilled chicken breasts or as a side for baked tempeh.

INGREDIENTS | SERVES 6

1 mango, peeled and cut into ¼ pieces
1 peach, peeled and cut into ¼ pieces
1 cup finely chopped red onion
1 cup chopped, peeled cucumber
1 tablespoon balsamic vinegar
1 tablespoon lime juice
1 teaspoon chili powder
½ teaspoon cumin
1 tablespoon fresh cilantro, chopped
1 tablespoon parsley, chopped
¼ teaspoon salt

Mix all ingredients together in a medium bowl. Chill at least 4 hours before serving.

PER SERVING Calories: 45 | Fat: 1g | Protein: 1g | Sodium: 104mg | Fiber: 2g | Carbohydrates: 10g | Sugar: 7.2g

Pineapple, Mango, and Cucumber Salsa

Serve with toasted pita chips or grilled seafood.
Cut all of the fruits and vegetables into even ¼" pieces.

INGREDIENTS | SERVES 8

½ cup chopped pineapple
½ cup chopped fresh mango
½ cup chopped cucumber
1 medium tomato, chopped
3 tablespoons sliced scallions
⅓ cup chopped bell pepper
2 tablespoons minced jalapeño pepper
3 tablespoons fresh cilantro
½ teaspoon salt

Combine all ingredients together in a bowl. Refrigerate at least 4 hours before serving.

PER SERVING Calories: 32 | Fat: 0g | Protein: 0.6g | Sodium: 196mg | Fiber: 1g | Carbohydrates: 6.4g | Sugar: 5.2g

Zesty Black Bean Salsa

This fresh-tasting salsa is great served with fish or simply with chips.

INGREDIENTS | SERVES 10

1 cup chopped red onion

¼ cup chopped cilantro

¼ cup chopped parsley

3 tablespoons minced jalapeño pepper

1½ cups canned black beans, drained and rinsed

4 cups chopped tomato

3 tablespoons lime juice

2 tablespoons olive oil

1. Place onion, cilantro, parsley, and jalapeño in food processor; chop finely.

2. In a medium bowl, combine onion mixture, black beans, and tomatoes.

3. In a small bowl, whisk together lime juice and olive oil. Pour over ingredients; mix well.

4. Chill well before serving.

PER SERVING Calories: 91 | Fat: 3g | Protein: 4g | Sodium: 125mg | Fiber: 4g | Carbohydrates: 13g | Sugar: 2.5g

Citrus Salsa

For a change of taste, substitute orange juice for the lemon and lime juices.
Chop all of the vegetables into ¼" pieces.

INGREDIENTS | SERVES 12

2 large ripe tomatoes, chopped

1 medium white onion, chopped

3 garlic cloves, minced

1 jalapeño pepper, seeded, ribs removed, minced

¼ cup fresh cilantro

¼ cup lime juice

1 teaspoon lemon juice

1 tablespoon dry white wine

1 teaspoon chili powder

½ teaspoon ground black pepper

Combine all ingredients together in a bowl. Refrigerate for at least 1 hour before serving.

PER SERVING Calories: 36 | Fat: 0g | Protein: 1g | Sodium: 145mg | Fiber: 2g | Carbohydrates: 10g | Sugar: 5g

Cranberry Orange Relish

Serve this relish with any of the potpies or casseroles made with poultry.

INGREDIENTS | SERVES 12; SERVING SIZE: ½ CUP

16 ounces fresh cranberries
1½ cups orange sections
2 teaspoons orange zest
¼ cup brown sugar
¾ cup sugar
1 teaspoon cinnamon

1. Chop the cranberries and orange sections in food processor using the pulse setting until coarsely chopped. Transfer to saucepan.

2. Bring cranberry mixture, orange zest, brown sugar, and sugar to boil over medium heat. Cook for 2 minutes.

3. Remove from heat; stir in cinnamon. Chill before serving.

PER SERVING Calories: 62 | Fat: 0g | Protein: 0g | Sodium: 3mg | Fiber: 2g | Carbohydrates: 16g | Sugar: 20g

Cranberry-Raisin Chutney

This chutney makes an elegant garnish for turkey or chicken casseroles.

INGREDIENTS | YIELDS ABOUT 3 CUPS; SERVING SIZE: 1 TABLESPOON

1 cup diced onions
1 cup diced peeled apples
1 cup diced bananas
1 cup diced peaches
¼ cup raisins
¼ cup dry white wine
¼ cup dried cranberries
¼ cup apple cider vinegar
1 teaspoon brown sugar
Sea salt and freshly ground black pepper to taste (optional)

1. In a large saucepan, combine the onions, apples, bananas, peaches, raisins, wine, cranberries, vinegar, and brown sugar. Cook over low heat for about 1 hour, stirring occasionally.

2. Cool completely. This salsa can be kept for 1 week in the refrigerator or in the freezer for 3 months, or canned using the same sterilizing method you'd use to can mincemeat.

PER SERVING Calories: 14 | Protein: 0.1g | Fat: 0g | Sodium: 0.5mg | Fiber: 0.5g | Carbohydrates: 3g | Sugar: 6g

Oregano Almond Pesto

*If your pesto is too thick, take a tablespoon of boiling water from
your pasta pot and stir it into the pesto to thin it out.*

**INGREDIENTS | MAKES 2 CUPS;
SERVING SIZE: 1
TABLESPOON**

2 bunches fresh oregano
½ bulb garlic
½ cup almonds
1 cup extra-virgin olive oil

1. Clean the oregano and remove the leaves from the stem. Peel and roughly chop the garlic.
2. Combine the oregano, garlic, and almonds in the bowl of a food processor. Pulse until well blended; pour in the oil, then blend until fairly smooth.

PER SERVING Calories: 37 | Fat: 4g | Protein: 0.2g | Sodium: 0.21mg | Fiber: 0.1g | Carbohydrates: 0.34g | Sugar: 0g

Mock Cream

Use in place of regular cream in any casserole dish for a fraction of the calories.

INGREDIENTS | YIELDS 1½ CUPS

2 cups skim milk
½ cup nonfat dry milk

Process the ingredients in a blender until mixed and use as a substitute for heavy cream.

PER SERVING Calories: 124 | Fat: 0g | Protein: 12g | Sodium: 515mg | Fiber: 0g | Carbohydrates: 18g | Sugar: 0g

Salsa Verde

Use this sauce as a condiment for baked white beans, on top of baked rice dishes, or with other Mexican casseroles.

INGREDIENTS | YIELDS 2 CUPS; SERVING SIZE: 2 TABLESPOONS

5 large tomatillos, husks removed
1 serrano chili
1 small white onion
¼ cup packed parsley
1 tablespoon chopped fresh oregano
3 tablespoons lime juice

1. Broil the tomatillos, chili, and onion 3" away from the heating element, turning with tongs, until they are spotty brown and softened.

2. Seed the chili and place in a food processor with the tomatillos, onion, parsley, oregano, and lime juice. Blend the salsa until puréed, but not quite completely smooth.

PER SERVING Calories: 10 | Fat: 0g | Protein: 0.2g | Sodium: 0.22mg | Fiber: 0.4g | Carbohydrates: 1.1g | Sugar: 0.67g

Basic Picante Sauce

For a less spicy sauce, keep the jalapeño pepper whole and remove it after simmering the mixture.

INGREDIENTS | YIELDS 3 CUPS

1 large white onion
1 fresh jalapeño pepper
6 medium ripe tomatoes
3 tablespoons vegetable oil
¼ teaspoon salt
¼ teaspoon granulated sugar
1 tablespoon fresh cilantro, chopped

Basic Picante Sauce Uses

Use this sauce as a side to any casserole that needs a bit more zing, or swirl into soups, beans, or stews for a kick of flavor.

1. Remove the skin from the onion and chop into ¼" pieces.

2. Remove the stems from the jalapeño and tomatoes and chop into ¼" pieces.

3. Heat the oil over medium heat in a large skillet. Add the onions and cook until tender, but not brown, 10 minutes. Add the remaining ingredients and turn the heat down to low. Simmer for 10 minutes, stirring occasionally until the flavors have combined.

PER SERVING Calories: 181 | Fat: 14g | Protein: 2.1g | Sodium: 206mg | Fiber: 3g | Carbohydrates: 9.7g | Sugar: 6.3g

Roasted Corn Salsa

This salsa adds zest to any baked fish or chicken dish.
Try it with baked tofu, too.

INGREDIENTS | SERVES 6

2 ears corn

1½ cups fresh tomatoes, skinned and chopped

½ cup red onion, chopped

3 tablespoons jalapeño pepper, finely chopped

1 tablespoon rice wine vinegar

¼ cup roasted red pepper, chopped

1½ tablespoons cilantro, chopped

1 teaspoon garlic, finely chopped

1 tablespoon lime juice

½ teaspoon cumin

2 teaspoons red wine vinegar

1. Husk the corn and grill it over a low fire. Cook for about 10–12 minutes until lightly browned and tender. Set aside to cool.

2. Combine the tomatoes, onion, jalapeño, rice wine vinegar, red pepper, cilantro, garlic, lime juice, cumin, and vinegar in a bowl.

3. When corn has cooled, cut kernels off the cob and add to remaining ingredients.

PER SERVING Calories: 104 | Fat: 1g | Protein: 4g | Sodium: 77mg | Fiber: 3g | Carbohydrates: 24g | Sugar: 4g

Condensed Cream-of-Mushroom Soup
(Mock Mushroom Sauce)

Use this soup as you would regular cream-of-mushroom soup in any casserole preparation.

INGREDIENTS | YIELDS EQUIVALENT OF 1 (10.75-OUNCE) CAN

¾ cup finely chopped fresh mushrooms

½ cup water

⅛ cup Ener-G potato flour

OPTIONAL INGREDIENTS:

1 teaspoon chopped onion

1 tablespoon chopped celery

1. In a covered microwave-safe container, microwave the chopped mushrooms (and the onion and celery, if using) for 2 minutes or until tender. (About ¾ cup of chopped mushrooms will yield ½ cup of steamed ones.) Reserve any resulting liquid from the steamed mushrooms and then add enough water to equal 1 cup.

2. Place all the ingredients in a blender and process. The thickness of this soup concentrate will vary according to how much moisture remains in the mushrooms. If necessary, add 1–2 tablespoons of water to achieve a paste. Low-sodium, canned mushrooms work in this recipe, but the nutritional analysis assumes that fresh mushrooms are used. Adjust the sodium content accordingly.

PER SERVING Calories: 92 | Fat: 0.5g | Protein: 3g | Sodium: 12.5mg | Fiber: 3g | Carbohydrates: 21g | Sugar: 1.7g

Roasted Red Pepper Salsa

While salsas are always delicious with tortilla chips, use them as flavorful sauces for baked grain dishes or baked meats and fish.

INGREDIENTS | SERVES 12

2 large red bell peppers
12 scallions, thinly sliced
¼ cup chopped fresh cilantro
¼ cup chopped, pitted olives
⅓ cup grated Parmesan cheese
¼ cup olive oil
4 tablespoons lime juice
½ teaspoon salt
½ teaspoon black pepper

1. Place the peppers directly over a gas flame, or broil about 3" from the heating element of the broiler. Turn with tongs until the pepper is blackened on all sides, then remove to a bowl, cover tightly with plastic wrap, and allow to steam for 20 minutes.

2. When the peppers are cool enough to handle, remove their skins and seeds and chop into ¼" pieces.

3. Combine all ingredients together in a bowl. Cover, refrigerate, and allow the flavors to blend for a few hours before serving.

PER SERVING Calories: 63 | Fat: 5.8g | Protein: 1.3g | Sodium: 160mg | Fiber: 0.5g | Carbohydrates: 3g | Sugar: 0g

Basic Chicken Stock

Prepare this stock for use in a specific recipe on the day you plan to cook, or make batches ahead of time, let cool completely, and freeze for a later use. Use this stock in place of canned broth in any recipe.

INGREDIENTS | YIELDS 1 GALLON; SERVING SIZE: 1 CUP

6 pounds chicken bones with meat
3 yellow onions
1 bulb garlic
3 carrots
3 large leeks
4 stalks celery
2 cups mushrooms
5 sprigs fresh thyme
½ bunch parsley
1½ gallons water
3 bay leaves
½ teaspoon peppercorns

1. Rinse the chicken in cold water and pat dry with paper towels. Peel and roughly chop the onions, garlic, and carrots. Roughly chop the leeks, celery, and mushrooms.

2. Add all the ingredients to large stockpot. Bring to a simmer and cook for 4–6 hours, uncovered.

3. Strain the broth through a fine-meshed sieve and discard all the solids. Use immediately, or let cool completely and freeze for later use.

PER SERVING Calories: 86 | Fat: 3g | Protein: 6g | Sodium: 343mg | Fiber: 0g | Carbohydrates: 8g | Sugar: 4g

Basic Beef Stock

Use this rich stock in place of beef broth in any casserole recipe.

**INGREDIENTS | YIELDS 1 GALLON;
SERVING SIZE: 1 CUP**

6 pounds meaty beef bones
5 yellow onions
2 shallots
1 pound carrots
1 bunch celery
5 sprigs fresh thyme
½ bunch fresh parsley
3 bay leaves
1½ gallons water

1. Heat the oven to 400°F and place the beef bones in a large roasting pan. Roast, turning the bones often, until they are golden brown, 30–40 minutes.

2. While the bones are roasting, peel and roughly chop the onions, shallots, and carrots. Clean and roughly chop the celery. Rinse the herbs.

3. Add all the ingredients to a large stockpot and bring to a simmer. Cook for 8 hours, uncovered, then strain the broth through a fine-meshed sieve and discard the solids. Use immediately or let cool completely and freeze for later use.

PER SERVING Calories: 31 | Fat: 0g | Protein: 5g | Sodium: 475mg | Fiber: 0g | Carbohydrates: 3g | Sugar: 1g

Basic Vegetable Stock

*This vegetable stock is easy and great for use in many casserole recipes.
Keep some stored in your freezer so that you can use it anytime.*

**INGREDIENTS | YIELDS 1 GALLON;
SERVING SIZE: 1 CUP**

4 pounds yellow onions
1 pound carrots
1 pound parsnips
1 bunch celery
1 bunch fresh parsley
½ bunch fresh thyme
4 bay leaves
6 peppercorns
2 gallons water

1. Peel and roughly chop the onions, carrots, and parsnips. Clean and roughly chop the celery. Clean the parsley and thyme.

2. Place all the ingredients in a large stockpot and simmer for 2 hours.

3. Strain the broth through a fine-meshed sieve and discard the vegetables and herbs. Use immediately or let cool completely and store for later use.

PER SERVING Calories: 38 | Fat: 0g | Protein: 0g | Sodium: 11mg | Fiber: 1g | Carbohydrates: 5g | Sugar: 1.4g

TVP Tomato Sauce

*Serve this tomato sauce over pasta or polenta, or add to
sautéed vegetables for a complete vegetarian meal.*

INGREDIENTS | YIELDS ABOUT 6 CUPS; SERVING SIZE: ¼ CUP

1 cup TVP

1 cup hot vegetable stock

2 tablespoons olive oil

1 large sweet onion, minced

2 garlic cloves, minced

¼ teaspoon crushed red pepper

4 cups canned Italian plum tomatoes with juice

2 teaspoons dried oregano

½ teaspoon sugar

¼ teaspoon salt

⅛ teaspoon pepper

3 tablespoons chopped fresh basil

1. Combine the TVP with the broth in a medium bowl. Soak for 6–7 minutes, then drain.

2. Heat the olive oil in a large saucepan over medium-high heat. When hot, add the onions, garlic, and red pepper. Cook until the vegetables become tender and translucent, about 5 minutes.

3. Purée the tomatoes in a food processor, then add them to the pan with the TVP, oregano, sugar, salt, pepper, and basil.

4. Simmer, partially covered, until the sauce thickens slightly and the flavors harmonize, about 45 minutes.

PER SERVING Calories: 36 | Fat: 1.7g | Protein: 2.4g | Sodium: 72mg | Fiber: 1.1g | Carbohydrates: 3.3g | Sugar: 1.5g

Basic Tomato Sauce

*This simple tomato sauce can be used in any of the recipes where prepared tomato sauce or jarred
marinara is called for. Make a double batch, then freeze until needed.*

INGREDIENTS | YIELDS ABOUT 5 CUPS; SERVING SIZE: ¼ CUP

2 tablespoons olive oil

2 cups coarsely chopped yellow onion

½ cup grated carrots

2 garlic cloves, minced

4 cups canned Italian plum tomatoes with juice

1 teaspoon dried oregano

¼ teaspoon sugar

¼ teaspoon salt

⅛ teaspoon pepper

3 tablespoons chopped fresh basil

1. Heat the olive oil in a large, deep skillet or saucepan over medium-high heat.

2. Add the onions, carrots, and garlic; sauté until the onions are transparent. (For a richer-tasting sauce, allow the onions to caramelize or reach a light golden brown.) Purée the tomatoes in a food processor.

3. Add the tomatoes, oregano, and sugar to the onion mixture along with the salt, pepper, and basil.

4. Simmer, partially covered, for 45 minutes. Process the sauce in the food processor again if you prefer a smoother sauce.

PER SERVING Calories: 24 | Fat: 1.4g | Protein: 0.35g | Sodium: 33g | Fiber: 0.53g | Carbohydrates: 1.9g | Sugar: 1.2g

Basil Pesto

*Swirl this pesto into baked bean dishes for an interesting flavor twist,
or toss with pastas just before baking.*

**INGREDIENTS | YIELDS ABOUT 3 CUPS;
SERVING SIZE: 1
TABLESPOON**

¾ cup pine nuts

4 cups tightly packed basil leaves

½ cup freshly grated Parmesan cheese

3 large garlic cloves, minced

¼ teaspoon salt

1 teaspoon freshly ground black pepper

½ cup extra-virgin olive oil

Blanching Herbs

Blanch herbs before chopping or blending to help them keep their bright green color. Simply bring a pot of water to boil, dip the herbs in for a few seconds, then shock them in a bowl of ice water. Pat them dry with paper towels before using.

1. Preheat the oven to 350°F. Spread the pine nuts on a baking sheet. Bake for about 5 minutes; stir. Continue to bake for 10 minutes until nuts are golden brown and highly aromatic, stirring occasionally. Let nuts cool completely; chop finely.

2. Fill a heavy medium saucepan halfway with water. Place over medium heat; bring to a boil. Next to pot, place large bowl filled with water and ice. Using tongs, dip a few basil leaves into boiling water. Blanch for 3 seconds; quickly remove from boiling water and place in ice water. Repeat process until all basil has been blanched, adding ice to water as needed. Drain basil in colander and pat dry with a towel.

3. In a blender or food processor, combine the basil, pine nuts, cheese, garlic, salt, pepper, and all but 1 tablespoon olive oil; process until smooth and uniform. Pour into airtight container and add remaining olive oil to top to act as a protective barrier. Pesto can be stored in the refrigerator for up to 5 days.

PER SERVING Calories: 37 | Fat: 4g | Protein: 1g | Sodium: 14mg | Fiber: 0g | Carbohydrates: 1g | Sugar: 0g

Three-Herb Pesto

Use combinations of your favorite herbs and nuts for a different flavor.
Enjoy swirled into stews or soups and over casseroles for a bit of extra herb flavor.

INGREDIENTS | YIELDS ABOUT 3 CUPS; SERVING SIZE: 1 TABLESPOON

¾ cup pine nuts
2 cups tightly packed basil leaves
1 cup tightly packed parsley leaves
1 cup tightly packed cilantro leaves
½ cup freshly grated Parmesan cheese
3 large garlic cloves, minced
¼ teaspoon salt
1 teaspoon freshly ground black pepper
½ cup extra-virgin olive oil

Freezing Pesto

If you find yourself with an abundance of leftover herbs, make pesto! Line a rimmed baking sheet with wax or parchment paper, and dollop a tablespoon of pesto in neat rows. Freeze the sheet, peel the frozen pesto off the paper, and store in a plastic bag for later use.

1. Preheat the oven to 350°F. Spread the pine nuts on baking sheet. Bake for about 5 minutes; stir. Continue to bake for 10 minutes until nuts are golden brown and highly aromatic, stirring occasionally. Let nuts cool completely; chop finely.

2. Fill a heavy medium saucepan halfway with water. Place over medium heat; bring to a boil. Next to pot, place a large bowl filled with water and ice. Using tongs, dip the herb leaves into boiling water. Blanch for 3 seconds; quickly remove from boiling water and place in ice water. Repeat process until all basil has been blanched, adding ice to water as needed. Drain herbs in colander and pat dry with a towel.

3. In a blender or food processor, combine the pine nuts, basil, parsley, cilantro, Parmesan cheese, garlic, salt, pepper, and all but 1 tablespoon olive oil; process until smooth and uniform. Pour into airtight container and add remaining olive oil to top to act as a protective barrier. Pesto can be stored in the refrigerator for up to 5 days.

PER SERVING Calories: 58 | Fat: 5.7g | Protein: 1.6g | Sodium: 45mg | Fiber: 0.32g | Carbohydrates: 0.77g | Sugar: 0g

Mock White Sauce

This recipe for white sauce has all the body of a full-fat sauce with just a few calories.

INGREDIENTS | YIELDS ABOUT 1 CUP; SERVING SIZE: ½ CUP

1 tablespoon unsalted butter
1 tablespoon flour
¼ teaspoon sea salt
Pinch of white pepper
1 cup Mock Cream (see recipe in this chapter)

Mock Sour Cream

In a blender, combine ⅛ cup nonfat yogurt, ¼ cup nonfat cottage cheese, and ½ teaspoon vinegar. If you prefer a more sour taste, add another ½ teaspoon of vinegar. The type of vinegar you use will affect the taste as well. Apple cider vinegar tends to be more sour than white wine vinegar, for example.

1. In a heavy medium nonstick saucepan, melt the butter over very low heat. The butter should gently melt; you do not want it to bubble and turn brown. While the butter is melting, mix together the flour, salt, and white pepper in a small bowl.

2. Once the butter is melted, add the flour mixture to the butter and stir constantly. (A heat-safe, flat-bottom spoon safe for nonstick pans works well for this.)

3. Once the mixture thickens and starts to bubble, slowly pour in some of the Mock Cream. Stir until it's blended in with the roux. Add a little more of the Mock Cream and stir until blended. Add the remaining Mock Cream and continue cooking, stirring constantly to make sure the sauce doesn't stick to the bottom of the pan.

4. Once the sauce begins to steam and appears that it's just about to boil, reduce the heat and simmer until the sauce thickens, about 3 minutes.

PER SERVING Calories: 61 | Fat: 3g | Protein: 3g | Sodium: 190mg | Fiber: 0g | Carbohydrates: 6g | Sugar: 0g

Red Chili Sauce

This is the classic enchilada or burrito sauce.
Feel free to make this sauce with the chilies of your choice.

INGREDIENTS | YIELDS 2½ CUPS

12 dried ancho chilies

1 small white onion

3 garlic cloves

3 large tomatoes

4 cups water

¼ teaspoon salt

1 teaspoon granulated sugar

Ancho Chilies

Ancho chilies are actually mature dried poblano peppers—they are slightly hotter than the mild poblano, but still rather tame. Find them in the international foods aisle of your grocery store or in Latin markets.

1. Preheat the oven to 250°F. Place the chilies on a rimmed baking sheet and toast in the oven for 8 minutes. Transfer to a bowl filled with warm water and allow to rehydrate. Remove the stems and seeds from the chilies.

2. Peel the onion and chop into small pieces. Peel the garlic and chop the tomatoes into small pieces.

3. Combine all the ingredients in a medium pot. Cover and simmer on medium heat for 30 minutes. Every 5 minutes, remove the cover and push the chilies back down into the liquid.

4. Transfer the mixture to a blender and carefully purée. Strain the mixture to remove any skins, then simmer an additional 5 minutes in a skillet to thicken the sauce slightly.

PER SERVING Calories: 136 | Fat: 3.5g | Protein: 5.5g | Sodium: 137mg | Fiber: 9.7g | Carbohydrates: 24g | Sugar: 2g

CHAPTER 15

Desserts

Baked Apples Stuffed with Nuts and Raisins

*Baked apples are a delightful, spicy, and warm treat in the colder months.
Serve them for breakfast or dessert!*

INGREDIENTS | SERVES 2

2 large apples, such as Macintosh, Rome, or Granny Smith

2 teaspoons brown sugar

½ teaspoon cinnamon

2 teaspoons chopped walnuts

2 teaspoons raisins

1 teaspoon butter

1. Preheat the oven to 350°F and spray a 1-quart casserole dish lightly with nonstick spray.

2. Remove the center portions of the apples using an apple corer or small knife, being careful not to cut through the bottom of the apple. Place the apple in the prepared casserole dish and add enough water to barely cover the bottom of the dish.

3. Mix together the brown sugar, cinnamon, walnuts, and raisins and stuff the mixture into the apples. Top each apple with ½ teaspoon of butter.

4. Bake the apples until they become tender, about 25 minutes.

PER SERVING Calories: 181 | Fat: 8g | Protein: 1g | Sodium: 22mg | Fiber: 3g | Carbohydrates: 28g | Sugar: 19g

Apple-Strawberry Crumble

*Don't throw out the apple peel in this recipe—it's full of fiber! Instead,
munch on it while the crumble is baking, or chop it up and add it to a salad.*

INGREDIENTS | SERVES 4

2 cups Granny Smith apples, peeled and chopped

2 cups chopped strawberries

¼ cup Egg Beaters

1 ripe banana, mashed

1 cup oatmeal

¼ cup brown sugar

½ teaspoon cinnamon

1. Preheat the oven to 350°F and spray an 8" × 8" casserole dish lightly with nonstick spray.

2. Combine the apples and strawberries in the prepared casserole dish. Stir in the Egg Beaters, banana, oatmeal, brown sugar, and cinnamon.

3. Bake the crumble until the fruit is tender and the topping browns and bubbles, about 25–30 minutes.

PER SERVING Calories: 231 | Fat: 1.6g | Protein: 4.1g | Sodium: 66mg | Fiber: 6.3g | Carbohydrates: 55g | Sugar: 32g

Sweet Potato Pudding

Sweet potatoes are a good source of fiber, vitamin B6, and potassium and are a very good source of vitamins A and C. They are naturally sweet and make an excellent dessert when paired with orange and brown sugar.

INGREDIENTS | SERVES 8

6 sweet potatoes, peeled and cubed
⅓ cup butter, melted
1 cup dark brown sugar
2 large eggs
2 large egg whites
⅔ cup orange juice
1 tablespoon grated orange zest
1 tablespoon vanilla

1. Preheat the oven to 350°F and spray a deep 2½-quart casserole dish lightly with nonstick spray.

2. Steam the sweet potatoes until tender, about 20 minutes. Place the potatoes into a large bowl and mash until very smooth.

3. Add the butter, brown sugar, eggs, egg whites, orange juice, orange zest, and vanilla to the bowl; mix until thoroughly combined. Pour mixture into the prepared casserole dish.

4. Bake the pudding until it puffs slightly and just barely wobbles in the center, about 40 minutes.

PER SERVING Calories: 286 | Fat: 8.9g | Protein: 4.9g | Sodium: 173mg | Fiber: 3g | Carbohydrates: 48g | Sugar: 32g

Oven-Roasted Pears

These pears are delicious served simply with a drizzle of crème fraîche, but they also make a welcome addition to a salad and cheese course.

INGREDIENTS | SERVES 4

4 ripe Bosc pears
1½ cups Marsala wine

1. Preheat the oven to 400°F and spray a 9" × 13" casserole dish lightly with nonstick spray.

2. Slice the pears in half and remove the seeds and stem. Place them in a single layer in the prepared casserole dish and pour the Marsala wine over them.

3. Bake the pears uncovered, basting every 20 minutes, until they are tender, 40–50 minutes. Add a splash of water if the Marsala evaporates too quickly and the dish becomes dry.

4. Remove the pears from the oven and baste them several times as they cool.

PER SERVING Calories: 217 | Fat: 0.5g | Protein: 1g | Sodium: 4mg | Fiber: 3g | Carbohydrates: 31.5g | Sugar: 12g

Tropical Pineapple and Mango Crisp

*Frozen pineapple and mango work just as well as fresh in this recipe—
just don't used canned fruit as it will taste tinny and become too soft during baking.*

INGREDIENTS | SERVES 8

2 cups mango, peeled, cored, and chopped

3 cups pineapple, peeled, cored, and chopped

2 tablespoons lemon juice

¼ cup sugar

½ teaspoon powdered ginger

½ teaspoon nutmeg

1½ cups quick-cooking oatmeal

½ cup whole-wheat flour

½ cup brown sugar

⅓ cup butter, melted

1. Preheat the oven to 350°F and spray a 9" × 9" casserole dish lightly with nonstick spray.

2. Combine the mango, pineapple, lemon juice, sugar, ginger, and nutmeg in the prepared casserole dish.

3. Combine the oatmeal, whole-wheat flour, and brown sugar in a medium bowl and mix well. Add the melted butter and mix until crumbly. Sprinkle the mixture evenly over the fruit.

4. Bake until the fruit bubbles and the topping browns and crisps, 40–45 minutes. Let the crisp cool for 15 minutes before serving.

PER SERVING Calories: 285 | Fat: 8.7g | Protein: 3.6g | Sodium: 115mg | Fiber: 2.5g | Carbohydrates: 47g | Sugar: 31g

Slow-Roasted Summer Fruit

*Served warm or cold, roasted fruit makes an excellent topping for angel food cake, yogurt,
or granola. Stir it into hot cereal or bake it into puddings for natural sweetness and fiber.*

INGREDIENTS | SERVES 4

2 cups strawberries, hulled and thickly sliced

1 cup nectarines, pitted and sliced

1 cup blueberries

1 cup raspberries

¼ cup white grape juice

¼ cup sugar

⅛ teaspoon salt

1. Preheat the oven to 375°F and spray a 9" × 9" casserole dish lightly with nonstick spray.

2. Combine the strawberries, nectarines, blueberries, raspberries, white grape juice, sugar, and salt together in the prepared casserole dish.

3. Bake the fruit on the middle oven rack until it is bubbly and the juices have thickened, about 30–35 minutes.

PER SERVING Calories: 149 | Fat: 0.68g | Protein: 1.1g | Sodium: 79mg | Fiber: 5.7g | Carbohydrates: 37g | Sugar: 28g

Peach Bread Pudding

Nothing says summer like the first peach of the season. If ripe peaches are not in season, you may substitute canned, drained peaches packed in juice, or frozen peaches. Do not substitute canned peaches packed in heavy syrup.

INGREDIENTS | SERVES 9

2 cups 1% milk

2 tablespoons butter

2 eggs

⅓ cup egg whites

1 teaspoon vanilla

2 teaspoons cinnamon

⅓ cup brown sugar

6 slices whole-wheat bread, cubed

2 cups sliced fresh peaches

1. Preheat the oven to 350°F and lightly spray a 9" × 9" casserole dish with nonstick spray.

2. Heat the milk in a small saucepan and melt the butter in the milk. Cool the milk and butter mixture until just slightly warm.

3. Beat the eggs, egg whites, vanilla, cinnamon, and brown sugar together in a large bowl. When combined, add the cooled milk and butter mixture.

4. Place the cubed bread in the prepared casserole dish, then arrange the sliced peaches on top of the bread cubes. Pour the egg mixture over the bread and peaches. Bake the pudding on the middle rack of the oven until the center of the pudding is set, 40–45 minutes.

PER SERVING Calories: 164 | Fat: 5g | Protein: 7g | Sodium: 175mg | Fiber: 2g | Carbohydrates: 23g | Sugar: 12g

Summer Fruit Cobbler

Any combination of fresh fruit will work well with this recipe.
Try blueberries, blackberries, peaches, mangoes, or plums for a total of 4 cups of fruit.

INGREDIENTS | SERVES 8

6 tablespoons sugar

¾ cup plus 2 tablespoons whole-wheat pastry flour

1 teaspoon cinnamon

1½ cups raspberries

1½ cups fresh peaches, sliced

1 cup strawberries, sliced

1½ teaspoons baking powder

½ teaspoon salt

2½ tablespoons canola oil

2 tablespoons milk

2 tablespoons egg whites

Cobblers: An American Classic

Food historians credit westward-bound nineteenth-century American pioneers with the invention of fruit cobblers. These simple deep-dish pies feature baked fruit covered with a biscuit-like topping. Easier to put together than a traditional pie or cake, cobblers could be made in a Dutch oven on the open trail.

1. Preheat the oven to 350°F and spray a 9" × 9" casserole dish lightly with nonstick spray.

2. Mix together ¼ cup of the sugar, 2 tablespoons of the flour, and the cinnamon in a small bowl. Place the fruit in the prepared casserole dish, then sprinkle evenly with the sugar mixture.

3. Sift together the remaining ¾ cup flour, 2 tablespoons sugar, baking powder, and salt in a medium bowl. Add the oil, milk, and egg whites; stir together until just mixed.

4. Drop the dough by spoonfuls over the fruit. Bake the cobbler on the middle oven rack until the fruit is tender and the dough is golden brown, 25–30 minutes.

PER SERVING Calories: 152 | Fat: 5g | Protein: 3g | Sodium: 248mg | Fiber: 4g | Carbohydrates: 26g | Sugar: 10g

Baked Pear Crisp

The rum in this recipe enhances the sweet vanilla and rich butter flavors. If you want to cook without alcohol, you may substitute an equal amount of pineapple juice concentrate for the rum, and use a nonalcoholic vanilla flavor substitute.

INGREDIENTS | SERVES 4

2 pears

2 tablespoons frozen, unsweetened pineapple juice concentrate

1 teaspoon vanilla extract

1 teaspoon rum

1 tablespoon butter

⅛ cup Ener-G brown rice flour

⅓ cup firmly packed brown sugar

½ cup oat bran flakes

1. Preheat the oven to 375°F and spray a 9" × 13" casserole dish lightly with nonstick spray. Core the pears and cut them into ½" chunks. Place the chunks in the prepared casserole dish.

2. In a glass measuring cup, microwave the frozen juice concentrate for 1 minute, then stir in the vanilla and rum; pour over the pears.

3. Using the same measuring cup, microwave the butter on high until melted.

4. Gently toss the brown rice flour, brown sugar, and oat bran flakes with the butter in a bowl; spread the mixture evenly over the pears.

5. Bake the crisp on the middle oven rack until it bubbles and just begins to brown, 25–30 minutes.

PER SERVING Calories: 200 | Fat: 3.5g | Protein: 1.5g | Sodium: 5mg | Fiber: 3g | Carbohydrates: 42g | Sugar: 12g

Strawberry-Rhubarb Cobbler

Serve this summery dessert with a dollop of Greek yogurt sweetened with honey or a scoop of vanilla ice milk.

INGREDIENTS | SERVES 9

FRUIT
4 cups chopped rhubarb
2 cups thickly sliced strawberries
¼ teaspoon lemon zest
¾ cup sugar
2 tablespoons cornstarch
2 tablespoons water

COBBLER TOPPING
¾ cup whole-wheat pastry flour
1 tablespoon sugar
¼ teaspoon ginger
1½ teaspoons baking powder
½ teaspoon salt
2½ tablespoons canola oil
2 tablespoons milk
2 tablespoons egg whites

1. Preheat the oven to 375°F and spray an 8" × 8" casserole dish lightly with nonstick spray.

2. In a mixing bowl, combine the rhubarb, strawberries, lemon zest, and ¾ cup sugar. Dissolve the cornstarch in water and pour over the fruit, stirring to combine. Place the fruit mixture in the prepared casserole dish.

3. Sift together the flour, 1 tablespoon sugar, ginger, baking powder, and salt. Add the oil, milk, and egg whites. Stir the dough together until just mixed, then drop it by spoonfuls over the fruit.

4. Bake the cobbler until the fruit becomes tender and the dough turns golden brown, 25–30 minutes.

PER SERVING Calories: 218 | Fat: 3.4g | Protein: 2g | Sodium: 139mg | Fiber: 2.3g | Carbohydrates: 40g | Sugar: 27g

Rhubarb

Although it has been used for centuries for its medicinal properties, rhubarb only became popular in culinary applications once refined sugar became cheaply and readily available in the seventeenth century. Save for its ruby-red color, rhubarb looks similar to celery and is typically made into jams, pies, and sauces. Rhubarb leaves are toxic and should not be eaten.

Blackberry Cobbler

This recipe can also be made from raspberries, blueberries, cherries, or a combination, which is sometimes called jumbleberry. The berry juice soaks into the biscuits, giving them extra flavor.

INGREDIENTS | SERVES 8

WHOLE-WHEAT HONEY BISCUITS
1½ cups all-purpose flour
1½ cups whole-wheat flour
4½ teaspoons baking powder
1 teaspoon salt
6 tablespoons cold butter
1¼ cups buttermilk
1 tablespoon honey

COBBLER
8 cups blackberries
¼ cup flour
¾ cup sugar
1 egg, beaten

1. Combine all-purpose flour, whole-wheat flour, baking powder, and salt together in a large bowl. Cut cold butter into the flour with a pastry cutter until the butter pieces are no larger than small peas. Stir together buttermilk and honey; add to the flour mixture, stirring until the dough just comes together. Pat the dough into a 1" thickness on a floured board and cut into 2" circles with a cookie cutter or drinking glass.

2. Preheat the oven to 350°F and spray a 9" × 13" baking dish lightly with nonstick spray.

3. Toss the blackberries, flour, and sugar together in the prepared casserole dish.

4. Bake the blackberries for 25 minutes; remove them from the oven and place the unbaked biscuits on top of the hot berries.

5. Brush the biscuit tops with the egg wash and return the cobbler to the oven to bake until the berry mixture thickens and bubbles and the biscuits puff and brown, about 25 minutes.

PER SERVING Calories: 202 | Protein: 3.5g | Fat: 2.5g | Sodium: 157mg | Fiber: 7.2g | Carbohydrates: 44g | Sugar: 26g

Raspberry-Rhubarb Crisp

This crisp can be baked ahead of time and reheated later.
It's even delicious when served cold!

INGREDIENTS | SERVES 8

FRUIT

6 cups chopped rhubarb
¼ cup flour
1 cup sugar
2 cups raspberries

COBBLER TOPPING

1 cup ground almonds
¼ cup rolled oats
1½ cups flour
½ cup brown sugar
¼ cup sugar
1 teaspoon cinnamon
½ teaspoon salt
¾ cup unsalted butter, cut in chunks

1. Preheat the oven to 350°F and spray a 9" × 13" casserole dish lightly with nonstick spray.

2. Toss the rhubarb with ¼ cup flour and 1 cup sugar. Add the raspberries, toss gently, and then place the mixture into the prepared casserole dish.

3. In a large bowl, combine the almonds, oats, 1½ cups flour, brown sugar, ¼ cup sugar, cinnamon, and salt. Add the butter chunks and mix to a sandy consistency with an electric mixer. The topping is ready if it clumps together easily when squeezed.

4. Cover the raspberry-rhubarb mixture evenly with the topping and bake until the juices start to bubble up and thicken and the topping becomes browned and crisp, about 1 hour.

PER SERVING Calories: 538 | Fat: 25.5g | Protein: 8g | Sodium: 167mg | Fiber: 7g | Carbohydrates: 73g | Sugar: 24g

Stuffed Apricots

These warm apricots are delicious served with vanilla ice milk or crème anglaise. For an alcohol-free version of this dish, substitute an equal amount of apricot or peach nectar for the white wine.

INGREDIENTS | SERVES 4

4 ripe apricots
⅓ cup sugar
¼ cup soft butter
1 egg white
¼ cup ground almonds
⅛ cup bread crumbs
½ cup white wine

1. Preheat the oven to 350°F and spray a casserole dish large enough to fit 8 apricot halves snugly in one layer lightly with nonstick spray.

2. Cut the apricots in half and remove the stones. Place the apricot halves cut side up in the prepared baking dish.

3. In a bowl, cream the sugar and butter together until fluffy. Beat in the egg white, then stir in the almonds and bread crumbs.

4. Place a scoop of the almond filling on top of each apricot, then pour the white wine around the apricots.

5. Bake the apricots, uncovered, basting every 10 minutes with the liquid at the bottom of the pan, until the fruit is tender and the topping is brown, about 45 minutes.

PER SERVING Calories: 255 | Fat: 15g | Protein: 3g | Sodium: 98mg | Fiber: 2g | Carbohydrates: 24g | Sugar: 12g

Rum-Raisin Rice Pudding

*This brown-rice pudding can be served warm
with vanilla frozen yogurt or chilled with a bit of whipped topping.*

INGREDIENTS | SERVES 6

½ cup raisins

½ cup dark rum

3 cups milk

1 cup uncooked brown basmati rice

½ cup sugar

1 teaspoon vanilla

1 tablespoon grated orange zest

1 mashed banana

½ cup cream

Fruit Puddings

Bread, rice, and tapioca puddings all taste amazing with the addition of fresh or stewed summer fruit. This is a fantastic way to use up fruit that is on the verge of becoming overripe or simply at the height of summer when gardens or orchards are bursting with fruit that must be used quickly.

1. Preheat the oven to 325°F and spray an 8" × 8" casserole dish lightly with nonstick spray. Combine the raisins and rum and allow the fruit to plump while you prepare the rest of the casserole.

2. Mix the milk and brown rice in a saucepan and bring the mixture to a boil, stirring occasionally. Cover, reduce the heat to low, and simmer the rice for 15 minutes.

3. Remove the rice from the heat and stir in the raisins, rum, sugar, vanilla, orange zest, banana, and cream. Spoon the rice pudding into the prepared casserole dish and cover with foil.

4. Make a hot water bath by putting a large roasting pan on the middle oven rack and placing the casserole dish inside. Carefully pour boiling water into the larger roasting pan so that the water comes halfway up the sides of the casserole dish.

5. Bake the pudding for 15 minutes, then remove the foil. Bake, uncovered, until the center of the pudding is just slightly wobbly and the rice very tender, about 15 minutes more. Carefully remove the pudding from the water bath and serve warm. Or cool the pudding to room temperature, cover, and chill it in the refrigerator.

PER SERVING Calories: 391 | Fat: 10g | Protein: 7.5g | Sodium: 198mg | Fiber: 2g | Carbohydrates: 58.5g | Sugar: 29g

Hasty Pudding

Hasty pudding is a colonial American porridge that is made "hastily" in contrast to the time-intensive, elaborate steamed puddings from England.

INGREDIENTS | SERVES 8

5½ cups milk
½ cup cornmeal
1 teaspoon vanilla
½ cup molasses
1 teaspoon salt
1 cup sugar
½ cup unsalted butter, cubed
1 teaspoon ground dry ginger
1 teaspoon cinnamon
1 cup dried cherries
1 cup fresh corn kernels
1 cup raisins
½ cup cream

1. Preheat the oven to 350°F and spray a 9" × 9" casserole dish lightly with nonstick spray.

2. Scald 1 cup of milk in a saucepan, add the cornmeal, and stir over medium heat until it thickens.

3. Remove the mixture from the heat and add all the remaining ingredients except the cream and 1½ cups milk, to the cooked cornmeal. Stir to combine and pour the mixture into the prepared baking pan.

4. Pour the cream and 1½ cups of milk over the top of the mixture to prevent a skin from forming during baking.

5. Bake the pudding uncovered for 30 minutes, then stir the pudding and bake for 30 minutes more.

PER SERVING Calories: 624 | Fat: 28g | Protein: 10g | Sodium: 120mg | Fiber: 3g | Carbohydrates: 87g | Sugar: 55g

Scalding Milk

Many older recipes call for you to "scald," or heat milk almost to boiling, which essentially accomplished two things. First, it killed bacteria, preventing the milk from souring. Second, it destroyed the enzymes naturally found in milk that keep it from thickening in recipes. Nowadays, all commercially sold milk is pasteurized, which eliminates the original need for scalding. Heating the milk, however, does help to melt butter, dissolve sugar, and speed the cooking process, which is why modern recipes still call for scalding.

Baked Apples

You can use almost any kind of apple for baking, but the tart, firm-fleshed Granny Smith is an excellent choice for this recipe.

INGREDIENTS | SERVES 4

4 apples
⅓ cup brown sugar
¼ cup chopped pecans
1 teaspoon grated lemon zest
1 teaspoon ground cinnamon
¼ cup dried cranberries
¼ cup butter, melted
⅔ cup apple juice

Cooked Fruit

Just about any type of fruit can be grilled, roasted, poached, and/or baked. Cooking fruit makes it easier for children and people with digestive or swallowing disorders to eat—just make sure to remove all skin, stems, and seeds before cooking.

1. Preheat the oven to 350°F and spray an 8" × 8" casserole dish lightly with nonstick spray.

2. Remove the stem and core of the apples with an apple corer or small knife, being careful not to cut through the bottom of the apple. Place the apples in the prepared casserole dish.

3. Combine the brown sugar, pecans, lemon zest, cinnamon, and dried cranberries and use this mixture to fill the holes in the apples. Drizzle the melted butter over the filling.

4. Pour the apple juice into the baking dish and cover with foil.

5. Bake the apples for 30 minutes, then uncover and baste them with the apple juice. Return the apples to the oven until the juice reduces slightly, about 10 minutes more.

PER SERVING Calories: 337 | Fat: 18g | Protein: 1g | Sodium: 127mg | Fiber: 3.8g | Carbohydrates: 42g | Sugar: 30g

Apple-Pear-Nut Crisp

Make this recipe throughout the autumn and winter for a healthy dose of vitamin C and lots of fiber!

INGREDIENTS | SERVES 8

2 apples, cored and sliced

3 pears, cored and sliced

2 tablespoons lemon juice

¼ cup sugar

1 teaspoon cinnamon

½ teaspoon nutmeg

1½ cups quick-cooking oatmeal

½ cup flour

¼ cup whole-wheat flour

½ cup brown sugar

⅓ cup butter, melted

Baking Fruit

When choosing fruit for baking, pick specimens that are fairly firm and not too ripe. The baking process breaks down the cell structure of the fruit, so if you start with soft fruit, it will bake down to mush. Firm, tart apples like Granny Smith and Cortland are good choices for baking. Bosc or Anjou pears hold their shape when cooked.

1. Preheat the oven to 350°F and spray a 9" × 9" casserole dish lightly with nonstick spray.

2. Combine the apples, pears, lemon juice, sugar, cinnamon, and nutmeg in the prepared casserole dish.

3. Combine the oatmeal, flour, whole-wheat flour, and brown sugar in a medium bowl and mix well. Add the melted butter and mix until crumbly. Sprinkle the mixture evenly over the fruit.

4. Bake until the fruit bubbles and the topping browns and crisps, 40–45 minutes. Let the crisp cool for 15 minutes before serving.

PER SERVING Calories: 354 | Fat: 10g | Protein: 5g | Sodium: 62mg | Fiber: 6.5g | Carbohydrates: 45g | Sugar: 23g

Chocolate-Zucchini Bread Pudding

This is an excellent way to use up the end-of-summer zucchini.
Serve warm out of the oven with a scoop of vanilla frozen yogurt.

INGREDIENTS | SERVES 9

2 cups 1% milk

2 tablespoons butter

2 eggs

⅓ cup egg whites

1 teaspoon vanilla

2 teaspoons cinnamon

⅓ cup brown sugar

6 slices whole-wheat bread, cubed

1½ cups grated zucchini

½ cups mini chocolate chips

Squash

There are two types of squash: summer and winter. Summer squash includes varieties such as zucchini and yellow squash, which are tender throughout and take minimal time to cook. Winter varieties generally do not have edible skin and must be cooked for a substantial amount of time until their flesh becomes tender.

1. Preheat the oven to 350°F and lightly spray a 9" × 9" casserole dish with nonstick spray.

2. Heat the milk in a small saucepan and melt the butter in the milk. Cool the milk and butter mixture until just slightly warm.

3. Beat the eggs, egg whites, vanilla, cinnamon, and brown sugar together in a large bowl. When combined, add the cooled milk and butter mixture.

4. Toss the cubed bread, zucchini, and chocolate chips together in the prepared casserole dish. Pour the egg mixture over the bread and zucchini, lightly pressing on the cubes so that they become saturated. Bake the pudding on the middle rack of the oven until the center of the pudding is set, 40–45 minutes.

PER SERVING Calories: 210 | Fat: 8.6g | Protein: 5.4g | Sodium: 179mg | Fiber: 1.2g | Carbohydrates: 29g | Sugar: 14g

Apple-Walnut Bread Pudding

Fragrant and spiced, this recipe welcomes all of the pleasant aromas and flavors of autumn.

INGREDIENTS | SERVES 9

2 cups 1% milk

2 tablespoons butter

2 eggs

⅓ cup egg whites

1 teaspoon vanilla

2 teaspoons cinnamon

⅓ cup brown sugar

6 slices whole-wheat bread, cubed

2 apples, peeled, cored, and diced

½ cup chopped toasted walnuts

1. Preheat the oven to 350°F and lightly spray a 9" × 9" casserole dish with nonstick spray.

2. Heat the milk in a small saucepan and melt the butter in the milk. Cool the milk and butter mixture until just slightly warm.

3. Beat the eggs, egg whites, vanilla, cinnamon, and brown sugar together in a large bowl. When combined, add the cooled milk and butter mixture.

4. Toss the cubed bread, apples, and walnuts together in the prepared casserole dish. Pour the egg mixture over the bread and apples, lightly pressing on the cubes so that they become saturated. Bake the pudding on the middle rack of the oven until the center of the pudding is set, 40–45 minutes.

PER SERVING Calories: 205 | Fat: 9.3g | Protein: 7.3g | Sodium: 191mg | Fiber: 1.6g | Carbohydrates: 22g | Sugar: 8.5g

Pumpkin Rice Pudding

This pudding is silky with the autumnal flavor of pumpkin.
Enjoy with a scoop of ice cream or a bit of whipped topping.

INGREDIENTS | SERVES 4

3 cups milk

1 cup uncooked brown basmati rice

½ cup sugar

1 teaspoon vanilla

1 tablespoon grated orange zest

1 cup cooked canned pumpkin

½ cup cream

Cooked Pumpkin Substitutes

This recipe also works well with other types of cooked squash such as kabocha, butternut, or acorn. Simply steam the squash and mash well until it is very smooth. If the squash is slightly stringy or fibrous, pass it though a fine-meshed strainer before using.

1. Preheat the oven to 325°F and spray an 8" × 8" casserole dish lightly with nonstick spray.

2. Mix the milk and brown rice in a saucepan and bring the mixture to a boil, stirring occasionally. Cover, reduce the heat to low, and simmer the rice for 15 minutes.

3. Remove the rice from the heat, and stir in the sugar, vanilla, orange zest, pumpkin, and cream. Spoon the rice pudding into the prepared casserole dish and cover with foil.

4. Make a hot water bath by putting a large roasting pan on the middle oven rack and placing the casserole dish inside. Carefully pour boiling water into the larger roasting pan so that the water comes halfway up the sides of the casserole dish.

5. Bake the pudding for 15 minutes, then remove the foil. Bake, uncovered, until the center of the pudding is just slightly wobbly and the rice very tender, about 15 minutes more. Carefully remove the pudding from the water bath and serve warm. Or cool the pudding to room temperature, cover, and chill it in the refrigerator.

PER SERVING Calories: 286 | Fat: 7.3g | Protein: 9.4g | Sodium: 124mg | Fiber: 2g | Carbohydrates: 47g | Sugar: 27g

Plum and Peach Crisp

Make this recipe at the height of stone-fruit season with fruit that is just slightly firm.
You may remove the skin from the fruit first or bake it with the skins for a little extra fiber.

INGREDIENTS | SERVES 8

FRUIT
1 pound plums, pits removed and sliced
1 pound peaches, pits removed and sliced
¼ cup flour
½ cup sugar

CRISP TOPPING
1 cup ground almonds
¼ cup rolled oats
1½ cups flour
½ cup brown sugar
¼ cup sugar
1 teaspoon cinnamon
½ teaspoon salt
¾ cup unsalted butter, cut in chunks

1. Preheat the oven to 350°F and spray a 9" × 13" casserole dish lightly with nonstick spray.

2. Toss the plums and peaches with ¼ cup flour and ½ cup sugar and put the mixture into the prepared casserole dish.

3. In a large bowl, combine the almonds, oats, 1½ cups flour, brown sugar, ¼ cup sugar, cinnamon, and salt. Add the butter chunks and mix to a sandy consistency with an electric mixer. The topping is ready if it clumps together easily when squeezed.

4. Cover the fruit mixture evenly with the topping and bake until the juices start to bubble up and thicken and the topping becomes browned and crisp, about 1 hour.

PER SERVING Calories: 512 | Fat: 24g | Protein: 7.4g | Sodium: 154mg | Fiber: 4.4g | Carbohydrates: 70g | Sugar: 43g

Chocolate Rice Pudding

This chocolate pudding is sure to satisfy even the most die-hard chocolate fanatic.
Serve with a dollop of whipped topping.

INGREDIENTS | SERVES 4

3 cups milk

1 cup uncooked brown basmati rice

½ cup sugar

1 teaspoon vanilla

1 tablespoon grated orange zest

1 tablespoon unsweetened cocoa powder

1 cup semisweet chocolate chips

½ cup cream

1. Preheat the oven to 325°F and spray an 8" × 8" casserole dish lightly with nonstick spray.

2. Mix the milk and brown rice in a saucepan and bring the mixture to a boil, stirring occasionally. Cover, reduce the heat to low, and simmer the rice for 15 minutes.

3. Remove the rice from the heat and stir in the sugar, vanilla, orange zest, cocoa powder, chocolate chips, and cream. Spoon the rice pudding into the prepared casserole dish and cover with foil.

4. Make a hot water bath by putting a large roasting pan on the middle oven rack and placing the casserole dish inside. Carefully pour boiling water into the larger roasting pan so that the water comes halfway up the sides of the casserole dish.

5. Bake the pudding for 15 minutes, then remove the foil. Bake, uncovered, until the center of the pudding is just slightly wobbly and the rice very tender, about 15 minutes more. Carefully remove the pudding from the water bath and serve warm. Or cool the pudding to room temperature, cover, and chill it in the refrigerator.

PER SERVING Calories: 382 | Fat: 16g | Protein: 6.3g | Sodium: 81mg | Fiber: 0.5g | Carbohydrates: 56g | Sugar: 35g

Glossary

Al dente

This term literally means "to the tooth" and is used to describe cooked pasta that retains a bit of resistance when you bite into it. When precooking pasta to add to casseroles, cook it to the al dente stage, or just slightly shy of al dente, as it will continue to cook in the oven during baking.

Antioxidants

Substances, such as vitamins or other nutrients, that may protect cells from the damage caused by harmful molecules known as free radicals. Food sources of antioxidants are theorized to be more helpful than those found in supplements. Fruits, vegetables, whole grains, and seafood are high in antioxidants.

Bake

A dry heat method of cooking food in an oven where even, constant heat surrounds the food being cooked.

Blanch

To briefly cook food in boiling water, then plunge it into cold water to stop the cooking. Food is blanched to set its color, to loosen skins, or to help it maintain its shape during later cooking.

Bulgur

Whole-wheat kernels that have been steamed, dried, and crushed. Bulgur has a slightly chewy texture and is sold in coarse, medium, and fine grinds. Bulger is used in dishes such as tabouleh and kibbe.

Calorie

A calorie is the amount of energy needed to raise the temperature of 1 gram of water by 1° Celsius, and is used as a unit of measurement. Carbohydrates and proteins each contain 4 calories per gram, and fat contains 9 calories per gram.

Cannellini bean

A white bean used in Italian cooking that has a creamy texture and is slightly larger than a navy bean.

Canola oil

A type of oil high in monounsaturated fat that is made from rapeseed. Its name, derived from "Canadian oil, low acid," is thought to be more marketable than "rapeseed oil."

Carotenoid

A plant pigment that provides the red, orange, and yellow colors of many fruits and vegetables. Carotenoids act as antioxidants and can be turned into vitamin A by the body.

Cornstarch

A very fine white powder derived from the starch in corn and used to thicken sauces, make crispy coatings, and add body to soups and braises.

Deglaze

To release the caramelized bits of food in the bottom of a skillet or roasting pan by adding a liquid and stirring over heat.

Dice
To chop food into even-sized pieces ranging in size from ⅛ inch to ¼ inch.

Edamame
The Japanese name for immature (green) soybeans that are eaten fresh (not dried). They are sold with or without their pods and are available year-round in the frozen section of most natural food stores.

Fillet
A boneless piece of fish or meat.

Flageolet
A tiny, pale green French kidney bean that can be purchased dried or canned.

Flavonoids
A group of nutrients found in plants that act as antioxidants, may help regulate the immune system, and appear to help with brain function.

Homocysteine
An amino acid that is found in the blood. Too much homocysteine is related to an increased risk of heart disease. Folic acid from vegetables and fortified grains can help to keep homocysteine levels low.

Insoluble fiber
A type of fiber that does not dissolve in liquid and helps the body to eliminate waste through the intestines. It may be protective against cancer and comes from plant sources.

Inulin
A type of carbohydrate that helps to promote a healthy intestinal tract and can help to lower cholesterol.

Julienne
To cut food into very thin strips resembling matchsticks.

Legume
A type of plant in the Fabaceae family that is notable for its ability to fix nitrogen in soil. Notable legumes include beans, lentils, peanuts, and peas.

Lipid
A class of molecules that includes fats, oils, waxes, steroids, and cholesterol.

Lycopene
A nutrient in the carotenoid family that helps reduce the risk of prostate cancer and may reduce the risk of heart disease. Red fruits and vegetables such as tomatoes and watermelon have high levels of lycopene.

Mince
To finely chop so that the texture of food is very small and uniform in size.

Organic food
Foods that are produced without chemical fertilizers and pesticides and do not contain genetically modified organisms.

Phytonutrients
Chemicals found specifically in plants that provide health benefits beyond those provided by the vitamins, minerals, protein, carbohydrates, and fat in food.

Processed food

Foods that have been altered from their natural state by methods such as canning, freezing, refining, refrigeration, dehydration, and aseptic processing. Processing foods allows them to be stored for greater lengths of time. In some cases, the nutritional value of foods is diminished by processing (making white flour); in others, it remains high (canning of tomatoes).

Reducing

The process by which liquid is evaporated and concentrated so that the flavors become stronger and more assertive.

Registered dietitian

A credentialed health care professional with specific training in nutrition completed at the bachelor's level or higher who has completed a supervised practice program and passed a registration examination.

Roast

A dry heat method of cooking by which foods are cooked in the oven at a high temperature.

Roux

A mixture of fat and flour that is cooked to varying degrees of flavor and color that is used to thicken sauces, soups, and stews.

Simmer

To gently cook a liquid food at just below the boiling point.

Trans fat

A type of fat that is made in an industrial process that adds hydrogen to liquid vegetable oils, thereby making them solid at room temperature.

Vitamins

An organic compound required by an organism in tiny amounts for normal growth and development. Most vitamins cannot be synthesized by the body.

Healthy Eating Web Resources

American Dietetic Association
A source for science-based food and nutrition information from the world's largest organization of food and nutrition professionals.
www.eatright.org

American Heart Association
The mission of the American Heart Association is to build healthier lives free of cardiovascular disease and stroke. Their website includes guidelines for healthier eating and the latest news about heart disease.
www.heart.org

The Centers for Disease Control and Prevention, Division of Nutrition, Physical Activity, and Obesity
Nutrition and health resources from the Nutrition division of the Centers for Disease Control and Prevention.
www.cdc.gov/nccdphp/dnpao

Food and Nutrition Information Center
The FNIC website provides links to current and reliable nutrition information from both governmental and nongovernmental sources.
http://fnic.nal.usda.gov

Food Safety and Inspection Service
A variety of food safety tips and fact sheets from the Food Safety and Inspection Service.
www.fsis.usda.gov

International Food Information Council Foundation
IFIC, the International Food Information Council Foundation, provides food safety, healthy eating, and nutrition information.
www.foodinsight.org

Let's Move
Resources for children, parents, schools, and everyone in between on eating healthy and being active from the incentive started by First Lady Michelle Obama.
www.letsmove.gov

USDA Food and Nutrition Service
A website that provides information on all the government's food assistance programs, as well as nutrition resources.
www.fns.usda.gov/fns

USDA Nutrient Data Laboratory
A database that lists the nutrient composition of more than 7,500 foods and dietary supplements.
www.nal.usda.gov/fnic/foodcomp/search/

Standard U.S./Metric Measurement Conversions

VOLUME CONVERSIONS

U.S. Volume Measure	Metric Equivalent
⅛ teaspoon	0.5 milliliters
¼ teaspoon	1 milliliters
½ teaspoon	2 milliliters
1 teaspoon	5 milliliters
½ tablespoon	7 milliliters
1 tablespoon (3 teaspoons)	15 milliliters
2 tablespoons (1 fluid ounce)	30 milliliters
¼ cup (4 tablespoons)	60 milliliters
⅓ cup	90 milliliters
½ cup (4 fluid ounces)	125 milliliters
⅔ cup	160 milliliters
¾ cup (6 fluid ounces)	180 milliliters
1 cup (16 tablespoons)	250 milliliters
1 pint (2 cups)	500 milliliters
1 quart (4 cups)	1 liter (about)

WEIGHT CONVERSIONS

U.S. Weight Measure	Metric Equivalent
½ ounce	15 grams
1 ounce	30 grams
2 ounces	60 grams
3 ounces	85 grams
¼ pound (4 ounces)	115 grams
½ pound (8 ounces)	225 grams
¾ pound (12 ounces)	340 grams
1 pound (16 ounces)	454 grams

OVEN TEMPERATURE CONVERSIONS

Degrees Fahrenheit	Degrees Celsius
200 degrees F	95 degrees C
250 degrees F	120 degrees C
275 degrees F	135 degrees C
300 degrees F	150 degrees C
325 degrees F	160 degrees C
350 degrees F	180 degrees C
375 degrees F	190 degrees C
400 degrees F	205 degrees C
425 degrees F	220 degrees C
450 degrees F	230 degrees C

BAKING PAN SIZES

American	Metric
8 x 1½ inch round baking pan	20 x 4 cm cake tin
9 x 1½ inch round baking pan	23 x 3.5 cm cake tin
1 x 7 x 1½ inch baking pan	28 x 18 x 4 cm baking tin
13 x 9 x 2 inch baking pan	30 x 20 x 5 cm baking tin
2 quart rectangular baking dish	30 x 20 x 3 cm baking tin
15 x 10 x 2 inch baking pan	30 x 25 x 2 cm baking tin (Swiss roll tin)
9 inch pie plate	22 x 4 or 23 x 4 cm pie plate
7 or 8 inch springform pan	18 or 20 cm springform or loose bottom cake tin
9 x 5 x 3 inch loaf pan	23 x 13 x 7 cm or 2 lb narrow loaf or pate tin
1½ quart casserole	1.5 litre casserole
2 quart casserole	2 litre casserole

Index

We Have
EVERYETHING®
on Anything!

The Everything® list spans a wide range of subjects, with more than 500 titles covering 25 different categories:

Business	History	Reference
Careers	Home Improvement	Religion
Children's Storybooks	Everything Kids	Self-Help
Computers	Languages	Sports & Fitness
Cooking	Music	Travel
Crafts and Hobbies	New Age	Wedding
Education/Schools	Parenting	Writing
Games and Puzzles	Personal Finance	
Health	Pets	